SCM STUDYGUIDE TO THEOLOGICAL REFLECTION

SCM STUDYGUIDE TO THEOLOGICAL REFLECTION

Judith Thompson

with Stephen Pattison and Ross Thompson

scm press

© Judith Thompson, Stephen Pattison and Ross Thompson 2008

The Authors have asserted their right under the Copyright, Designs
and Patents Act, 1988, to be identified as the Authors of this Work

British Library Cataloguing in Publication data

A catalogue record for this book is available
from the British Library

978 0 334 04055 2

First published in 2008 by SCM Press
13–17 Long Lane,
London EC1A 9PN

www.scm-canterburypress.co.uk

Second impression 2010

Typeset by Regent Typesetting, London
Printed and bound in Great Britain by
Antony Rowe Ltd, Chippenham SN14 6LH

Contents

Preface   vii

Introduction   1

Part 1: What is PTR?   15

1 What Theological Reflection is – and what it isn't   17

2   PTR in Practice: Some Simple Paradigms   35

3 Ways and Means: A variety of PTR Approaches and Models   50

Part 2: The Elements of PTR and its Basic Resources   73

4 The Place of Scripture in PTR   75

5 God, Gaps and Glory – The *Kairos* Moment   97

6 PTR in the Context of Daily and Community Life – *Chronos*   113

7 PTR and Personality: Differences in Thinking, Feeling, Learning
   and Doing   128

Part 3: The Wider Perspective   151

8 PTR and Theology   153

9 PTR, Ethics, Institutions and the Wider World   175

10 PTR for Life – Not Just for Courses   195

Part 4: A Toolkit for PTR   209

Notes   233
Core Texts   237
Index of Biblical References   239
Index of Names and Subjects   241

Preface

This book began its life through a small research project entitled *Theological Reflection for the Real World* (Pattison *et al.*, 2003), and has been written in response to cries for help from groups of ministerial practitioners and generations of students. Having signed up to the crucial place of theological reflection at a hypothetical level in their study and practice they have found a frustrating lack of clarity about what it is in reality or how to go about it.[1]

Study days arranged with my co-authors, but mainly Stephen Pattison, for practitioners in Worcester, Cardiff, Bristol and Birmingham, revealed a universal longing among participants to relate their lives in general and ministerial practice in particular more closely to fundamentals of faith and belief. They had no problems at all about this in theory but many experienced real difficulty in doing so in the ordinary and extraordinary events, decisions and actions of daily life and work.

Whether this book succeeds in demonstrating and exemplifying the skill and process of theological reflection (TR) sufficiently clearly and engagingly to meet this need, and whether it takes sufficient account of the multiplicity of ways in which people reflect, its readers will decide for themselves. Our hope is that at the very least it will provide a useful contribution in making the specific activity to which we have given the acronym PTR (Progressing Theological Reflection) (see Chapter 1.1) more accessible, more employable, more vital and more fun. But if it proves to be a useful tool for anyone who longs to enable faith and life to interact with vitality and integrity in the decisions and events of daily living and wrest from the struggle of doing so new fruits of godly insight, wisdom, zest for life, and practical commitment, then the effort of writing it will have been well rewarded.

Such clarity as I have reached and been able to convey about the process and methodology, as well as intriguing richness, robustness and truth-bearing beauty of the crucial activity of theological reflection owes much to others. It has been enabled by pondering, practising and striking sparks of wisdom, through struggle and humour with a number of people over several years. In this respect a particular debt of gratitude is due to both my co-authors. Though most of the writing of this book, apart from Chapters 8 and 9, has been mine, none of it would have been written at all, and it would certainly never have been finished, without the companionship, intellectual stimulus, encouragement, humour and tough criticality, respectively, of each of my co-authors: Stephen Pattison, formerly Head of the School of Religious and Theological Studies at Cardiff University and now Professor of Religion, Ethics and Practice in the Department of Theology at the University of Birmingham; and Ross Thompson, formerly Tutor at Cardiff as well as ministerial colleague over many years, now an author in Christian spirituality, and also my life-partner and husband.

Many other people have contributed, directly and indirectly, to the development of the ideas and examples in this book – including parishioners and church members in Bristol,[2] five generations of students at the School of Religious and Theological Studies at Cardiff University and at St Michael's College, Cardiff, and colleagues at both institutions, especially Paul Ballard, John Holdsworth, Gareth Williams, John Weaver and Michael Wilson. I am similarly indebted to friends and colleagues in BIAPT (British and Irish Association of Practical Theology) and participants in the Theological Reflection Symposium held at St Michael's College, Cardiff, in September 2004, especially to Elaine Graham, Frances Ward, Heather Walton, Andrew Todd, Zoe Bennett, Helen Cameron, John Foskett and Duncan Ballard. Duncan – formerly as a student and more recently as my parish priest, companion-in-struggle and TR partner, and in his enthusiasm for computer-mediated theological reflection – has contributed more than he may realize. Heather Walton and Andrew Todd deserve special gratitude for having read and commented on the whole book, as do two students in the early stages of accredited ministry, Christine Holzapfel and Ruth Atkinson, who worked through the entire book and most of the exercises with me. Comments and suggestions from them and from others mentioned above have been invaluable in sharpening, pruning and improving the text, but responsibility for any shortcomings remains my own. And thanks are due also to Tony Seldon for the pictures in the toolkit.

I am also deeply grateful to my parents and family and many friends and mentors whose love and lives have enriched my appreciation of God, the universe and everything, and thus contributed fundamentally to my passion in affirming the interrelatedness of life and faith.

Judith Thompson
St Barnabas' Day 2008

Introduction

1 Getting started.
2 Connecting faith and practice.
3 Theological Reflection (henceforward TR) in Christianity and other faiths.
4 Understanding TR – the basics.
5 Taking care of the reflector.
6 An overview of this book.
7 Using this book.

1 Getting started

Theological reflection is, quintessentially, an experiential activity which can only be assimilated, appreciated and mastered by the doing of it. So, rather than begin by telling you what it is – if you don't already know – and why its significance is almost universally accepted by theological educators and practitioners, we invite you to try it out for yourself. This should whet your appetite for more, if the process is new to you. If you are a seasoned theological reflector, it may revitalize and reaffirm your experience and practice.

You are encouraged to engage with the exercise below, and the other exercises in this book, so that the work to enrich your use of this skill is always rooted in practice.

A basic 5-Step exercise in theological reflection

Write brief notes, rather than paragraphs, for each step of this exercise:

1 **Focus** on whatever has been the best thing that has happened to you or for you so far this week. Write a short phrase to identify it and make it specific.

2 **Fill out** the memory of that event as richly as you can: include the sights and sounds around you at the time, the context of the event and its significance for yourself and others, and its relationship to other events in your own life, and in the wider world. You might find it helpful to draw pictures or write your notes as a flow diagram or make a table with headings for each aspect of your account (which could then be linked with your discoveries in Step 3).

3 **Find connections** between elements of your reliving of the experience and texts, parables, prayers and events from the religious tradition you are most familiar with. Savour and enter into the narrative of what comes to mind in this way, using brainstorming, spidergrams or whatever form of representation enables you to explore the connections and feelings that arise for you. Ponder these things and offer it all in prayer in whatever way feels appropriate.

4 **Return to the event** that you began with but look at it from the perspective of Step 3. Allow the 'flavours', nuances or clear insights from your explorations to surprise and intrigue you as you look afresh at the experience you had. Wonder and ponder on any resulting changes in your view of that event, and record anything especially significant.

5 **Action:** note down two or three actions, however small, that your reflection leads you to consider taking as a way of living out the truth of what you have discovered. Note also how you would hope to respond should something similar happen in the future. Finally, make a definite commitment to undertake at least one of the actions you have noted.

There are many different ways of approaching theological reflection, some of which are described in Chapter 1. The exercise you have just completed is only one way in to this life-giving and energizing (but often misunderstood) method of interrelating life and faith. You may not much like writing things down, and may prefer more visual or tactile ways of reflecting. Whatever mix of methods you use, theological reflection (TR), if practised methodically and habitually, can provide a constantly renewing source of discernment and vision for anyone who is serious about developing the practice of faith in the decisions, actions and processing of everyday life and ministry.

2 Connecting faith and practice

In a nutshell, TR is a process by which explicit connections are made between belief and practice. Its evolution as a distinct theological activity is outlined in Chapter 1, but of course a concern to put faith into practice began long before the twentieth century, and has a very long history in all faith communities. In the Christian tradition, it finds expression in the injunction in the Letter of James that the faithful should 'be doers of the word and not hearers only' (James 1.22) and St Paul's insistence that the 'fruits of the spirit' are evident in the lives of believers (Gal. 5.22; Eph. 5.9). The irony is that it is perfectly possible to be a fervent believer in living out faith in practice and still not notice blatant contradictions between, for example, assertions of one's duty to love one's enemy, feed the hungry and forgive indefinitely, and what one actually does in practice. It was the conspicuous mismatch between Christian ideals and social practice in Latin America that gave rise to liberation theology, a major contributor to the development of TR, as described in Chapter 1.3.

Moments such as this, of personal or communal crisis, often seem to provide the triggers which enable individuals and faith communities to recognize the inconsistencies between attitudes, assumptions and habits that have become embedded in their patterns of praxis, and the fundamental tenets of the faith they subscribe to. Executions, imprisonment, torture and crusades are in blatant contradiction with belief in a God of love. But while many of the contradictions between belief and practice are less spectacular, far more undoubtedly occur at a day-to-day level in communities of faith than are recognized or even noticed. A few examples of this for you to ponder are provided in the following exercise.

Exercise: challenging apparent inconsistencies between proclamation and practice

1 Jesus said, 'call no man on earth Father, for you have one father who is in heaven' (Matt. 23.9). Jesus seems to have been encouraging his followers to think of themselves as one equal family united in their love of their heavenly father without hierarchies of any kind – even those traditionally based on family seniority. But most families use this word, or an equivalent, to name the male parent, and some churches have generated the habit of using 'Father' as a title for those in (benevolent) authority over them. (Cf. Alison, 2001, pp. 56–85; Wink, 1992, p. 119.)

   How do you respond to the raising of this question in relation to (i) families, (ii) church practice?

2 God's exaltation of the humble and meek and of the weak and the poor in spirit is a recurring biblical theme, as is 'putting down' the rich and the powerful (Luke 1.52). The faithful are repeatedly enjoined to live together as brothers and sisters.

   What issues does this raise for you in relation to current practice in your church or faith community?

3 Jesus taught his disciples to 'take no thought for tomorrow' (Matt. 6.25–34) but to trust in our heavenly father's providence.

   What contradictions do you notice between what Jesus is saying here, and how we order the life of our churches and our own lives, and how do you account for such contradictions?

4 In the church or faith community to which you belong, there are, doubtless, many instances where accepted practice fails to take account of explicit and implicit teaching and preaching in text and proclamation. Brainstorm as many examples as you can where accepted practice in your faith tradition seems to be at odds with the tradition itself.

The examples given above and others you have thought of illustrate how easy it is to ignore divergences between our practice and both minor and major tenets of the faith we proclaim. Those who regularly, habitually and unthinkingly belie the teachings of their faith by what they do and say, may often be very sincere believers, devout in their pattern of prayer and worship and commitment to religious practice, and they may be quite unaware of such contradictions. The Church has been described as *semper reformanda,* and certainly it has always been, and always will be in need of reformation. Theological reflection, as exemplified in this book, offers a simple yet effective way of enabling ongoing reformation and reconsideration of thought and practice applicable to any faith community.

Equally important is the issue of how what we do and experience feeds back into our interpretation of belief. Indeed, it is arguable that theology itself evolved in one form or another through reflection on practice and experience (see Graham *et al.*, 2005; Wilson, 1988; Tracy, 1981).[3]

In the New Testament theology arises out of the practical wisdom of Jesus and the efforts of Paul to build up the Church. In the Fathers, experience and practice generally precede doctrine, a case in point being Augustine's doctrine of original sin, which emerged out of the practice of infant baptism. The doctrines of the incarnation in Athanasius, and the Trinity in the Cappadocian Fathers, were intrinsically linked with the experience and practice of participation in God in the liturgy and elsewhere, while in modern times the Trinity has been 'rediscovered' in the practical search for equality in community. Not until the Middle Ages did theology begin to establish itself as a theoretical, systematic discipline in its own right; only then was a theological academy established, separate from the practical searchings of 'unprofessional' Christians.

The guru's cat

When the guru sat down to worship each evening, the ashram cat would get in the way and distract the worshippers. So he ordered that the cat be tied during evening worship.

Long after the guru died the cat continued to be tied during evening worship. And when the cat eventually died, another cat was brought to the ashram so that it could be duly tied up during evening worship.

Centuries later, learned treatises were written by the guru's disciples on the essential role of a cat in all properly conducted worship.

(De Mello, 1983, p. 79)

But doctrines tend to become gurus' cats (see box), preserved for their vener-able age and widespread acceptance rather than the long-forgotten practical content! However, whenever in TR a connection is made between a doctrine and practice, not only is practice transformed, but the doctrine itself is seen in a new light. The theological cat can then begin to wake up, shake off its bonds and purr.

In many ways, despite its long antecedents, TR is still in the early days of its history and development. It currently forms a key component in many mod-ules in practical theology as studied in universities, colleges and courses; and it forms a regular part of the life of a few Christian communities, notably within the Roman Catholic Church in parts of Ireland and North America (Gros, 2001). But it is not as yet a recognized and established element in the daily life and practice of churches and faith communities generally. It is hoped that this book will provide a useful guide in contributing to this development.

3 TR in Christianity and other faiths

As is evident from the outline of its history above, TR as a distinct activity has grown within the context of the Christian tradition, and, certainly in its early days, with specific reference to ministerial education. More recent develop-ments (Pattison, 1997b; Heskins, 2001; Green, 2002; Killen and de Beer, 2002) have stressed its crucial importance for all the faithful, laity as well as clergy, in honest appraisal and critical self-awareness, in bringing the practice of daily living closer to the vision and teaching of the Christian faith. The gestation of this book, therefore, has been from within the field of Christian ministerial education. However, the theory and application of this process as presented here is intended to be transferable to any group of believers of any faith com-munity – and even, perhaps, secular 'faith communities', as in *The Faith of the Managers* (Pattison, 1997a). The issues of the vital importance of connecting faith and practice are, after all similar, though the belief systems and traditions with which practice is correlated may be different.

The authors of this book would be particularly glad to hear from members of other faith communities who can relate the use of TR as described here to their own experience; and to enable the development of ways in which the rela-tionship between different faith communities could be enriched by working together in such projects, locally or nationally. Examples of using TR in other faith traditions would be a welcome enhancement to any future edition of this publication. But as it stands at present, examples are drawn from the authors' own experience and research within the Christian tradition. It is our firm belief and hope that, by describing and illustrating the elements of the process of TR from the standpoint of one tradition, this book can make TR more readily transferable to other traditions, and thus make a real contribution to interfaith dialogue and understanding (see further Chapter 8.5).

4 Understanding TR: the basics

At this stage it is necessary to begin to state more clearly what TR is and how it works. It may interest, amuse or alarm you to know that although TR exercises have been a requirement in most practical theology and ordination courses for more than twenty years, no clear definition of what TR actually is has yet been agreed. Research has shown how immensely frustrating and deskilling students have found being expected to operate in this vacuum (Pattison, Thompson and Green, 2003, pp. 123–4). This reaction is hardly surprising since there can be few things more frustrating than being told that you have to do something though no one will tell you what it is or how to do it, or how to judge for yourself how well you have done it – only criticism if you don't get it right.[4] Too often, it seems, people cannot really see what they are being invited to do and how this really can add value to their lives, thought and faith.

For this reason considerable importance is attached to the process of defining and describing TR in this book. This process is developed in Chapter 1.5 and is revisited in Chapter 10.2, by which time you will be able to refine your understanding and definition more precisely from the experience gained by working through the exercises in this book. TR must be known by its fruits: and it is hoped that you will discover this fruitfulness for yourself.

It would seem helpful to identify three broad understandings of the TR process, and to clarify the focus of this book in relation to them.

1 Some people use 'theological reflection' fairly loosely to mean any ruminative activity making connections between life and faith, and speculating about other ways of being and thinking in relation to belief. This use of the

term is descriptive rather than prescriptive: there are no 'rules' for doing it or evaluation. It is simply a description of a cognitive process that takes place quite spontaneously, though not necessarily with much rigour or criticality, among faith community members.

2 Others use TR as an umbrella term, almost synonymous with practical theology, to cover any thought-out activity that seeks to correlate theological concerns and insights with current social issues and events.

3 A third use of the term describes a much more precise, disciplined activity, undertaken methodically and rigorously by ministers, lay people or practitioners of any faith who are seeking, consciously and deliberately, to integrate belief and practice. This activity relates insights and resources from a theological tradition, specifically and carefully, to contemporary situations and vice versa, so that a mutually enlightening reappraisal may result. Pointers are sought to action which leads to a response which is more authentically true to the faith tradition on which it is based.

It is this third, rather more precisely defined use of the designation 'theological reflection' that is the main focus of this book, to which we have given the acronym PTR to distinguish it from the other two more general uses of the term. A fuller explanation for the use of this term, and the specific range of activities to which it refers, is given in Chapter 1.1.

5 Taking care of the reflector: a warning

This book, and the practice of PTR which it describes and exemplifies, will be of no help whatever to anyone who is not prepared first of all to care for themselves by allowing adequate time and space for rest, recreation and prayer. One of the very first groups encountered in the early days of the project that formed the background to this book illustrated this necessity very clearly. At the end of a weekend exploring current practice and new possibilities in TR, when invited to name new (to them) methods of theological reflection that they would explore over the coming year the participants identified activities such as hill-walking, going to India, dancing, creating music, having time away with a partner, timetabling space for reflection, going to the pub in a group. All of these seemed valuable commitments to make, and were affirmed as such, and were in themselves an acknowledgement of the absolute necessity of recreative space as a prerequisite for the practice of reflection – but they were not, in themselves, methods of theological reflection.

Maslow's hierarchy of needs (Maslow, 1970) suggests that only when our basic physiological and safety needs have been met, so that we have adequate nourishment, rest and shelter and a sense of security and stability, can human beings have spare energy to devote to relating, belonging and a sense of confidence and self-worth and thence to the kind of maturity that enables self-acceptance, objectivity, creativity, an awareness of the transcendent (and much more). Maslow is concerned here with the overall development of the human personality. But in a similar way, surely, it is true that, until fundamental physical and bodily needs are met, including rest and recreation, and the needs for security, relationship and a sense of belonging and worth, we will simply not have the time or strength or mental capacity available to make possible the kind of open-minded but demanding searching, lateral thinking and lively interaction with text, tradition and community that theological reflection requires.

Seeking to discover and translate into real life God's truth for us today in relation to particular situations through the hermeneutic of scripture and tradition requires a lively freshness of heart and mind on the part of the seeker, as well as diligence and commitment in searching and questioning, and a readiness to let go into uncertainty for as long as may be needed. (Trying to force an answer too quickly is likely to destroy the process.) The agent in this process is not a machine but a fragile human being whose physical, emotional and spiritual needs have to be met – every bit as much as would a machine's needs for fuel, lubricant and proper care – if these rewarding tasks are to be well carried out. The commandment to 'do no labour' on the Sabbath day may be flexibly interpreted these days, but accepting that we are divinely commanded to take proper time off from work and commitments for rest and space and peace and renewal, as well as prayer and worship, is one that all the faithful, but perhaps clergy in particular, need to take very seriously (Litchfield, 2006; see also Chapter 5.3).

6 An overview of this book

For the sake of clarity, this book is divided into 4 parts:

Part 1 What is PTR?

Part 1 describes and explores the process of PTR and provides a number of definitions and worked examples.

- Chapter 1 describes, briefly, a variety of approaches to TR generally and, more specifically, the process of PTR and its place in relation to reflective practice in other professions and to liberation theology and ministerial practice. Definitions and marks of good practice are considered.
- Chapter 2 consists of worked examples of PTR to stand as simple paradigms for the core process understood and developed in this book.
- Chapter 3 brings together a variety of models and formulae which have been used for PTR and invites you to begin to adopt and develop an approach for your own use.

Part 2 The Elements of PTR and its Basic Resources

Part 2 identifies the key elements present in any PTR endeavour and suggests how they may be effectively used in the process.

- Chapter 4 explores the use of the Bible or other sacred text and its key role in PTR. A variety of ways of accessing its depths and wisdom are identified so that the whole PTR process may be rooted in the heart of the religious tradition.
- Chapters 5 and 6 focus on how the reflector, as she focuses on a specific situation or issue, may be open to receive divine guidance, whether in a *kairos* moment of inspiration (Chapter 5) or by means of *chronos*, a more gradual process of revelation through time and the ordinary events of reflective living (Chapter 6).

- Chapter 7 looks at some of the ways in which personality traits and attributes are likely to be part of the reflective process for each individual.

Part 3 The Wider Perspective

Part 3 examines how PTR is situated in its theological, socio-political and everyday context. To enable this:

- Chapter 8 explores the place of PTR within theology as a whole, asking what it can teach us about God and about humanity.
- Chapter 9 considers how it may be related to and contribute to issues and events in the wider world and how it may be used to evaluate and challenge institutions and political structures and our part in them.
- Chapter 10 affirms and demonstrates that PTR is 'for life and not just for courses' and explores ways in which PTR can enrich the Church and help it engage with the wider world.

Part 4 A Toolkit for PTR

The toolkit provides a number of techniques, diagrams, games and activities to help reflectors engage creatively and effectively with this process in ways that are both refreshing and enjoyable yet also demanding or even disturbing. Particularly at times when you feel rather stuck or lacking in inspiration, dipping into the toolkit may help rekindle your imagination and enable your mind and heart to begin to dance again with the life of the Spirit.

7 Using this book

This book is intended to allow for flexibility in its use. It provides a basic reference book on the theory and practice of the disciplined use of PTR (see 4.3 above and Chapter 1.1) for anyone studying modules and courses designed to develop or extend the use of the skill. It is also intended for pastoral practitioners who wish to brush up their skills or enhance their learning of PTR gleaned in their initial training, by relating it more specifically to the context in which they are now working.

It is also hoped this book will be of value for any group of adherents of any faith, with or without accredited leadership, who simply wish to explore together with care and commitment a process which will enable them to evaluate more rigorously how well their day-to-day living out of their faith measures up to what its texts and traditions proclaim. It could, for example, provide a useful resource for any church- or faith-based study group, looking for a different approach in growing together in belief and practice.

Discipline is key to the whole of the enterprise described in this book: not the kind of discipline that instils fear or leads to rigidity; but rather the kind of discipline that empowers athletes, musicians and scientists to hone and develop skills and aptitudes that enable expertise and excellence in their respective fields. Scientists must pay meticulous attention to detail; musicians must practise until they become as one with the piece they are playing; athletes must exercise unfailingly to maintain a peak level of fitness. In the same way he or she who wishes to become proficient in theological reflection needs to make it a fundamental part of thinking and feeling in daily living as well as in practical action and decision-making – and in the academic study of practical theology, when this is undertaken. Only so can a reflective practitioner guard against the subtle dangers of solipsism and unconscious prejudging that can so easily undermine critical thinking and lead to self-delusion.

Therefore, as emphasized earlier, readers are encouraged to tackle the exercises provided as they work through this book to enhance both their reflective and critical cognitive processes and their powers of emotional discernment.

If possible, it is likely to be stimulating and energizing to engage with the exercises in a group, rather than alone, whether in a class or study group or as a result of a more informal arrangement among colleagues, church members or friends (see also Chapters 6.5 and 7.6). Anyone reading this book as a lone enterprise who feels that such a shared approach would not be possible is invited to check this out. You may feel somewhat embarrassed asking around among colleagues or church members if they would meet at intervals to work through this book with you. But if you persevere, you may find yourself agreeably surprised by the results of doing so. This is not only because, in a great many situations of reassessment and appraisal, two heads (or more) will be found to be better than one, particularly in noticing blind spots and personal bias, but also because it is often intriguing and fascinating to discover the different approaches and insights that others may have to the same set of data. It may well be that God's spirit can come alive to us more readily when we pool our mental and emotional resources in this way. As Jesus put it, 'When two or three are gathered together in my name, there am I in the midst' (Matt. 18.20).

When this book is used in university settings as a reference book for the teaching of particular modules it is hoped that many of the exercises will provide a basis for class discussions or written work. Course tutors will, of course, make their own selection and adaptations from among the exercises offered. Students could also work through them in more informally arranged groups, or on an individual basis.

Above all, however, it is hoped that anyone using this book to develop their PTR skills will find the practice both habit-forming, stimulating and life-and-faith-enhancing to such an extent that they will happily acquiesce with the title of Chapter 10 and conclude that theological reflection is indeed for life – not just for courses.

PLEASE NOTE

1 The observation necessary for the exercise which provides the basis for the discussion in Chapter 5.5 needs to begin at least a month in advance. Readers are encouraged to read the rubric for that exercise and begin keeping brief records as suggested.
2 The 'verbatim report' for the exercise in Chapter 3.3 needs to be prepared for at any time in advance of the study of that section.
3 Part 4 of this book, 'A Toolkit for Theological Reflection', is intended for use alongside the other parts, and there are several references to it in the text of Parts 1–3. It is suggested that readers begin to acquaint themselves with the toolkit straight away, reading it in parallel to Parts 1–3.

Further reading (see also core texts at the end of the book)

Alison, J. (2001), *Faith Beyond Resentment*, London: Darton, Longman & Todd.

Kinast, R. (1996), *Let Ministry Teach*, Collegeville: Liturgical Press.

Graham, E., Walton, H. and Ward, F. (2005), *Theological Reflection: Methods,* London: SCM Press.

Graham, E., Walton, H. and Ward, F. (2007), *Theological Reflection: Sources,* London: SCM Press.

Green, L. (2002), *Let's do Theology*, London and New York: Continuum.

Gros, J. (2001), *Theological Reflection: Connecting Faith and Life*, Chicago: Loyola University Press.

Heskins, J. (2001), *Unheard Voices*, London: Darton, Longman & Todd.

Killen, P. and de Beer, J. (2002), *The Art of Theological Reflection*, New York: Crossroad.

Litchfield, K. (2006), *Tend My Flock*, London: Canterbury Press.

Maslow, A. (1970), *Motivation and Personality*, 2nd edn, New York: Harper & Row, pp. 29–35.

De Mello, A. (1983), *The Song of a Bird,* Anand, India: Gujarat Sahitya Prakash.

Pattison, S. (1997a), *The Faith of the Managers,* London: Cassell.

Pattison, S. (1997b), *Pastoral Care and Liberation Theology*, London: SPCK.

Pattison, S., Thompson, J. and Green, J. (2003), 'Theological Reflection for the Real World. Time to Think Again', *British Journal of Theological Education*, vol. 13, no. 2, pp. 119–31.

Tracy, D. (1981), *The Analogical Imagination: Christian Theology and the Culture of Pluralism*, New York: Crossroad.

Weaver, J. (2007), *Outside-in: Theological Reflections on Life*, Macon GA: Smyth and Helwys.

Whitehead, J. and E. (1995), *Method in Ministry: Theological Reflection and Christian Ministry*, Lanham, Chicago, New York, Oxford: Sheed & Ward.

Wilson, M. (1988), *A Coat of Many Colours: Pastoral Studies of the Christian Way of Life*, London: Epworth.

Wink, W. (1992), *Engaging the Powers: Discernment and Resistance in a World of Domination*, Minneapolis: Fortress Press.

Part 1

What is PTR ?

Part 1 describes and explores the process of PTR and provides a number of definitions and worked examples.

- Chapter 1 describes, a variety of approaches to TR generally, and specifically, the process of PTR and how it relates to reflective practice in other professions, to liberation theology and to ministerial practice. Definitions and marks of good practice are considered.
- Chapter 2 consists of worked examples of PTR to stand as simple paradigms and provide a point of reference for the core process understood and developed in this book.
- Chapter 3 brings together a variety of models and formulae which have been used for PTR and invites you to begin to adopt and develop an approach for your own use.

1

What Theological Reflection is – and what it isn't

1 Approaching an understanding of TR and introducing PTR.
2 PTR and reflective practice in other professions.
3 PTR and liberation theology.
4 PTR and ministerial practice.
5 Defining and refining.
6 Transformation and other marks of good practice in PTR.
7 PTR and transferability.

1 Approaching an understanding of TR and introducing PTR

It is difficult to date precisely the birth of theological reflection as a discrete methodological form within the field of practical theology, but it seems to have developed through the coming together of insights from three parallel, though not contiguous, related movements in the twentieth century: liberation theology, which evolved in Latin America in the 1950s and 60s; the Clinical Pastoral Education Movement, which grew from the work of Anton Boisen (see also Aden, 1990) in the 1920s onwards; and various attempts to formalize and enhance the application of reflective practice in professional training programmes developed from the work of the philosopher John Dewey (1991). This crystallized in the experiential learning cycle developed by Daniel Kolb (1984) and others in the 1980s, and within the growing discipline of practical theology, to the development of the pastoral cycle as a core model for reflective practice (see pp. 51ff).

The development of practical theology as a distinct theological field is itself recent. Theology as taught in theological colleges for ministerial formation at least until the 1960s consisted almost entirely of historical, biblical, doctrinal and ethical studies. The newly ordained were left to their own devices to bridge the temporal, conceptual and cultural gap between their studies at college and the life and events of the individuals and communities among whom they were then sent to minister. Gradually 'pastoralia' and then 'pastoral studies' were tacked on as an extra to the main body of material studies. It wasn't until the late twentieth century that it was more generally recognized as a significant part of ministerial training and formation and even then it remained – and still remains – optional in some routes or courses.

Theological reflection is central to, and perhaps even the defining element of, practical theology, but is not synonymous with it. It is the means by which connections are made between other aspects of theological discipline and its application in pastoral practice, and the process by which pastoral events and situations are reviewed in the light of theological understanding. The implications of this are explored further in the sections which follow.

A recent book that is particularly useful in illustrating different approaches to TR is *Theological Reflection: Methods* (Graham *et al*, 2005). This work begins with a plea for a more holistic approach in the teaching and learning of theology such that biblical, historical and systematic theology should be presented and assimilated contextually and integrated with TR at all levels. It then distinguishes seven different approaches to TR, most of which have long antecedents (see box).

Seven approaches to TR summarized

1 **'Theology by heart': the living human document**
   Experiences of God mediated and evaluated through personal experience, particularly through journalling and the telling of personal stories
   and attempts at self-understanding.
2 **'Speaking in parables': constructive narrative theology**
   Listening to a variety of accounts from alternative and unexpected
   sources and stories and relating these imaginatively to traditional
   perspectives.
3 **'Telling God's story': canonical narrative theology**
   Looking at the world in the perspective of God's revelation and discernment as suggested and illustrated in the biblical narrative.
4 **'Writing the body of Christ': corporate theological reflection**
   An examination of the ways in which congregations could, or do, create their own corporate narrative by consciously or unconsciously using
   particular themes, practices and metaphors, such as that of 'the body
   of Christ' and other particular images and symbols in discussion and
   liturgy.
5 **'Speaking of God in public': correlation**
   Theological reflection understood as a critical conversation between
   the Christian tradition and culture as expressed in the fruits of intellectual, technological, artistic and social development.
6 **'Theology-in-action': praxis**
   The work of discipleship understood as perceiving God's work in history and enabling it in the present through making his incarnational
   love real in pastoral and practical care and in working for justice alongside the suffering and the marginalized.
7 **'Theology in the vernacular: local theologies**
   This approach attempts to enable the understanding and expression
   of Gospel truths, stripped of dominant cultural accretions, to be translated and developed in different local and temporal cultures.

The approaches to TR outlined in the box are descriptive rather than prescriptive. The authors of *Theological Reflection: Methods* are not setting out to
demonstrate what TR is and how it should be practised, but rather to examine,

classify and shed light on processes already at work in historical and contemporary situations and identify and describe what they have observed.

The purpose of this present book is different. It is to make guidelines available to experienced and inexperienced students of practical theology, and anyone preparing for ministry, or wanting to examine the integration of faith and practice in their lives more systematically; guidelines in the practice of the kind of TR which will help them to engage with 'lively ecstatic theology that dances, puzzles, stimulates, delights, strikes sparks from contemporary experience and transforms individuals and communities' (Pattison, 2000 p. 219).

The most helpful approach for this purpose, of those outlined above (Graham *et al.* 2005), is that described as 'Theology-in-action' (though there is some overlap in the detail, with some of the other approaches described). This TR approach we have here refined and defined more closely in order to distinguish it clearly from other forms of theological reflection, and have called it PTR, or 'Progressing Theological Reflection', for short. We have tried to encapsulate its key characteristics under the 'Five Ps' as in the box below.

PTR : Theological Reflection with five **P**s

PTR denotes theological reflection which is:
Progressing – moves on, transforms, starts at one place and leads on to another; enables new life.
Particular – focused on specific events and situations rather than general ideas and theories.
Potent/**P**rophetic – seeking to know and be and do God's truth, mediated through scripture, tradition, prayer and, perhaps, revelation, for this particular situation.
Practical – rooted in the here and now and resulting in definite action.

To appreciate the full richness of this 'praxis' tradition, and its practical value, it is helpful to relate it to its cousins in other professions, and to its antecedents in liberation theology. These subjects form the nucleus of the rest of Part 1 of this book. Part 2 considers the elements and resources for PTR. In Part 3 there is a shift from focusing on PTR as the gold standard of pastoral practice to a consideration of its wider contribution in the context of theological wisdom and political struggle.

2 PTR and reflective practice in other professions

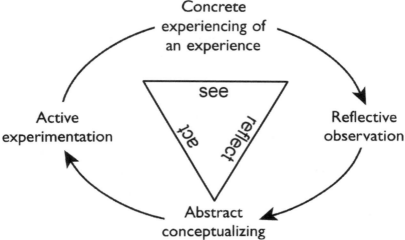

Figure 1: Kolb's learning cycle (simplified).

PTR is, among other things, a specific approach to theological reflection from a critical distance, with as much objectivity as possible. Reflection with a critical perspective has, of course, existed for as long as human beings have been able to think about and articulate what they do and why they do it: but, with the work of philosopher John Dewey in the 1930s, in the field of education reflective practice began to be a conscious and deliberate part of professional training. Gradually, other writers refined and developed Dewey's rather linear and individualistic pattern for reflection into a process with distinct phases which could be transferred and replicated. In 1984 Daniel Kolb formulated this into an 'experiential learning cycle' (Figure 1) which forms the basis for many similar models that have been developed since – including the pastoral cycle (see Figures 2 & 3 on pages 23 and 56). Such cycles, at their simplest, have three phases:

SEE – REFLECT – ACT

though many have a fourth, allowing an extra dimension of reflection, specifically relating it to the particular discipline in which it is being used:

EXPERIENCE – REFLECTION – THEORY – ACTION

In the 1980s Donald Schön (1983; 1987) was particularly influential in establishing reflective practice as a crucial component of professional performance. He drew an important distinction between reflection-in-action (when the practitioner would have to draw on internalized theory to make an in-the-moment decision) and reflection-on-action, which allows for a retrospective review, leading to an evaluation of action and new learning for future occasions.

There are four fields of professional practice, besides that of Christian ministry, in which reflective practice has become established as normative, each with a slightly different form of practice: education, medicine, social work and counselling.

In counselling, reflection takes place largely through regular in-depth meetings with a supervisor in the role of a critical friend who can offer both support and ask pertinent and searching questions. In social work, a similar function is served by regular team meetings in which colleagues raise with each other issues and critical questions which enable re-evaluation to feed into the next phase of action. In medicine and education, similarly, there are regular meetings with colleagues, guided by means of reflection. The practice in all four cases has developed from the Action–Reflection model, into a specific, focused process. It is an equivalent focused process for practical theology that PTR, as described in this and the next two chapters, is intended to provide.

3 PTR and liberation theology

The place of theology in PTR is critical since this is the element of TR which clearly distinguishes it from other forms of reflective practice. Liberation theology is particularly significant, since it is based on a distinctive method of relating theology and practice which has many similarities with the secular development of reflective practice outlined in the previous section. Liberation theology evolved initially in the Roman Catholic Church in Latin America over roughly the same period as the development of reflective practice in other professions. It was in that context that, even as early as the sixteenth century, Bartolomé de las Casas had denounced (1974) the oppression of the native Americans practised by many who claimed to be bringing the Christian gospel to the benighted. Such voices of criticality, though largely ignored by those in power, then had a long history, and, eventually, elements of it connected with the practice of

Action–Reflection groups developed among progressive Catholics in the 1960s. These groups, in turn, became strongly influenced by the model of experiential learning developed initially by the Belgian priest Joseph Cardijn, who worked between the wars (Green, 1990, pp. 23–4), and then by Paulo Freire (1996). Drawing on Marxist principles for empowering the poor through critical engagement with their direct experience and a commitment to work for change, this model encouraged participants, not simply to reflect, but to work for the transformation of the reality in which they found themselves, and thus take control of their own lives.

Crucial in this process was the Marxist notion of *praxis*, which means not simply 'practice' but action informed by a correct analysis of the situation. The leaders of this movement, now known as liberation theologians, such as Gustavo Gutiérrez (1984, 2001), Juan-Luis Segundo (1982), and Leonardo Boff (1996, 1997) were very clear that they were not trying to undertake an exercise in applied theology (i.e. beginning with theological principles and then trying to put them into practice) but one which began and ended in practical engagement. Theology, they argued, is not in the business of dispensing timeless certainties but of informing and inspiring faithful praxis. Segundo even asserted, in the teeth of most traditional approaches: 'Christians should not redefine social praxis by starting with the gospel message. They should do just the opposite. They should seek out the historical import of the gospel by starting with social praxis' (Segundo, 1982, p. 85).

Figure 2: Pastoral cycle according to Segundo.

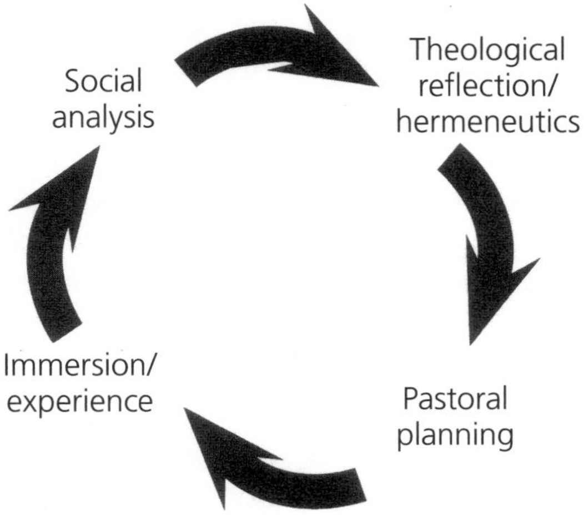

Social analysis

Theological reflection/ hermeneutics

Immersion/ experience

Pastoral planning

Segundo's version of the pastoral cycle (Figure 2; from Graham *et al.*, 2005, p. 188) illustrates this process, the working out of which not only leads to new action and practical commitment, but also enables participants to recognize their own complicity in the social matrix of 'structural sin' which helps to cause the problems under scrutiny.

The pastoral cycle familiar in current western approaches to TR over the last 30 years has tended to become more anodyne and even rather abstract (a wonderful contradiction, given that the concept is specifically about practice) but it still retains some of the features of the liberation approach: particularly that of beginning and ending in praxis and including a 'thick description' (see Chapter 3.1.b) of the social context in which the event takes place. Both the value and the difficulty of using PTR to analyse and influence institutions and social structures is further explored in Chapter 9.

4 PTR and ministerial practice

All faiths, to a greater or lesser extent, emphasize the importance of *orthopraxis* (right action) as well as *orthodoxy* (right belief or worship). Just as, in doctrine, some faiths and denominations within them are more prescriptive than others in terms of what the faithful should believe, so some are more precise than others about how faith should be translated into daily living. While such regulations apply to all believers of a particular expression of faith, those who exercise accredited ministry are expected to exemplify very clearly, by what they do, say and are, the truths which the faith proclaims, both within and on behalf of their faith community.

There will be many instances in the life of a church – or any faith community – when what is done or said or decided upon, or the manner in which it is done, seriously fails to live up to the fundamental teachings and beliefs that it proclaims. Such failures will impact not only on the relationships between groups and individuals within that particular faith community, but also on connections and perceptions in the wider community – for which the church's actions tend to speak louder than words (Cameron *et al.*, 2005). For these reasons, but perhaps even more importantly, in order to be true – in the case of a church – to the message of the Christian gospel, regular, prayerful and analytical reflection on practice is essential. A careful and disciplined use of an appropriate model of PTR by the church leaders, and indeed by the whole church community, is one way of ensuring that such evaluation takes place regularly. The exercise below gives you an opportunity to see what this might mean in practice. As well as, or instead of, the two examples given, you might identify a current issue in your own church which would benefit from such a process of reflection and evaluation.

Situation 1

The Bouncy Castle, hired at considerable expense, for the church fete, turns up late. The minister, wearing her dog collar, angrily berates the poor driver – who was genuinely delayed by a distressing accident. As a result of her own anxiety that, because of its lateness, the bouncy castle may end up making a loss, she uses language and voice tone at which both the driver and amused bystanders become rather shocked, and, as a result of which, the minister herself subsequently feels very ashamed. Although the fete was a resounding success in terms of the money it raised overall and the interaction with members of the local community, the minister found herself, at the end of the day, not only exhausted but depressed and demoralized.

Situation 2

The church building on the edge of a fairly large council estate is the subject of frequent petty vandalism and minor theft. Groups of young people quite often come in noisily during church services and sometimes climb onto the theoretically inaccessible church roof. Flowers are picked and shrubs decapitated, and broken glass, empty cans and litter of all kinds left in the small tarmac area in front of the church and the rather unkempt garden around it. These related problems are a recurring matter of heated discussion at church meetings. Some members would like the police to be called whenever young people come near the premises and insist that they should be kept away from the building at all times (without specifying how this might be done!); others believe passionately that the church and the gospel are open to all, especially the young, the wayward and the vulnerable and those on the margins, and that a youth club and special events should be set up especially for them (again, the resourcing of such projects is unspecified). Matters come to a head after one particularly alarming incident, and the minister and church stewards are at their wits' end.

Exercise

On your own or, preferably, in a small group, imagine that you are an established member of the church involved in one or both of these situations and describe a process of PTR that will shed some light on understanding what is happening and what action might be taken next, and how this may be done with integrity of belief and practice. If possible, compare your reflective process with that of others and record your learning from the exercise.

5 Defining and refining

It is easier to say what PTR isn't than what it is! What PTR clearly isn't is reacting defensively to a challenging situation by finding as many texts and references-to-tradition as possible to 'prove' the rightness of your position, without any attempt to stand back from it and submit it with an open mind in prayer and critical and theological analysis. Indeed, any kind of 'proof-texting' is always a danger signal. PTR, as emerges in Chapter 4, requires a deeper and richer engagement with sacred text, and is a much more subtle, deeply engaging, delicate, intricate and beautiful activity than that of offering superficial 'proofs'.

Nor is PTR the quest to find theological words with which to 'baptize' practices, theories and conclusions that have been arrived at on completely untheological grounds, so that they look religious and can be used to claim authority for their users. This is an ideological misuse of PTR which seeks to defend rather than explore experience. It is sometimes found in church debates where the word 'theology' may be used to browbeat opponents into accepting that, as far as God is concerned, they are in the wrong. Even at a local pastoral level the use of 'theology' or theological concepts in practice and in conversation can sometimes be a way of avoiding people and the realities they are having to deal with, rather than going deeper into things. When people are facing serious illness or other painful circumstances, for example, some Christians provide theological rationales for its being God's will – thus protecting themselves, and believing they are protecting their faith, rather than sharing fully and honestly the other person's distress. PTR invites us to allow experience to question our received traditions, in order to be led to renewed theological understanding every bit as much as allowing theological understanding to enlighten experience and influence future action.

Equally, PTR isn't personal, psychological or sociological reflection on an event or experience in the absence of any theological understanding, themes or perspectives. What differentiates *theological* reflection from reflection in other fields and contexts is precisely that whatever the issue under scrutiny, and however unrelated it may seem at first sight to themes in sacred text and tradition, a rigorous exploration is undertaken to discover how a theological perspective may illuminate, interrogate and suggest alternative ways of acting, in a process that also sheds new light on that theological perspective. One test of good PTR is an interillumination between theology and practice that leaves neither unchanged (see Chapters 4 and 8).

So much for what PTR *isn't*. You may, by now, have a clear sense of what theological reflection *is*. Whether you have or not, you are invited to do the following exercise:

Exercise

Before turning the page to see various definitions of TR that have been offered by a number of practical theologians, write your own definition of PTR in about fifty words. If possible, do this exercise in pairs or small groups, and then compare the merits of the different definitions suggested. Keep a copy of your initial definition and see how it evolves as you work through the material in this book.

Definitions of theological reflection

Definition 1

The process of bringing to bear in the practical decisions of ministry the resources of the Christian faith (Whitehead and Whitehead, 1995, p. ix).

Definition 2

A *critical conversation* which takes place between the Christian tradition, the student's own faith presuppositions and a particular contemporary situation (Pattison 2000, p. 136).

Definition 3

The cognitive component of piety … the insightfulness and knowledge that runs out of and shapes the attitudes and dispositions of the self in its apprehension of God and the world in relation to God (Osmer, 2005).

Definition 4

The discipline of exploring our individual and corporate experience in conversation with the wisdom of a religious heritage. The conversation is a genuine dialogue that seeks to hear from our own beliefs, actions and perspectives, as well as from those of the tradition. It respects the integrity of both. Theological reflection, therefore, may confirm, challenge, clarify and expand how we understand our own experience and how we understand the religious tradition. The outcome is new truth and meaning for living (Killen and de Beer, 2002, p. 51).

Definition 5

The habitual, conscious, methodical and purposeful correlation of some of the insights and resources of the theological tradition with contemporary situations and practice, resulting in a continuous process of critical awareness, transformation and action (Pattison and Thompson, unpublished).

Exercises

1 For each of these five definitions, note carefully:
   • what elements they have in common;
   • what elements are particular to each definition;
   • what elements are present or absent in each case.
2 Now analyse your own definition and those of others you are working with in the same way, and compare them with those offered in the box above.
3 In the light of your analysis of these definitions of TR, refine your own definition to express as accurately as you can, for now, the process that you hope to engage with whenever you undertake PTR, whether as a module requirement or for your own benefit, or with other members of your church or faith community.

---

6 Transformation and other marks of good practice in PTR

While it is clearly helpful to find a satisfying definition of your understanding of PTR, that doesn't necessarily mean that you will immediately become perfect at doing it in practice! You need a means of looking critically at your reflective process, with objectivity and acuity to help you assess whether what you have done equates with what you set out to do. The series of questions listed in the box below are designed to help with such an evaluation of any PTR exercise (in real life, as well as the ones in this book). The questions are designed to elicit responses in relation to any piece of work in this field, and suggest criteria for high aspirations which though probably unattainable, help to keep a clear model of ideal usage in mind. You are unlikely ever to score a list of straight 'Yeses' but if the number of 'Noes' exceeds the number of 'Yeses' this may indicate that you need to let go of preconceptions and enter more fully into open-minded and adventurous exploration in your engagement with PTR.

Heather Walton's marks of good practice in PTR (Walton, 2006)[5]

1 Is it compelling, interesting, desirable, exciting? (Is it sexy?)

2 Does it 'wrestle with an angel in the night', not letting go until it yields a blessing? (Gen. 32.22–32)? Does it strike sparks from the flint of tradition ? (Are you wrestling with tradition?)

3 Does it involve a real encounter with 'alterity', something that is alien to you, does it emerge from a collision with strangeness or a stepping out into the unknown, never to return (part of an Abrahamic pilgrimage – Gen. 12.1–4)? (Are you engaging with the other?)

4 Is it alarming and worrying? Does it leave you wondering what others might think or include fearsome revelation? (Is it scary?)

5 Does it touch the pain of the world? Does it connect with the image of picking out glass from the world's wounds, weeping as God weeps? (Does it hurt?)

6 Does it contribute to healing, reconciliation, justice? (Does it help?)

7 Does it have simplicity and grace – analogous to the 'beauty' used as a criterion in the scientific community? (Is it beautiful?)

8 Does it have the qualities of part of an authentic journey drawing closer to the heart of God? (Does it lead you to an open space?)

9 Does it sparkle? Have life? Is it integrative, growing authentically from tradition while being rooted and grounded in praxis? (Does it help to glorify God and lead the participants to worship and love?)

The use of questions such as those provided in the box can help to remind practitioners that PTR must always be a matter of genuine critical enquiry, engagement with 'otherness' and being ready to let go of the familiar and to reach out into the unknown. 'Transformation' is the key concept that sums up the kind of experience that the questions highlight. Reflectors need to expect to be changed in terms of previously held views or assumptions, and expect to see things in new light and a wider, deeper context. For this to happen, it is necessary when bringing a particular situation to the scrutiny of theological reflection to approach it with real wondering and open-mindedness. This isn't always easy to do, particularly if the matter under review is one about which you have long held a very definite view, well rooted – so you have always believed – in scripture and tradition, or if you have vested interests at stake. PTR entails letting go of assurance and foregone conclusions, embracing uncertainty, mystery and not-knowing, and being ready for surprise and revelation – and even the recognition of having previously been wrong. Such 'negative capability' (see Chapter 5.3) is not easy, but the process of transformation rarely is.

There are plenty of examples in life and in scripture of people who have experienced such transformation. Consider for example: Jonah on the way to Nineveh, the disciples on the road to Emmaus, Philip and the Ethiopian Eunuch, Peter at Joppa, Martin Luther, George Fox, John Wesley, Oscar Romero, Albert Schweitzer, and, perhaps, Karl Barth. On the whole, of course, transformation through the consciously undertaken process of PTR is likely to be on a smaller scale, and less dramatic, though no less significant. A minister who has reached an impasse on a particular issue and is falling victim to creeping despair suddenly sees things quite differently, and finds a new way of working. On the surface, nothing has changed. The issues are the same, the people involved are the same and the pervading sense of intransigence is the same; but through an experience of transformation, how it is perceived and understood, and possibilities for future development and action, have become significantly different.

Exercise

- Make brief notes on the process of transformation for some of those listed above, and identify the key elements in this process. In what ways are they similar and dissimilar?
- Identify others, whether historically or recently or from your own direct or indirect life experience, who have had comparable transforming encounters. Compare the key features of these with those in the previous exercise.
- How might these key features be similar to and how might they be different from the key elements involved in the transformative process in PTR?

7 TR and transferability

Such transformative moments are often intense, emotional and, almost by definition, subjective. The potential for self-delusion is all too apparent. For this reason, another key hallmark of authentic PTR is its 'transferability'. In the moment of transformation, the reflective process needs to be open-ended, unrestricted and creative, open to the movement of the Spirit – in whatever way this is understood. But following that, by means of systematic process, it needs careful evaluation. In other words, though the process of enlightenment may be intense, personal and internal, for the results of that process to be trusted and considered safe to act upon, the experience needs to be capable of being shared with others, reviewed from a critical distance and externalized – a process that is no less part of the work of the Spirit. Only so can the insights, new ways of thinking and acting become transmissible and applied in practice. How this may be done is discussed further in Chapter 10.3.

Summary

This chapter has:

- noted the spectrum of TR approaches explored in a recent publication (Graham *et al.*, 2005) and, from among them,
- identified 'praxis' or 'theology-in-action' as that which is closest to the method explored and described in this book, to which we have given the acronym PTR to differentiate it clearly from other approaches;
- related PTR to its antecedents in the methodology of reflective practice in other professions and, specifically, in the field of liberation theology and to the development of the pastoral cycle (see also Chapter 3);
- pinpointed with a couple of examples and an exercise the importance of PTR in relating life and faith in ministerial practice;
- offered a variety of definitions of TR in the search for an appropriate definition of PTR for the reader's use;
- provided a checklist of the marks of authentic PTR; and
- noted the importance both of transformation, and a shift in perception and action as a result of the process; and of its transferability for use by others and in other situations.

Thus equipped with a brief description of the history of the evolution and theory of TR we turn, in Chapter 2, to three worked examples of its use in practice, which, between them, provide a paradigmatic reference point for what is meant by PTR in this book.

Further reading (see also Core Texts at the end of the book)

Aden, L. (1990), *Turning Points in Pastoral Care: The Legacy of Anton Boisen and Seward Hiltner*, Grand Rapid: Baker Books.

Boff, L. (1997), *Ecclesiogenesis: The Base Communities Reinvent the Church*, Maryknoll NY: Orbis Books.

Boff, L. and C. (1996), *Introducing Liberation Theology*, New York: Orbis Books.

Cameron, H., Richter, D., Davies, D. and Ward, F. (eds) (2005), *Studying Local Churches: A Handbook*, London: SCM Press.

Cochrane, J. (1999), *Circles of Dignity: Community Wisdom and Theological Reflection*, Minneapolis: Ausburg Fortress Press.

Croft, S. and Walton, R. (2005) *Learning for Ministry: Making the Most of Study and Training*, London: Church House Publishing.

Dewey, J. (1991), *How we Think*, New York: Prometheus Books.

Freire, P. (1996), *Pedagogy of the Oppressed*, Harmondsworth: Penguin.

Freire, P. (2005), *Education for Critical Consciousness*, London and New York: Continuum.

Graham, E., Walton, H. and Ward, F. (2005), *Theological Reflection: Methods*, London: SCM Press.

Green, L. (1990), *Let's Do Theology*, London: Continuum.

Green, L. (1990), *Let's Do Theology*, London: Mowbray. Later editions published by Mowbray (2000) and Continuum (2001).

Gutiérrez, G. (1984) *We Drink from our Own Wells: The Spiritual Journey of a People*, London: SCM Press.

Gutiérrez, G. (2001), *A Theology of Liberation*, London: SCM Press.

Killen, P. and de Beer, J. (2002), *The Art of Theological Reflection*, New York: Crossroad.

Kolb, D. (1984), *Experiential Learning: Experience as the Source of Learning and Development*, New Jersey: Prentice Hall.

Las Casas, Bartolemé de, 1974, *In Defence of the Indians*, Northern Illinois University Press.

Moon, J. (2004), *Reflection in Learning and Professional Development*, Abingdon: Routledge Falmer.

Mudge, L. and Poling, J. N. (eds) (1987), *Formation and Reflection: The Promise of Practical Theology*, Philadelphia: Fortress Press.

Osmer, R. (2005), *The Teaching Ministry of Congregations*, Louisville KY: Westminster John Knox Press.

Pattison, S. (1989), *Some Straw for the Bricks*, in Pattison and Woodward (2000), pp. 135–45.

Pattison, S. (2000), *A Critique of Pastoral Care*, third edition, London: SCM Press.

Pattison, S. and Woodward, J. (2000), *The Blackwell Reader in Pastoral and Practical Theology*, Oxford: Blackwell.

Schön, D. (1983), *The Reflective Practitioner: How Professionals Think in Action*, New York: Basic Books.

Schön, D. (1987) *Educating the Reflective Practitioner: Toward a New Design for Teaching and Learning in the Professions*, New York: Basic Books.

Segundo, J.-L. (1982), *The Liberation of Theology*, Maryknoll NY: Orbis Books.

Walton, H. (2006), lecture delivered at the Conference of the British and Irish Association for Practical Theology, Manchester, July.

Whitehead, J. and Whitehead, E. (1995), *Method in Ministry: Theological Reflection and Christian Ministry*, Lanham, Chicago, New York, Oxford: Sheed and Ward.

2

PTR in Practice: Some Simple Paradigms

Chapter 1 has outlined various approaches to TR and within them focused in particular on the theology-in-action praxis approach. A variety of definitions have been considered, together with some of the characteristics that the process of PTR can be expected to enable.

There are a number of models that can be used as a basis to develop your own approach, some of which are described in Chapter 3. This chapter confines itself to three examples, described in outline, but with the element of theological enquiry described in some detail. In our experience, those seeking to put theological reflection into practice find identifying a situation for reflection and building a 'thick descriptor' around it (see Chapter 3.1.b) relatively straightforward, but then often struggle (or simply omit) to relate the matter to and engage with scripture and theological tradition. The examples which follow demonstrate ways in which this may be done. They are not perfect and are unambitious in the issues addressed, but together, provide a basic paradigm for the process of PTR, which, as you will remember, is:

Progressing – moves on, transforms, starts at one place and leads on to another; enables new life;
Particular – focused on specific events and situations rather than general ideas and theories;

> **Potent/Prophetic** – seeking to know and be and do God's truth, mediated through scripture, tradition, prayer and, perhaps, revelation, for this particular situation;
> **Practical** – rooted in the here and now and resulting in definite action.

Like most of the examples and exercises given in this book, the situations are drawn from real life experience, but suitably disguised to protect the anonymity of the people and places involved. The examples in this chapter illustrate PTR being used in different ways: first, to help make an important decision; second, to help a community review their community project; and third, to aid an individual's reflection on her spiritual journey.

Example 1

Sean was a keen young curate whose vicar had encouraged him to take responsibility for one of three churches in the parish – a rather miserable Victorian 'daughter church', which had probably always been surplus to requirements and now looked marooned and out of place on the very large outer-city council estate that had grown up round it. It was draughty and rather ugly (in Sean's view) with rigid, dark pews, unsatisfactory heating, no available meeting room separate from the worship area (making children's activities during the service almost impossible), and an average Sunday congregation of 15 who struggled to pay the bills and 'parish share' to keep it going. Sean liked a challenge, but his response to the situation was rather different from what Mary, the vicar, had in mind. Believing in meeting people where they are, Sean had taken to visiting the local pub (not far from the church) fairly regularly, and had become quite friendly with the landlord and his family. Rita, the landlord's wife, told him she used to come to church quite regularly when her children were small, and occasionally since then, but now the pub had started doing Sunday lunches it was difficult to take the time off. 'But why not hold a service in the pub sometimes,' she said, mischievously, 'then I could be included again?' The idea appealed to Sean immediately, and he asked her to talk it over with her husband, Darren, to see if it might be a serious possibility. So it came about that Sean found himself asking Mary if she would allow him to give the idea a trial run on Mothering Sunday.

Mary wasn't very happy about the idea. She saw herself in the tradition of early twentieth-century High Church Anglican priests who had sought to bring to inner-city areas a beauty of worship which could lift participants out of the grind and dreariness of their everyday lives, enabling them to glimpse and share something of the glory of God when they came to church. Using the pub as a place of worship seemed the antithesis of this model, and in danger of giving the wrong message, with under-age drinking becoming a serious problem on the estate. Sean's enthusiasm was persuasive, and not wanting to stifle his first initiative, she reluctantly agreed to let it go ahead, having obtained the Bishop's permission on a one-off basis.

The service was timed for 11.30, finishing in time for Mothering Sunday lunch bookings. Rita and Darren made sure it was well publicized and it caught the imagination of many of the regulars: support, participation and appreciation was impressive, and the service itself, a simple family service with appropriate songs to well-known tunes, flowers for all and an engaging address, had a liveliness about it rarely seen in the church building. There was a spontaneous request for a more regular event, at least monthly, and Sean began to dream of closing the church building completely and using the pub instead!

Mary was pleased that the Mothering Sunday service had been well received, but did not want it to become a regular event. She was a traditionalist at heart, and felt very uneasy about losing the sense of awe and otherness that were part of entering a church building (nineteenth-century gloom, in Sean's view). If she was honest, Mary was also uncomfortable about losing control of the way worship was prepared for and presented, and disliked being thought of as trying to be 'trendy'. Sean and Mary had a useful debrief on the Mothering Sunday service, but when Mary questioned whether it had really been worship of God, transcendent and immanent, or simply Mothers' Day entertainment, Sean could feel himself becoming angry, especially as it began to look as if a monthly service was out of the question.

He suggested, and Mary readily agreed, that rather than get stuck in opposing arguments they should do some PTR around the issue. As they worked together to build a 'thick descriptor' they both began to feel much calmer. They included social, cultural and psychological issues, and a recognition of spiritual emptiness and malaise in society in general and the bleakness and fear evident on the estate where they worked in particular. They also acknowledged the real and perceived cultural and emotional gulf that existed between life on the estate and the traditions, values and practices of the church.

They then moved on to seek enlightenment from scripture and tradition. Tradition was ambiguous with, on the one hand, a compelling strand of Puritanism, asceticism, the temperance movement, Sunday observance and the emphasis on the holiness and 'otherness' of God. On the other hand, fellowship, rejoicing together and meeting people where they are and on their own terms had been a hallmark of evangelism from St Paul at Athens onwards, including the embracing – with subtle changes – of pagan festivals, secular music and the comfortable Christianizing of what became the Holy Roman Empire, and much else in the various periods of revival. Early Methodism had been characterized by a heroic readiness to reach out to people where they were – but also insisted on abstinence from alcohol. Being 'in the world but not of the world' (John 15—16) had always been a difficult challenge for the Church.

However, Jesus' 'bias to the poor', his call to sinners rather than the righteous, and his readiness to associate with, welcome, and receive from prostitutes and sinners, were recurring gospel themes. The turning of water into wine at the wedding at Cana (John 2), in addition to its symbolic significance, seemed to suggest permission for lively conviviality. Jesus clearly had no time for the outward 'correct' trappings of religion – the official places and procedures for worship. Rather than worshipping 'in Jerusalem', Jesus said 'true worshippers will worship the Father in spirit and in truth' (John 4.21–25). Luke 18.9–14 was relevant but ambiguous. It was clearly the 'sinner' who went away whole and healed and in a right relationship with God, rather than the pious and fastidious Pharisee: though it was as a result of going to the Temple to pray that all this had come about.

As they prayed and pondered over all this, it was Mary rather than Sean who said that, on balance, following up the initiative in the pub seemed more in keeping with what they had encountered in their reflection than putting an end to it. For his part, Sean had become more aware of the possible misunderstandings and misinterpretations of such a physical shift from church to pub, and the need to proclaim the gospel rather than just have a merry time with a slightly churchy flavour. They agreed to proceed in this way:

- to seek agreement of the church council and diocesan authorities to go ahead cautiously with a monthly family service in the pub on a year's trial basis;
- to try to ensure that worship in the pub contained within it opportunities for quiet prayer and reflection and encounter with God, with the 'entertainment' element not more than 50 per cent and always closely related to the theme of the day;
- to keep two forms of 'journal':
  - a book for people at the pub to write in it prayer requests and responses to the monthly service;
  - a journal kept by Sean and others who helped to lead the worship on their own experience and reflections on what happened each month and on developments between services connected with it;
- to keep a supply of cards in the pub, inviting anyone who wished, to attend the weekly service in church, or its Wednesday coffee morning, or/and to contact Sean or Mary to talk over issues raised for them;
- to review matters regularly with Darren and Rita and others who emerged as regular attenders at the pub service;
- to seek assistance from diocesan resources and to make contact with the 'Fresh Expressions' initiative, based in Oxford, which offered experience, training and resources for innovative and alternative approaches to worship; and to visit other churches trying similar approaches;
- To review the matter every six months with each other, and with the church council.

Example 2

The situation detailed below arose in a village we will call Little Winterton in an ecumenical project based on St John's Anglican Church which is centrally situated close to the shops, the pub and the post office. Little Winterton has about 3,000 inhabitants and is a compact village, well serviced by local amenities, including a doctor's surgery, a garage, a mini recycling site, and even a library and information centre; and has a number of fairly flourishing local organizations such as a gardening club, a film club and amateur dramatics. The churches (Methodist, Quaker and Anglican) work increasingly closely together and share in a number of projects together, one of which is the focus of this study.

Just over a year ago, and after months of planning, it was decided to provide a weekly drop-in coffee morning on a Friday from 10 to 12.30 at the back of St John's Church, which has a glass partition separating it from the rest of the building, enabling it to be separately heated and made into quite a pleasant area available for meetings and events throughout the week. The aims of the Friday coffee morning were simply to provide hospitality and friendship for anyone who wished to come, both as an end in itself, and also as a simple attempt at outreach to those who didn't presently attend church and might be encouraged to think about doing so. A rota of people undertook to make the place as warm and welcoming as possible, and to maintain supplies of tea and coffee etc, and a separate rota of keen cooks provided cakes and biscuits. Nine Anglicans, five Methodists and two Quakers took their turn on the rotas and everyone welcomed the chance to work together in this way. Prices were kept as low as possible, subsidized by a little bring-and-buy stall. The aim was to break even and cover heating expenses, rather than to make money. It was well advertised with posters and leaflets around the village, and from the start was quite well patronized and well appreciated, with, on average, between ten and twenty people attending each week, and sometimes more.

Now that the project has been running for a year it was felt appropriate to hold a mini AGM and annual review, which was well attended. Both the vicar and the Methodist minister came, as well as church wardens and council members; almost everyone on the rotas came, and even one or two 'punters', all of whom had been invited.

A student, Anna, who happened to be on placement with the churches at the time, suggested that, once the nuts and bolts of the meeting had been concluded, people might be encouraged to raise any issues they felt needed airing to improve the overall development of the project in relation to its original aims, and to spend some time in prayer and reflection on these matters. The original aims had never formally been spelt out, and the discussion began with a brainstorm to tease out what they might be. The agreed list eventually looked like this:

1 to offer a ministry of welcome and hospitality to all who came;
2 to deepen existing friendships and to allow new ones to develop;
3 to provide an opportunity for new people, or people on their own, to meet and begin to get to know others living in the locality;
4 to enable helpers and visitors to relax and enjoy each other's company;
5 to encourage people to come inside the church and discover more about it, and the other local churches, for themselves;
6 to make it easier for visitors to become aware of what went on in church and what it stood for;
7 to provide a ready opportunity for those who wished to do so to learn more about the Christian faith and consider what meaning it might have in their own lives.

The group began by considering the overall context in which their little project was set, and identified a number of factors which seemed significant:

- the myth of the cosy village
- twenty-first-century relative isolation
- distrust of strangers
- sentimentality versus faith
- suspicion of traditional certainties and the Christian 'metanarrative'
- the history of the village and its recent expansion to include social housing
- shift in Sunday culture to exclude worship
- the emptiness of some people's lives
- the over-busyness of many

- need for friends and companions
- perceptions of 'us' and 'them'.

This generated a lot of discussion, and, at Anna's suggestion, a search for themes and images:

- a plant growing in stony and unfertile ground
- the search for an oasis in an arid desert
- living water/dry bones
- wandering in the wilderness
- Jesus in the stranger
- emptiness/abundance
- good news for the poor.

The group then divided into twos and threes to consider these themes, images and passages from the Bible and from the Christian tradition that seemed to relate to any or all of these issues. (A wide selection of Bibles, concordances and other books were provided.) After half an hour, these were shared, and included:

- grass that fades, God's word lives for ever (1 Pet. 1.24–25)
- rivers in the desert (Isa. 43.19–20), rivers of living water, baptism
- river of water of life flowing through the street of the city and yielding fruit (Rev. 22.1–2)
- singing the Lord's song in a strange land (Ps. 137.4)
- showing hospitality to strangers – entertaining angels unawares (Heb. 13.1–2)
- St Francis' welcome to all and delight in whatever is
- the ideal of monastic hospitality through the ages
- Jesus' being known in the breaking of bread (Luke 24.13–35)
- the visit of the angels to Abraham (Rublev's icon)
- people coming from all over the earth to sit at table in God's kingdom (Luke 13.29), messianic banquet (Luke 14.15–24)
- where two or three are gathered in my name, there am I in the midst of them (Luke 18.20)
- 'Love one another as I have loved you' (John 13.34), 'Love the aliens, for you were aliens in the land of Egypt' (Deut. 10.19)
- rejoice in the Lord (Ps. 32.11 and many others); 'I was glad to go into the

house of the Lord' (Ps. 122.10), 'rejoice with those who rejoice; weep with those who weep' (Rom. 12.15)
- food as a symbol of God's provision, abundance, rejoicing; a symbol of order; of spiritual nourishment
- ambiguity of the wilderness – a place apart for prayer and a place of evil, danger and decline – of deprivation and revelation.

The group were surprised to discover how absorbing and fruitful it felt to follow up themes, images and ideas generated in this way, and would happily have continued with the exercise for much longer. Having shared and explored further the results of what they had discovered with each other in the whole group, they then set about trying to crystallize all this into tangible pointers for developing their project in the future. These were:

- increased confidence in the value of what they were doing, small as it was, in continuing the tradition of godly welcome and hospitality;
- a deeper valuing of the opportunities for developing friendship and companionship with one another and with their guests;
- a sense of awe that the presence of Christ 'in the midst' of their little gathering might be a reality;
- recognizing that their visitors brought 'gifts' and were not just the passive recipients of hospitality;
- finding ways of 'rejoicing' and 'weeping' with each other and their visitors – celebrating birthdays and special events, marking anniversaries and times of loss and sadness;
- encouraging the sharing of gifts and talents;
- being ready to offer the opportunity for prayer and informal worship as part of the Friday morning 'package';
- taking special care of those who might easily feel left out;
- greater honesty among the helpers when they experienced difficulty working with each other, so that issues could be addressed and resolved

Not all of these new or revised perspectives and aspirations could be translated immediately into practical action. The group agreed to keep this list and use it at intervals to measure developments within the project. In the meantime, they committed themselves to:

- Pray regularly for everyone involved in the project, and have a 'prayer requests' poster available for anyone's use.
- Make the weekly coffee morning from 10 to 12 (instead of 12.30) but with these additions:
  - first Friday each month – finish with informal Eucharist, around the coffee tables, 12–12.30
  - third Friday each month – finish with informal prayer and song, 12–12.30
  - second and fourth Fridays to encourage participants in the later part of each morning to share with each other whatever anyone might like to offer – craft activities; poems; music; song; telling stories; short sketches; holiday experiences; other passions and interests.
- When there was a fifth Friday in the month, anyone who wished would be invited to stay from 12 to 12.30 to share as honestly as possible with each other about how the project was going, and to address any particular issues or difficulties that may have arisen; and make suggestions for developments.
- To develop a sense of a 'shared journey' among helpers and visitors, allowing friendships to develop, different ideas and approaches to be encouraged, and the sharing of joys and sorrows; to respect and value differing standpoints and perceptions – including those that questioned the church and the way it worked. (Because this commitment was the least tangible it was agreed to give it extra high priority.)
- To arrange an opportunity three times a year, when everyone involved in the project could meet for prayer, reflection and time together. No one would be expected to attend, but everyone would be welcome. The experience of today's reflection helped them to decide to use the time in a disciplined, structured way, and it was agreed to invite someone they knew in a neighbouring church who was experienced in this kind of approach to facilitate the first such meeting.

It was noted that in one way, these developments would make the project more overtly 'churchy' than had been originally intended; but at the same time the hidden agenda of encouraging church attendance had been replaced by a more open approach, allowing visitors to choose their own way and level of involvement on Friday mornings, and at other times.

Example 3

Ruth had served the Church all her adult life, and even as a child: first as a very committed lay person, then as an elder, then for many years as non-stipendiary minister while leading a very busy life as a headteacher. Retirement and the opportunity to spend more time with family and friends proved at first as joyous in reality as in anticipation. But gradually, Ruth became aware of feelings of malaise and emptiness. Her life continued to be busy with many requests for her as a speaker or contributor at meetings and conferences and for help in difficult pastoral or educational situations and to sit on various committees. But somehow, now that she no longer had a clear role, nor the authority to influence decisions and get things done, and was free to choose what she did and didn't take on, she had a strange sense of being adrift and loss of direction. 'It's almost', as she put it to a friend, 'as if I don't know who I am any more. Or maybe I never did, but was too busy to notice.' In her busy pre-retirement life, she had omitted to seek a new soul friend or spiritual director after the death of the person she had seen for many years. But having remedied this and begun to talk things over, she arranged to go on a two-day private retreat.

This helped her focus on a particular area of difficulty: prayer. Prayer for Ruth in her working life and ministry had often been rather rushed and had been pretty much focused on commending each busy day, and all the people she met, to God's love. She had found it easy enough to believe in God's love for others, and to seek guidance for herself, but realized she had rather avoided any sense of herself being in a loving relationship with God. As she looked out of the window in the retreat house prayer room, she felt hollow and rather desolate. She had used a PTR process often enough in her work and ministry, and it suddenly occurred to her that she could use it for her current situation. Having stayed with those uncomfortable feelings for some time, and noted down as much as she could about how and why this had come about – as the 'thick descriptor' (see Chapter 3.1.b) she then began to notice what she could see and hear. The relentless, purposeful hum of the motorway traffic in the distance reminded her of her former goal-directed life; the white clouds moving slowly and majestically across a clear blue sky seemed to suggest a – to her – unattainable contented acceptance of a God-given existence; but it was the birds, and the apparent differences in her subjective view of their 'moods', that particularly drew her attention. Some seemed to be flapping about rather aimlessly, some were clearly hunting or hovering for food; others seemed to be enjoying floating gently on the wind currents and just being alive.

Following her spiritual director's guidance, Ruth tried to put her usual goal-focused diligence on one side and approach all this in a more relaxed way than was customary for her. She decided to use her feelings and her observations as a basis for theological reflection, and made these notes, as a result of her prayer, study and reflection on these themes:

- Wandering in the wilderness:
  - Forty years in the wilderness needed to be endured (she read in *Lo and Behold*) 'to confront the anger of God, not to hurl it in others' faces, but in humility to confront it in ourselves, is to provide a knife to cut through the pious cant, and a fire to burn up our sentimentality and our complacency (Dennis, 1991, pp. 86–7).
  - Wilderness – place of revelation (Moses, Jacob, John the Baptist, Jesus).
  - Thirst – longing for God (Ps. 63.1).
  - Lost sheep (Luke 15.4). (Ruth had never noticed before that the 99 sheep – and presumably the lost one, too – were left 'in the wilderness'.)
  - Wilderness becoming a fruitful field (and vice versa; Isa. 32.15; Jer. 4.26).
  - Jesus' fasting and temptation (Matt. 4.1–11).
  - Desert Fathers found God especially in vast empty landscapes; *Extreme Pilgrim* – a programme Ruth had watched intermittently on television – showed this finding of God in desolate places still.
  - Letting go of attachments.
- Groaning and travailing: Ruth happened to pick up a copy of *Five for Sorrow, Ten for Joy* (Ward 1971) in the retreat house library, and found herself reading words which struck a chord with her current feelings:

  > There is … in the Church today a sharp, unsatisfied longing for God, the desire for freshness in Christian utterance … and an intense, perturbed self-questioning. This also is the presence of God. It has

been part of Christian experience of God from the beginning. St Paul writes about [how we] can only groan and fumble to express ourselves in struggles and longings that seem to be part of a great universal travail. It was his view that God is particularly present and deeply working there.

- Clouds: again and again, clouds seemed to symbolize the hidden but powerful presence of God:
  - pillar of cloud; God present but hidden; thick cloud on Mt Sinai (Exod. 19.16; 24.16)
  - clouds filling the Temple (1 Kings 8.10–11; 2 Chron. 5.13–14)
  - Isaiah 19.1–2: 'the Lord rides on a swift cloud'
  - Psalm 104: 'clouds his chariot'
  - transfiguration; ascension: a cloud obscuring Jesus
  - Cloud of Unknowing.
- Birds – night/sinister, vultures unclean; quails; snare of fowler; Psalm 124.7, soul escaped like bird out of snare; wings of dove – fly away and find rest; birds neither sowing nor reaping; sheltering wings; healing in his wings; God's wisdom in migration (Job 39.26), Jer 8.7; doves in Song of Songs; solitary desolate.
  - St Francis.
- Be still and know that I am God.

Ruth spent a couple of hours immersed in the wealth of material her images had suggested, browsing among the books in the library and reflecting. As she did so, and discovered or recalled so many instances in scripture and in the Christian tradition when others had experienced times of spiritual emptiness and desolation, and then found God in unexpected places – like Elijah on the mountain, finding God not in the whirlwind or earthquake or fire, but in the still, small voice (1 Kings 19.12). She began to feel she was in good company! Rather than a fraud and a failure, she felt as if she belonged to a huge company of people through the ages who had come close to God through doubt and struggle. As she prayed and wondered and looked out of the window at the now familiar landscape, she experienced a new sense of being held in God's loving embrace. It was not so much that she had rationally worked out in the light of the traditions she had explored that God was to be found in the wilderness and in loss of identity, as that the wealth of imagery had fused in her mind so that she could see the world around her in a new light. The same things surrounded her, but things that had seemed senseless, like the birds, or unattainable, like the clouds, now felt like parts of a Bible-shaped wilderness world to which she deeply belonged.

It seemed to her now that in her life until retirement, her very busy-ness on so many good and godly matters had, strangely, prevented her from ever encountering God in any meaningful way. She had had to keep all the strands of her life carefully under control in order to get everything done and stay on top. What had seemed to her recently a frightening state of loss of identity and purpose, and a state of spiritual emptiness was actually the means by which she could become open to God in a different way, allowing herself to be carried home, like the lost sheep. She no longer saw that image as sentimental but as representing a tough new calling to recognize her own need, and be more responsive to others' needs, rather than approaching everything and everyone with ready-made solutions.

In the light of all this, she resolved to:

- spend at least an hour in prayer or/and the same kind of exploratory reflection on at least three days each week;
- continue to enjoy – rather than be burdened by – such times of prayer and reflection; and to be alert to finding God in all things and meeting Christ in encounters with others;
- talk with her minister about reducing her church commitments retaining only those which were really needed from the church's point of view – not worrying about her own overt role, or lack of it;
- cut down the number of committees and conferences she attended, and say 'no' whenever possible to new requests;
- find someone to befriend and other ways of helping through the local volunteer bureau, approaching these things in a spirit of openness and wondering, without expecting to provide solutions;
- sell or dispose of some of the physical clutter of her life and live generally more simply, even monastically, to give her life more of a feel of travelling light through the wilderness;
- review the result of these commitments with her spiritual director in a month's time, and again six months later.

In all of these examples the encounter with scripture and tradition made a significant difference to the perceptions and decisions and actions of those involved. In each case, you may like to consider other theological resources that could have been used, and how they might have affected the outcome. You could also reflect on how these experiences might, in the long run, contribute to new theological perspectives.

Further reading (see also Core Texts at the end of the book)

Dennis, T. (1991), *Lo and Behold: The Power of Old Testament Storytelling*, London: SPCK.

Ward, N. (1971), *Five for Sorrow, Ten for Joy*, London: Epworth Press.

3

Ways and Means:
A Variety of PTR
Approaches and Models

In Chapter 1 a brief outline was provided of the evolution of TR in general and PTR in particular; and Chapter 2 provided some worked examples of PTR in practice. This chapter looks in more detail at some of the main models of PTR as currently taught and practised in theological colleges, departments and courses. These include:

1 The pastoral cycle: origins and development.
  a Kolb's learning cycle
  b The cycle in liberation and pastoral theology
  c Potential use in other faiths
  d A recent development of the cycle (Andrew Todd).
2 The pastoral cycle: variations
  a The reflective spiral (Laurie Green)
  b A five-phase cycle (Emmanuel Lartey)
  c Critical conversation (Stephen Pattison)
3 Clinical Pastoral Education
4 Reflection through insight and spiritual wisdom (Killen and de Beer)
5 Narrative reflective practice (Gillie Bolton, Heather Walton, Frances Ward)

1 The pastoral cycle: origins and development

a Kolb's learning cycle

As has already been noted (Chapter 1.2) the pastoral cycle, which forms a useful basis for the theoretical understanding of reflective pastoral practice, is derived from a similar approach in other fields illustrated by Kolb's experiential learning cycle, Figure 1 on p. 21.

According to this model there are four definite stages in the learning (Kolb links them to Piaget's developmental stages). Beginning with the identification of a specific 'concrete experience' the learner then distances herself sufficiently from it, mentally, to become an 'observer' of the situation, rather than an 'actor' in it, so that she becomes able to view the matter with analytic detachment. The next stage, that of 'abstract conceptualization', moves from impartial observation to the derivation and application of general rules and principles from and to the experience, which then allows the learner, at the final stage, to try out 'active experimentation' as she resumes the role of 'actor' but with new insight and choices. While this represents an over-simplification of how things happen in real life – particularly the neat four-step sequence – it is a useful model in stressing the importance for the learner of being able to move in and out of the roles of active participant and objective observer, something often of crucial importance in applying PTR in pastoral practice.

Exercise

Identify two or three 'mini events' in your life recently that have left you feeling uncomfortable. (For example, someone swearing at you when you slowed down while driving, not knowing which lane you needed to be in near a city centre junction; or perhaps you were the person who swore at such an offending driver and subsequently wished you hadn't; or a misunderstanding between you and a friend over a restaurant bill.) For each mini event:

1 Describe briefly your thoughts and feelings about the incident as it occurred.

2 Mentally switch into the role of an impartial observer of the situation and describe the event from that perspective.

3 Look carefully at the differences between 1 and 2 and see if you can abstract at least two 'rules' or general principles that could be useful to you whenever you are faced with a similar situation in future, so that you can begin to see things more objectively and choose how you respond, even while you are in the middle of it.

4 Imagine finding yourself in an almost identical situation in a few days' time. How would you respond differently?

5 What have you learnt from looking at experiences in this way, following the process of Kolb's learning cycle?

While everyone would surely benefit from being able to move in and out of the respective roles of active participant and detached observer in a difficult situation, it is often of particular importance in pastoral practice, where there is always a subtle danger that the person 'ministering' may unwittingly assume that their actions should be beyond question because they are doing God's work. The habitual use of the pastoral cycle can not only counteract this tendency, but also enrich and enliven the whole way of interpreting the interaction between faith and practice.

b The cycle in liberation and pastoral theology

A quick glance at Figure 2 on p. 23, comparing it with Kolb's learning cycle, Figure 1 on p. 21, gives the impression that the process is essentially the same, though there are different 'labels'. This impression is fairly accurate, but there is one significant difference which is crucial for PTR, namely, the element of theological insight from the reflector's faith tradition. In its simplest form, when represented diagrammatically, there is no discernible difference from that of Kolb's model, since these key elements are simply incorporated into the melting pot at the stages of reflective observation – including the production of a 'thick description' (see Box) – and abstract conceptualization (stages 2 and 3). In more detailed versions of this model (see below), the theological perspective has its own specific and separate phase in the cycle. This has the benefit of ensuring that theology doesn't get squeezed out amid all the other factors in the 'abstract conceptualization' phase. However, its being considered entirely separately in this way brings a certain self-consciousness into the process. Probably the most helpful way of getting over this difficulty in practice (as with the moving in and out of the 'actor' and 'observer' role described above) is to keep the theological element as a distinct part of the process at a theoretical level, while, in practice, moving freely between the different elements being considered, ensuring that theology is very much a live partner in the enterprise.

The 'thick description'

'Thick description' (or 'descriptor') is a core concept in theological reflection. It is a term introduced to anthropology by Clifford Geertz (1973) from the philosopher Gilbert Ryle (1970). Ryle's uses the example of a wink. A thin description would just say 'John winked', leaving the meaning of this event unclear. A 'thick description' would supply the context and interpretation, for example, 'John winked to indicate that he fancied me' or 'to show he knew my secret intention and would turn a blind eye to it' or 'because a fly had got into his eye'. In PTR it is important to fill out the bare facts of a situation with wider aspects of the context – sociological, psychological, historical and so forth – that might help to interpret it. The idea is to err on the side of excessive description, on the grounds that human behaviour is often ambiguous and explicable at several different levels at once, and we do not know which levels and aspects will provide food for reflection.

---

c Potential use by different faiths

The pastoral cycle, as it has so far been used in pastoral theology, has been studied and implemented almost exclusively from within the Christian tradition, but the cycle itself could equally well be applied in any faith tradition.

The elements of the cycle would be the same, but the content would be faith-specific. This was well illustrated in a television programme in the BBC *Dispatches* series in May 2006, which focused on pointers to reformation and future developments in Islam, and raised some fascinating parallels with the use of PTR in the Christian tradition. The presenter Tariq Ramadan and those he interviewed stressed that, in order to apply insights from Islam to modern life, sayings from the Qur'an and from traditional Islamic teachers had to be reflected on and reinterpreted for the very different social, practical and geographical circumstances in which many Muslims now live. Only thus, they said, could they be truly obedient to the ancient truths of their faith, instead of merely repeating a set of words and behaviours which did not touch the dilemmas and challenges faced daily by Muslims living in the modern western world. This is, of course, exactly the kind of thing that PTR is intended to enable its practitioners to do. Not all Muslims would be comfortable with such an approach, but for those who are, PTR provides a ready-made tool to assist in bringing fresh insight and vitality in their living out of their faith today.

The pastoral cycle in action

An outline example of the use of the pastoral cycle can be seen in the way a particular issue was resolved at a theological college. In the college chapel there was a tradition, going back at least a hundred years, that the tutors all sat in elevated seats at the back, with the principal's and vice-principal's seats distinguished by especially ornate carving, while the students sat on ordinary chairs in the main body of the chapel. Some members of staff felt uncomfortable about this but accepted the practice, until one day it was questioned by a new group of students, causing a certain amount of consternation. The situation was used as a focus for a group theological reflection, which provided the opportunity for a measured consideration of the issues involved. As may be imagined, the discussion was lively and not as systematic and clear cut as the summary below suggests. Although the sequence in discussion was fairly fluid (!), retrospectively the stages in this process were identified as follows:

1 **The clear identification of the issue.**
   This was agreed as the questioning of whether the long-standing tradition of having tutors in a place of worship sitting in a position and type of seating that identified them as superior and as exercising power and authority over the students was appropriate or authentic in a college which owed its existence to the formation and preparation of students for ministry in a church which proclaimed Christ as 'the one who serves' and who, in his life time, criticized the trappings of authority and power.

2 **The building of a 'thick description' around the issue.**
   Looking at context, perspective and some sociological and psychological factors. Matters raised included: changes in society about authority and hierarchy; psychological insights into the abuse of power; increasing informality in schools, colleges, institutions; overall trends towards egalitarianism; changing approaches to order and discipline.

3 **Ensuring that key insights from theology and faith tradition were included.**
   Relevant passages cited included: Matthew 20.25–28, 'whoever would be great must be your servant'; Luke 6.40, 'a disciple is not above his teacher' ; Luke 9.48, 'The least among you is the one who is great'. Authority-challenging episodes from the lives of the saints were also noted, such as Francis of Assisi's literally naked defiance of his father, and the Russian holy fool who challenged Ivan the Terrible, at great risk to his life! At the same time it was noted that church tradition has often been deeply hierarchical. Order of rank in processions is strictly observed, while the main point of placing the 'first' in power at the tail end of the procession is generally forgotten. Theologically the Fathers' rejection of hierarchy in the Trinity (as was manifest in the Neoplatonist versions they inherited) seemed relevant.

4 **Allowing these insights to illuminate and reframe the issue.**
   These insights were allowed to come into dialogue with one another, and it was admitted that the voices in favour of order and hierarchy ware strong. Nevertheless, the egalitarian strands seemed more distinctive and more ancient and more in tune with Jesus' teaching than the hierarchical, and in the group these voices prevailed, making the present ordering of chapel seem inappropriate.

5 **The identification of outcomes and appropriate action.**
The decision was made to abandon the staff pew and integrate staff
and students, keeping careful notes of any changes in personal and
collective knowledge and understanding that resulted, to be reviewed
at the end of the year.

d The 'classic' pastoral cycle in a new format

Andrew Todd[6] has refined the pastoral cycle to a version which forms the basis
of Figure 3. Todd defines theology as 'a seeking to know God in a situation' and
asserts that 'theological reflection is primary theology, not secondary'. Theological reflection does not simply apply a previous knowledge of God arrived

Figure 3: Pastoral cycle developed from Todd.

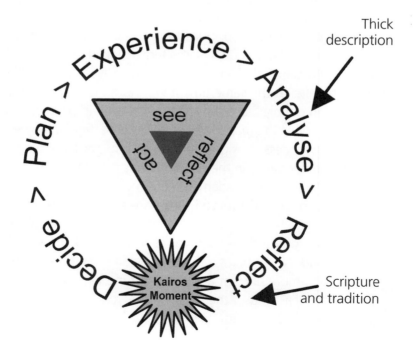

at in 'theology proper'; it is itself a process of coming to know God through reflecting on God's world in the light of resources from the tradition. Going round the circle from the top, the key stages are:

1 paying attention to the situation, to my point(s) of view, to other points of view.
2 asking, as well as historical, sociological, psychological and economic questions, the critical *theological* questions.
3 engaging in dialogue with the Christian tradition (and other traditions).
4 reflecting prayerfully and weaving together the different strands of experience and theological tradition. There will also be a right moment of insight (the *kairos*) enabling the move from reflection to action. Naming such a moment, which is explored further in Chapter 5, is a distinctive feature of Todd's approach.
5 following this through in reflective action.
6 leading on to a new situation, so the cycle moves on in what is effectively a spiral (cf. Laurie Green, below).

Though the diagrams and descriptions of the pastoral cycle vary, it is essentially the same process being described. In this book we have used (with permission) Andrew Todd's version, which is richest in helpful detail, and provides a new illustration of the 'classic' pastoral cycle as the basis for PTR. We now turn to some descriptions that suggest more substantial modifications of this 'classic' version, not just in description but in content.

2 The pastoral cycle: variations

If PTR is about relating belief and practice both spontaneously and also deliberately and consciously, it has probably always been practised by believers (even in as simple a matter as decisions about giving alms to beggars or caring for the sick and vulnerable). Gradually, and in a variety of contexts, it seems to have become a more deliberate and disciplined process, as has already been seen in Chapter 1. But it was not until the 1980s, building on the work of, for example, Bob Lambourne and Michael Wilson (1988) in Birmingham and that of the Whiteheads in Chicago (1995), that TR (or PTR as we have now named the more formalized approach to this activity) became firmly established as a crucial tool in the discipline of practical theology. The Whiteheads, interestingly, make no specific reference to Kolb's learning cycle, though their description of the reflective process and the key elements of it are very similar. They derive the model they are advocating more explicitly from the work of Paul Tillich (1968), David Tracy (1975, 1981), Bernard Lonergan (1973) and others, and from the clinical pastoral education methods (see below, section 3). The models they provide are not, therefore, directly parallel or based on the learning cycle, but are useful in stressing the importance of the different elements that need to be included in the reflective process in a way which is readily assimilated in the pastoral cycle model.

a Laurie Green's reflective spiral

Figure 4: Green's reflective spiral.

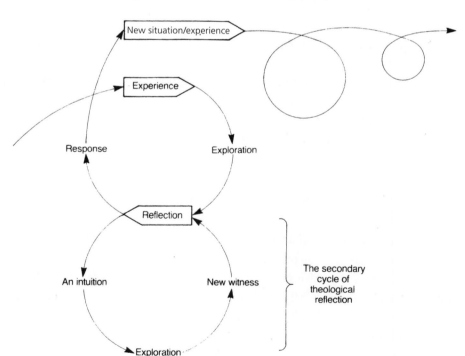

Another model for theological reflection, which evolved without explicit reference to the pastoral cycle but which is very similar to it, is the 'reflective spiral' of Laurie Green (2001, p. 95). This model (Figure 4) has two useful extra dimensions, one in time and one in thought. The effect of the 'spiral' is to make the model dynamic through time, suggesting that the cycle can be repeated many times in relation to both large and small aspects of a particular situation in response to shifts in the focus of attention. It is usually the case in learning and pastoral cycles that new practice creates a new situation to experience, suggesting that you always return to the cycle's starting point to begin again. Laurie Green's model allows the new point reached in the process to become a different new starting point, resulting in a spiral that moves through time, rather than just a cycle.

A further difference in Green's model is that theological tradition has its own 'secondary cycle' of theological reflection, so that when a theological idea illuminates with experience, new intuitions are created which can be explored and tested and then witnessed to in the community. This suggests a more active dialogue between tradition and experience than other models, particularly as it offers a whole extra cycle for the specific task of reflecting and responding to theological themes and issues. This could be a disadvantage if the theological perspective is completely split off from other perspectives (as if it should be 'uncontaminated' by worldly thoughts and considerations!); on the other hand, it has the clear advantage of ensuring – when the model is followed carefully – that the theological perspective is fully explored and developed through being applied in new ways.

b Emmanuel Lartey's five-phase cycle

Emmanuel Lartey (2000) provides a helpful summary of the three main strands that have contributed to the development of PTR and its place in practical theology, and provides his own model which attempts to integrate all three and also to add a further phase or dimension. As well as drawing in insights from social, political and psychological theory to correlate with those from the Christian tradition, there is also an opportunity for secular knowledge and perception to be interrogated by theological wisdom and insight, and vice versa. This, Lartey believes, provides a more robust framework for the pastoral cycle, which, in his version (p. 130), looks like Figure 5.

Figure 5: Lartey's five-phase cycle

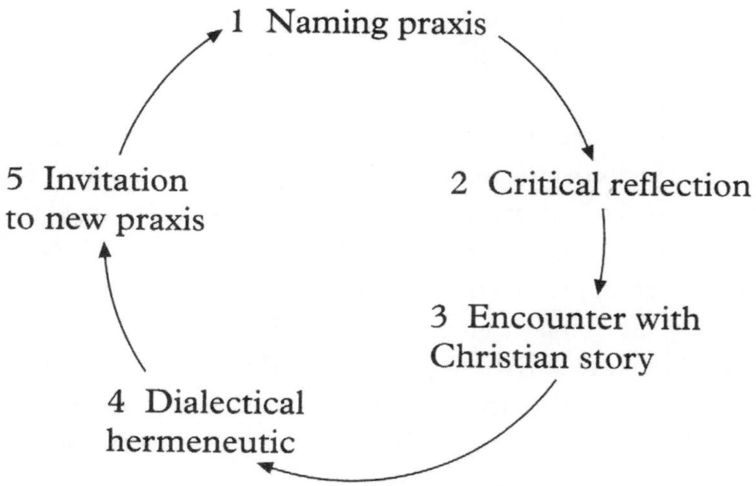

1 Naming praxis

5 Invitation
to new praxis

2 Critical reflection

3 Encounter with
Christian story

4 Dialectical
hermeneutic

The first two phases are similar to those of the classic cycle but the third and fourth phases, which he calls 'theological analysis' and 'situational analysis of theology', are the ones which require a two-way interrogation between the initial sociological understanding of the context in which the event took place, and theological perspectives, themes and insights which relate to it. Lartey suggests that by working in a group and enabling a lively exchange between participants around these two ways of perceiving and analysing the situation, an appropriate response will begin to emerge resulting from the 'visioning and re-visioning' that take place. This in turn will enable a responsible and suitable course of action to be agreed on and action taken.

Exercise

On a hospital visit, Angela encountered a family who were having to consider whether their elderly and confused husband/father should have his leg amputated because of the onset of gangrene. He was adamant that he did not wish to have the operation, but his family felt this was because of his confusion and lack of understanding of the issues involved. There was a danger, of course, that the operation itself might hasten the old man's death and a real question about whether he would ever be able to learn to walk with an artificial limb: but as far as the family was concerned there was only one possible choice, since, without the amputation, the gangrene would spread and his death would be inevitable and imminent.

Your task is to examine the issues following Emmanuel Lartey's model, enabling interrogation between the two perspectives (social and theological) and identifying an appropriate response. Keep your exploration of these issues at a theoretical level until the very last phase, that of 'responsible action' when you try to work out what you would say to the family if they sought your advice.

c Stephen Pattison's critical conversation

Pattison's model (1989) of a critical conversation between the ideas, beliefs and assumptions of the individual, those of the Christian tradition and the contemporary situation which is being examined is clearly based on that of the pastoral cycle, with the difference that, rather than suggesting a four-phase approach, he advocates giving careful attention to the three following strands:

- the contemporary situation which is being examined
- the beliefs, assumptions and perceptions provided by the Christian tradition (including the Bible)
- the reflector's own ideas, beliefs, feelings, perceptions and assumptions.

Having done this thorough preparation, keeping the three strands carefully distinct, the reflector, or group of reflectors, then enable a discourse to take place between the three strands, as if they were three different participants in a conversation. This method has the advantage of clarity and apparent simplicity. In practice it requires considerable discipline to retain the distinctive contribution of each of the three elements. As Pattison suggests, it may be helpful to imagine the three participants as three different people, or, in a group situation, to designate three different people to take on one role each and keep carefully to the role. For someone working alone, this could be more difficult, but it is still worth the effort.

Exercise

Using the 'critical conversation' approach outlined above, imagine you are a somewhat conservative and traditional Christian who has been approached by Andy, a relatively new member of the church community in his early twenties, who has fallen in love with another man who has been begging him for some time to come and live with him and to consider entering into a civil partnership. Andy longs to enter into this partnership as it is the first time in his life that he has ever felt really loved and cared for; but he has heard so many things about the Church's attitude to homosexuality that he is unsure. Make brief notes: in the role of the traditional Christian, on 'your' ideas, beliefs, feelings and perceptions of the matter; on elements of scripture and tradition that relate to this issue; and on the situation in its contemporary context. Encourage the three 'participants' – that is, perspectives – in this conversation to give their views clearly, and listen to each other carefully. Do not begin to formulate a response for Andy until you have really 'heard' and attended to all three strands as fully as possible. If you are doing this as a group exercise, it may be helpful to let three different group members represent, respectively, these three different perspectives with the rest of the group merely observing or asking questions for clarification. Only when this exploration stage is complete should open discussion between all group members begin, taking care to take into account all three different perspectives as you begin to work out how you would express this to Andy.

Note: The issue raised by this situation is one in which feelings tend to run high and careful reflection can easily go out of the window. Take special care, therefore, to keep your own feelings, fears, prejudices (in either direction) right out of the discussion until the very last stage: and, at that stage, acknowledge and describe them as objectively as you can (from a 'detached observer' perspective).

This is not to suggest that passions and emotions are unimportant, or that they have no place in the reflective process. They do, and this is considered more fully in Chapter 7, and is also important in the approach described in section 4 of this Chapter. The purpose of this exercise is to get a sense of how the critical conversation approach works in practice, and for this purpose it is important to keep a clear perspective on the three different elements of the conversation, and to listen carefully and objectively to each one.

3 Clinical pastoral education and the living human document

The particular approach to relating belief and practice developed by Anton Boisen, the founder of the clinical pastoral education movement, grew out of his own intense and painful experience as a psychiatric patient. He came to view psychotic episodes and mental illness as important indicators of dis-ease within society itself, and was passionately committed to the importance of listening to the patient and the patient's own understanding of his or her condition. He had to fight to get the psychiatrists responsible for his treatment to take any account of his own view of his experience (a problem that many psychiatric patients find still remains today); and, throughout the whole episode, he felt that there was a complete failure in connection between the language and theories of the 'experts' and the felt and expressed experience of those needing their help. In the same way, he believed, theological practitioners can be in danger of using a set of theories and language to discuss events in pastoral practice which seem to bear little or no relation to – and fail to be understood by – ordinary Christians seeking to live out their faith in daily life.

It was this dissatisfaction, and a desire to integrate theological theory with ordinary lived experience, that led him to develop the approach which become known as clinical pastoral education. Classically, this involved a careful and detailed analysis of a significant part of a pastoral encounter by means of a verbatim report, that is, a word-for-word report of a conversation between the pastor and the person she was seeking to help. This led to the concept of the 'Living

Human Document' – of turning life (or a very small part of it) into script – so that it could be considered and reflected on in depth by others as well as, whenever possible, those concerned in the encounter, allowing theological insights to be brought to bear on the issues involved.

The clinical pastoral education movement, although it has never taken centre stage in pastoral theological education in the UK, was one of the early influences in establishing the academic credentials of the discipline of pastoral theology, and has developed steadily if not dramatically ever since its beginnings in Chicago in 1925 (see Gerkin 1984; Foskett and Lyall 1988).

This approach to PTR obviously comes from different roots and belongs to a different family of reflective practice from those considered so far in this chapter, and cannot so neatly be expressed in diagrammatic form, but the exercise below shows how it can work in practice.

Exercise

NOTE: The material for this exercise needs to be prepared in advance of its use in class or group or pair discussion.

As you go about your pastoral encounters with others, be alert for a particular exchange that would be worth exploring. You might consider using a video or camcorder to capture an appropriate piece of raw material. When you have identified such an experience, take care to write it down word-for-word (verbatim) as accurately as you possibly can, in the form of a dialogue. Try to recall exactly what was said by yourself and others involved in the exchange, and resist the temptation, if you can, to improve on it as you write it down. The document should be no more than 500 words in length, so if you find yourself writing something much longer, select the 500 words from it that seem the most significant to form the basis of your discussion. When you have done this, identify three or four key theological insights that seem to have bearing on the content of the verbatim and make notes on what they seem to suggest. Either through discussion with others, or as a result of your own attempt at objective reflection, identify which interventions of yours in the dialogue seem to be appropriate, and which, with the insights that you now have, would have been different, and how.

4 Reflection through imagination and spiritual wisdom

This approach, which makes particular use of themes, imagination and feeling to develop reflective practice, following the work of Buttitta (1992), Fischer (1983) and Dillard (1988), has been made very accessible by Killen and de Beer, whose book (2002) you are strongly recommended to read. This describes an alternative creative method of PTR which some readers may find particularly appealing. The aim is to enable a 'conversation' between experience and religious tradition as described in definition 4 on p. 28, but this conversation is facilitated by identifying feelings underlying experience, and crystallizing these in images that connect with those of scripture and tradition.

In outline, this approach, like the previous one, is delightfully simple, though – also like the previous one – it is rather more complex to carry out in practice. To begin with, once a focus situation has been identified, the participants need to ensure that they start from a standpoint of genuinely open-minded and open-hearted *exploration*. It is important that it is neither a standpoint of *certitude* – that is, one in which a current interpretation is seen as 'absolute, unchanging and true' (p. 5) – or one of *self-assurance* in which 'we choose to be our own compass, map and guide and reject our need for any other' (p. 10). Either of these often unconsciously adopted standpoints will inevitably block any genuine exploration or transformative reflection.

Having thus cleared the mind of prejudgements of any kind, this approach takes us through the following stages, each with their corresponding image.

1 Enter or re-enter the experience identified.
2 Pay careful attention to both 'inner and outer' dimensions of the experience and to the *feelings* and bodily *sensations* aroused by it.

3 When those feelings and sensations have come into focus, allow an appropriate *image* to arise which gives shape and form to them.
4 Stay quietly with that image and others that may arise, gently allowing connections with theological *themes*, insights and narrative to emerge and then begin to resonate with elements of the identified situation shedding new light on your perception of it.
5 Identify new ways of thinking and acting based on these insights.

In the box below you will find an example of how it might work in practice.

Timothy had a pretty sleepless night after a difficult church council meeting and woke in the morning feeling thoroughly depressed and not a bit like going to work.

As he yawned and told his wife (who comes to church occasionally but isn't a committed Christian) how rough he was feeling and why, she commented how strange it seemed that an organization based on beliefs about love, liberation and newness of life should so often, in practice, have such a deadening and depressing effect on those who went along to its meetings.

As she spoke, a picture came into Timothy's mind of an old man bent nearly double under the weight of a heavy burden, struggling up a steep hill. Instead of dismissing this picture from his mind as irrational nonsense, Timothy remembered reading something about using images in PTR and decided to explore it further.

When he returned home from work that evening, in spite of his weariness, he was determined to see if such exploration might help. Using his concordance, he came up with the following biblical references:

- Exodus 1.11, which speaks of the new Pharaoh 'who did not know Joseph' deliberately inflicting impossible burdens on the people of Israel.
- Exodus 18.22, referring to Moses' delegation of the burden of acting as judge.
- Psalm 55.22 encourages the faithful to 'Cast your burden on the Lord, and he will sustain you'; while in Galatians 6.2 he read that 'bearing one another's burdens' fulfils the law of Christ.
- He also noted that in several places in Isaiah the word given in newer

translations as 'oracle' appears in the King James Bible and in the Revised Version as 'burden'.

- Matthew 11.30 offers the joyous possibility that in carrying Jesus' yoke we will find rest for our souls, for 'my burden is light'; while Matthew 23.4 describes the pharisees as binding heavy burdens which are 'hard to bear' on others, while themselves refusing to lift a finger to help.

Timothy also thought of other elements of the Christian tradition which used images of 'burdens', such as John Bunyan's *Pilgrim's Progress* and Negro spirituals. Pilgrim's burden, which at last fell off when he finally understood and accepted that Jesus' death had freed him, clearly represented the weight of sin; whereas that of the spirituals seemed more equivalent to the whole burden of life and living for those in slavery. Timothy also remembered Coleridge's Ancient Mariner who had to wear the life-enhancing albatross he had shot as a burden round his neck, as he watched his fellow sailors one by one perish of thirst in the becalmed waters. He curses the becalmed sea and the vile sea snakes he sees writhing in its murky depths. But then he notices a strange, fiery beauty in them, and 'blessed them unawares'. At last the albatross falls from his neck, the curse begins to lift and the winds begin to blow.

From all these passages Timothy gleaned a sense that burdens are heavier when we curse them, or our situation generally. They can begin to be light when we allow the Lord to carry them, when we bless them or our surroundings or when we share them. All of these are different kinds of opposite from the possessive and self-pitying clinging to our own burden, which can result in a deadening kind of enjoyment of our own resentment.

Timothy felt that this was what he had been doing and was determined to change. He resolved to:

- pray so as to 'cast his burden on the Lord'
- share the burden with others he could trust
- ensure enough rest and leisure to enable him to 'bless' the challenges that came his way, welcoming them as a kind of spiritual equivalent of physical exercise
- find a mentor to help him live up to these resolutions, and
- find ways of freeing others at his church from a similar sense of burden and despair (see Chapter 4.5 box).

5 Narrative reflection

A different way of using the imagination as an aid to reflective practice has been explored and documented by Gillie Bolton (2001) and related to the specific work of reflective practice in Christian ministry by, among others, Frances Ward (2005) and Heather Walton (2002, 2003, 2005). Discussing the poverty of the term 'reflective practice' as suggesting a mere reflection in a mirror of something that stays on this side of it, Bolton advocates:

> a creative adventure right through to *looking glass land* the other side of the silvering. Such reflective practice can take us out of the narrow range of experience and help us to perceive experiences from a range of viewpoints and potential scenarios. It can do this by harnessing a vital human drive – to create stories about our lives, and communicate them. (p. 43)

She advocates writing stories about our experiences, from different perspectives, real and imaginary, and in different genres, including poetry, and sharing such stories in groups. The effect of the different perspectives and genres is to jolt us out of our conventional ways of reading our experience, so that as we seek for new expressions we notice new things, and new ways of thinking, feeling and responding. It encourages a 'negative capability' (see Chapter 5.3) such that we can become truer to our experience through being fictional about it than we might if we tried to be painstakingly accurate and factual.

Of course, faith traditions and scriptures include an immense amount of narrative and poetry, so writing a story or a poem around our experience can make the interillumination with those traditions easier; arguably Jewish Midrash (Chapter 4.4) is precisely an imaginative writing in which our story and biblical story are rewoven together. There is no specific theological 'strand' in narrative reflection, and an important part of the process is to be able to 'let go' and write freely without censoring or forcing the direction of the story or the thoughts behind it. For some theological reflectors, writing in this way will result in theological insights appearing quite naturally in the narrative reflection. Others may find it helpful to let a piece of free narrative remain exactly as written, and then return to review it later in the light of deliberate theological perspective and insight. Reflecting on one's reflection in this way can be an extremely worthwhile activity; and one of the advantages of keeping the written narrative pieces carefully, is that one can return to them weeks, months or even years later, to look at anew in the light of subsequent experience.

Exercise

Write for exactly six minutes (set an alarm to be sure you keep to the time) on any issue or incident that is current for you. Write without thinking or censoring what comes into your mind, and in narrative form. There is no right way to do this, but until you have tried it, you won't begin to appreciate the value of it. So just do it! Share the results of what you have written with others, if possible, and see what you can begin to learn from it, and how the narrative of your experience relates to theological and biblical themes and stories.

Summary

This chapter has considered a variety of models for theological reflection and their use in practice:

- the pastoral cycle: its antecedents in the learning cycle, its adaptability for different faiths, and its development by Todd
- variations on that cycle provided by Green, Lartey and Pattison
- the rather different approach of the clinical pastoral education movement
- the freer approaches of imagination and spiritual wisdom, and
- narrative reflection.

It is suggested that you try all of these approaches at different times, as you begin to evolve your own preferred approach. It is important to steer a middle way between the alternatives of choosing one model for PTR and using it relentlessly for one's practice of PTR in all situations, on the one hand, and, on the other, being so ready to adopt a flexible approach that you use a mish-mash of all the approaches without any clear structure at all. While it is essential to allow thoughts and feelings to roam freely and imaginatively as part of the process, it is also important to relate them to a clear framework. The whole approach to PTR as described in this book takes the need for careful discipline in the reflective process as crucial, if it is to be a genuine tool for enabling critical evaluation and transformation linking belief and practice in daily life.

Further reading (see also Core Texts at the end of the book)

Aden, L. (1990), *Turning Points in Pastoral Care: The Legacy of Anton Boisen and Seward Hiltner*, Grand Rapids: Baker Books.

Bolton, G. (1999), 'Stories at Work: Reflective Writing for Practitioners', *The Lancet* 354, pp. 243–5.

Bolton, G. (2001), *Reflective Practice: Writing and Professional Development*, London: Chapman.

Buttitta, P. (1992), *The Still Small Voice that Beckons: A Theological Reflection Method for Health Ministry*, Chicago: Peter Buttitta.

Dillard, A. (1988), *Teaching a Stone to Talk*, New York: HarperCollins.

Fischer, K. (1983), *The Inner Rainbow: The Imagination in Christian Life*, New York: Paulist Press.

Foskett J. and Lyall, D. (1988), *Helping the Helpers: Supervision and Pastoral Care*, London: SPCK.

Geertz, C. (1973), 'Thick Description: Toward an Interpretive Theory of Culture', in (1973), *The Interpretation of Cultures: Selected Essays*, New York: Basic Books, pp. 3–30.

Gerkin, C. (1984), *The Living Human Document: Revisioning Pastoral Counselling in a Hermeneutical Mode*, Nashville: Abingdon.

Green, L. (2001), *Let's do Theology*, London and New York: Continuum. Figure 4 on p. 58 is reprinted with permission of the publisher, The Continuum International Publishing Group.

Killen, P. and de Beer, J. (2002), *The Art of Theological Reflection*, New York: Crossroad.

Kolb, D. (1984), *Experiential Learning: Experience as the Source of Learning and Development*, New Jersey: Prentice Hall.

Lartey, E. (2000), 'Practical Theology as a Theological Form', in Pattison and Woodward (2000), pp. 128–34. Figure 5 on p. 60 was first published in Contact 119, 1996, reproduced with the permission of Equinox Publishing.

Lonergan, B. (1973), *Method in Theology*, London: Darton, Longman & Todd.

Pattison, S. (1989), 'Some Straw for the Bricks', in Pattison and Woodward (2000), pp. 135–45.

Pattison, S. and Woodward, J. (2000), *The Blackwell Reader in Pastoral and Practical Theology*, Oxford: Blackwell.

Paver, J. (2006), *Theological Reflection and Education for Ministry: The Search for Integration in Theology*, Aldershot and Burlington VT: Ashgate.

Ryle, G. (1970), *The Concept of Mind*, Harmondsworth: Penguin Books.

Segundo, J.-L. (1982), *The Liberation of Theology*, Maryknoll NY: Orbis Books.

Tillich, P. (1968) *Systematic Theology*, Welwyn: James Nisbet.

Tracy, D. (1975), *Blessed Rage for Order: The New Pluralism in Theology*, New York: Seabury Press.

Tracy, D. (1981) *The Analogical Imagination: Christian Theology and the Culture of Pluralism*, New York: Crossroad.

Walton, H. (2002), 'Speaking in Signs: Narrative and Trauma in Practical Theology', *Scottish Journal of Healthcare Chaplaincy*, 5(2), pp. 2–6.

Walton, H. (2003), 'Women Writing the Divine', in P. Anderson and B. Clack (eds), *Feminist Theology of Religion: Critical Readings*, London: Routledge, pp. 123–35.

Walton, H. (2005) 'Literature and Theology: Sex in the Relationship', in D. Bird and Y. Sherwood (eds), *Bodies in Question*, Aldershot: Ashgate.

Ward, F. (2005), *Lifelong Learning: Theological Education and Supervision*, London: SCM Press.

Whitehead, J. and Whitehead, E. (1995), *Method in Ministry: Theological Reflection and Christian Ministry*, Lanham, Chicago, New York, Oxford: Sheed and Ward.

Wilson, M. (1988), *A Coat of Many Colours: Pastoral Studies of the Christian Way of Life*, London: Epworth Press.

Part 2

The Elements of PTR and its Basic Resources

Part 2 examines key elements in the PTR process to help you develop your own style of excellence in its practice.

- Chapter 4 describes a variety of authentic approaches to sacred texts in PTR, and cautions against others.
- Chapter 5 looks at the *kairos* moment of 'interillumination', in which text and experience shed light on each other.
- Chapter 6 looks at the contrasting issue of *chronos*, duration, and at establishing an enduring discipline of PTR.
- Chapter 7 looks at that key ingredient in PTR, the reflector herself, and ways in which personality may influence one's approach to PTR positively and negatively, so that you may be discerning in developing your approach.

Faith traditions vary in their evaluation of these elements. Most have sacred texts which they revere, but in some cases these are thought of as a general source of hallowed wisdom; in other cases – for example, the Qur'an in Islam, the Torah and Tanakh in Orthodox Judaism, and the Bible in some forms of Protestant Christianity – they are seen as the sole source of religious truth and values. Again, some traditions – Evangelical Christianity and Zen Buddhism, for example – emphasize *kairos* moments of conversion or awakening, while others emphasize the ongoing discipline of *chronos*. Chapter 8 examines these differences further, but since most traditions give some weight to all of these factors you will need to consider each carefully.

Of course the full range of resources available to PTR is much wider, including insights and understanding from other disciplines and especially from the whole theological search into the nature and revelation of God (Graham *et al.*, 2007). The immense issues of how PTR connects with this and the relationship of PTR to ethical issues and the wider world are left out here, but are given as much consideration as one chapter can allow in Chapter 8. Practice precedes theory, and it is important to suspend a natural concern for the 'big issues' until you have begun to acquire your own lively practice of PTR. Only then will you be able to assess its capacity – or otherwise – to cast light on ethics in today's world, and the broader applications of theological enquiry.

4

The Place of Scripture in PTR

The aim of this chapter is to help the reader consider and develop good practice in the use of scripture and sacred texts in PTR. To do this, the following are explored:

1 Some hermeneutical approaches.
2 Familiarity and friendship with sacred texts: a prerequisite for good PTR.
3 Using and abusing sacred text.
4 Midrash: 'Imaginatively performing the narrative' – an ancient approach.
5 Starting from scripture.
6 Imaginatively entering the narrative – as in Ignatius' Spiritual Exercises (see Ivens, 1998).
7 Identifying themes and subject areas.
8 Using images and motifs.
9 *Lectio divina* – meditation on particular texts.

1 Some hermeneutical approaches

Any use of texts in PTR will involve an implicit or explicit hermeneutic or interpretation, because to allow a text and a situation to interilluminate is in some sense to interpret each by means of the other. Hermeneutics is essential in PTR but as has already been said, relating it to the 'big issues' of today, and linking PTR to theories of revelation, are the task of later chapters. Right now our concern is what makes for good practice in the use of sacred texts in PTR, which clearly must draw on sound hermeneutics that have stood the test of time within the faith traditions.

While all religions have their sacred texts, even within any one faith tradition there have been many different methods of interpretation. In the Judaeo-Christian tradition alone, there have been the following approaches, among others, some of which we shall return to in greater depth:

1 **Midrash** – see section 4. This is a mainstream method in Judaism, but is to be found in Paul and other early Christian writers, especially the early Syrian tradition, until 'the three levels' (see below) came to replace it.
2 **Mystical and apocalyptic readings** – again, Jewish and early Christian – in which the text is read as a secret code or allegory for historical or mystical events.
3 **The three levels**, initiated by Origen and becoming mainstream in Christianity, in which the text has a surface literal meaning, a deeper ethical meaning, and a still deeper level of mystical meaning.
4 *Lectio divina* – a meditative approach developed in the monastic tradition. See section 8.
5 **Literal meaning**: the Reformers, in their desire to place interpretation in the hands of ordinary lay people rather than learned experts, shifted focus to what they took to be the plain literal meaning of the texts.
6 **Imaginative reading** – as developed in the Spiritual Exercises of Ignatius. See section 5.
7 **Original meaning.** In the nineteenth and twentieth centuries many theories of hermeneutics were developed. Quite often the word 'hermeneutics' is used to describe the kind of approach that was dominant in this period, which begins by trying to understand the original writer's identity, context and purpose in order to extract a 'meaning' that might be relevant today. This is a complex process demanding many kinds of knowledge – textual, historical, literary, psychological, sociological. While familiarity with the process is important for PTR, it is not itself an exercise in hermeneutics. Nor is PTR an 'archaeology' (Ford, 2007, p. 3) engaged in digging up ancient meanings but rather the discovery of theological meaning for life now.
8 **Literary meaning.** More recently (e.g. Dennis, 1991; Miles, 1991) the focus

has shifted away from original authors and contexts to sacred scripture in its present, much edited form, focusing on its power as a work of literature.

9 **Deconstruction.** Others have read the scriptures with a 'hermeneutic of suspicion', seeking the suppressed voices of women and the poor underneath the mainstream editorial current of patriarchy and power. Here the author is bracketed out, and it is the text that matters; what it says, often reading between the lines and despite the author's intention, may be the most important thing to note. Again, though it is good for the reader to know about deconstruction, and to carry with him into PTR some of the critical awareness it instils, PTR is not an exercise in this complex art.

Our task now is not to discuss the merits of each of these approaches, but to explore some of the approaches for what they have to offer for good PTR.

2 Familiarity and friendship with sacred texts

First and foremost, whatever the faith tradition, good practice depends on the theological reflector's being thoroughly steeped in that tradition and its sacred texts. Your prime task, in this respect, is to be as fully and deeply immersed as possible in text and tradition through steady participation in the life and worship of the faith community, and through a regularly maintained and carefully developed familiarity with its recognized sacred text or texts.

In the case of Christians – and there is an equivalent process in other faith traditions – the goal of such familiarity will be 'to shape and form the consciousness and character of the Christian community' (Pattison, 2000, p. 130). Alertness to the way truths of the tradition relate to a current situation and vice versa can only arise from a deep friendship with the text and the tradition surrounding it.

David Ford writes (2007, p. 3) of the 'wisdom interpretation' of scripture 'distilled from reading and rereading the Bible'. The Bible, he says, has been

extraordinarily generative for imagining, understanding, believing, hoping and living. Its interpretation has required the making of endless connections with past, present and future, and with a range of disciplines, spheres of life, aspects of self, religions, worldviews and experience. The very abundance of meanings, which are often in tension with or even in conflict with one another, calls for continual rereading and discernment ...

... and, we might add, the ongoing practice of PTR.

For a Christian reflector, therefore, having instant recall to chapter and verse for a wide range of biblical quotations may sometimes be useful. But it is vital for PTR purposes to be aware of the great biblical themes, and of subjects, images and motifs (see sections 7 and 8), all of which cut across the neat division of scripture into chapter and verse.

3 Using and abusing texts

The later sections in this chapter suggest a wide variety of imaginative ways of using sacred text in PTR. However, it is also possible to abuse scripture in ways that inhibit critical reflection.

The use of short biblical texts as a source of meditation (as in *lectio divina*, see section 8), as a basis for prayer, or as an inspiration for daily living has a long and worthy history in many branches of Christianity, as has its equivalent practice in other faiths. But such prayerful reflection is a whole world away from the activity known as 'proof-texting' in which, for example, a hapless student, desperate to find something that looks respectably theological to include in his prescribed piece of TR, finds a short text which seems to bear some relation to the matter under consideration, quotes it with minimal discussion, and considers his job done.

Even worse is the case where the person has already made up her own mind what the answer to a moral issue or dilemma is, and simply marshalls as many scriptural quotes as she can that appear to support her case. The quotes are sundered from their context in scripture, let alone the wider contexts; and the close attention to the situation that is integral to the PTR cycle is omitted. Here scripture is used as a way of avoiding serious reflection. As Oliver writes (2006, pp. 43–4; compare Reed, 2000):

Treating the Bible as some kind of literary pope that utters holy truth without regard for circumstance or context will only serve to close some issues that should be left open to the speaking of God. Simple resort to proof-texting, far from enabling the word of God to be clearly heard, undermines the whole idea of the Bible as revealing the word of God. The very idea of the word or the speaking of God carries the invitation to engage in conversation that can lead somewhere quite new.

An example of the misuse of sacred text is given in the box below.

As part of her church placement activity, Esther worked alongside parents and children involved in the small youth club. She got to know one family particularly well, and included their situation as one of the 'case studies' for TR in her assignment. In it she described how 12-year-old Kirsty, herself a volatile and troubled child, had become very worried about Tony, her 10-year-old brother. Tony hung around with a group of older boys who were known to be involved with drugs and were often in trouble. Having spent time with Kirsty and Tony and visited their parents, who seemed upset but rather resigned to the situation – as if there was really nothing that could be done about it – Esther felt that the best solution would be for these children to learn about 'putting on the whole armour of God' so that they could learn 'to stand against the wiles of the devil' (Eph. 6.11). She explained this to their parents, showing them the passage in the Bible. In her enthusiasm to help, Esther mistook their polite but mystified responses for understanding and agreement, and, as she prayed with them after they had talked together, believed that the problem was all but solved. She described this conversation with satisfaction in her case study, illustrating the use of PTR in pastoral practice.

Exercise

What was appropriate and what was inappropriate about Esther's use of the Bible and practice of PTR in this instance? How might Esther's colleagues, in discussion, help her to reflect on this piece of practice in general; and, in particular, what suggestions might they make about alternative approaches to the use of the Bible in this situation?

The temptation to misuse the Bible (or other sacred text) to suit our own ends always lurks, even for the academically rigorous. However, recognizing the influence of various ways of understanding how the Bible expresses God's Word, and the role of the Church, the minister and the individual believer, in enabling it to be revealed and heard, can assist in increasing awareness of these temptations. Gordon Oliver (2006, pp. 28–38) identifies four different views on this:

- The Bible – every word of it – *is the Word of God*, believed to be spoken by the Holy Spirit directly to those who wrote and compiled the scriptures. Such a view makes proof-texting quite legitimate, but, as Oliver argues, it hits problems when one text contradicts another, and where God is depicted commanding morally abhorrent actions such as human sacrifice and genocide.
- The Bible – as a whole – *reveals the Word of God*. This view requires us to recognize the whole human process involved in the formation of the Bible and that 'revelation' is a two-way process of giving and receiving, in which the church has a significant role as the receiving community.
- The Bible *contains the Word of God* – as in Article Six of the Anglican Thirty-Nine Articles (*Book of Common Prayer 1662*) which states that the Bible 'containeth all things necessary to salvation'. This suggests that parts of the Bible are not revelatory and our job is to find the parts that are. Most Christians probably find themselves in any case underlining mentally or literally the parts of scripture which are particularly treasured; but taken too far this can lead to any eclectic 'pick-and-choose' approach, ready to dismiss parts that seem too difficult or strange. The danger is that we may make up our own story of salvation out of our favourite passages.
- The Bible *is the sacramental Word of God* (Brown and Loades (ed.), 1996). On this view the emphasis shifts from using the Bible to receiving it. It suggests that just as a sacrament uses ordinary things – bread, wine, water – which when received in faith become communion with God, so the Bible, though in many ways an ordinary and fallible human document, can enable us to receive the Word of God. On this view there is more of a possible contrast between the text of scripture and the Word of God, as there is between the bread and wine, and the body and blood of Christ as suggested by Wright:

> Treated … as a sacramental affirmation which heightens the possible *contrast* between what scripture says and what God says, 'This is the word of

the Lord' affirms the gracious truth that God continues to speak through an amazing variety of fallible human viewpoints. (2002, p. 83, italics original)

Oliver's preferred image for understanding the relationship between the Bible and the Church is that of hospitality (Oliver, 2006, pp. 123–7), itself a rich recurring theme throughout both Old and New Testaments, frequently expressing a divine encounter. Most often the Church acts as host to the Bible as an honoured guest received with openness and curiosity, but exploring the Church as guest of the Bible is equally fruitful. 'Openness is about having emotional, psychological and spiritual space within oneself so that there is room for the stranger to come near and rest and be refreshed and offer the gifts of wisdom, encouragement and challenge that they bring' (p. 125).

Exercise

From the four bullet points above, identify the view you find most helpful and the advantages and pitfalls of each when using the Bible in PTR.

---

4 Imaginatively performing the narrative: Midrash

Rowan Williams (according to McCurry, 2007) argues that faith traditions are like symphonies and plays. Every time we 'perform' them, though we need to follow their text closely, a new and unique event takes place. His idea of treating sacred text as something fixed and immutable, and needing close attention, but also demanding imaginative recreation in a variety of 'performances', is precisely what we need in PTR where one hopes that fresh experience will lead to ever-different 'performances' of sacred text in our actions. In this context Laurie Green (1990, p.85) invites us to use dramatic reading, mime and role play to engage scripture in PTR (see also Toolkit 'Hypertext', 'Role Play' and 'Sculpting'). But the idea is not new in the least; it is fundamental to one of the oldest hermeneutical traditions we know of: Jewish Midrash.

The rabbis responsible for the Midrash were like the best modern film-makers. They read the text carefully, noticing extreme details in the text, down to matters of where the breathings came in the Hebrew. They believed the Torah was the immutable and eternal word of God, and were certainly not free to change or criticize such a sacred text. Despite that, they were remarkably free in using their imagination to fill in the details, often composing myths or *aggadah* (plural of *aggadot*). Just as there can be many different films based on one piece of history, so there were many different *aggadah* based on any given text.

For example, in the story of Adam and Eve and the fruit, the commentators noticed that whereas God simply commanded Adam not to eat the fruit or he will die (Gen. 2.15), when Eve reports this to the serpent she says that God had told them not to eat the fruit *or even touch it* or they will die (Gen. 3.3). How is this difference to be explained? Some rabbis argued that Adam must have added the extra restriction. The serpent then pushed Eve so that she touched the fruit and found she did not die, confirming that the serpent was right – the fruit was quite safe to eat – and Adam must have got it wrong! Thus one *aggaddot* evolved, which was favourable to Eve; others were the opposite!

The early Christian authors freely used the same techniques in their own interpretation of the scriptures. For example, when Paul declares that the rock from which the Hebrews drank in the wilderness was Christ, it sounds a very wild interpretation to us, but was quite in line with the interpretive techniques that Paul as a Pharisee would have learnt.

Jacob Neusner writes

> Midrash minimizes the authority of the wording of the text as communication, normal language … While it is always governed by the wording of the text, it allows for the reader to project his or her inner struggle into the text. This allows for some very powerful and moving interpretations which, to the ordinary user of language, seem to have very little connection with the text. (http://shamash.org/lists/scj-faq/HTML/faq/03-24.html)

This suggests Midrash needs to be used with care since it could be used simply to pour out personal feelings and responses, but with that caveat it might be an approach particularly suited to PTR in that it engages experience and leads to action in a way similar to that of the pastoral cycle. A possible Midrash approach might involve these stages:

1 Read the story carefully. Notice all the details of the phrases, both what is said, and what is left out; what is explained and what is left unexplained. The gaps are a very important part of the text (compare 'Negative space' in Toolkit).
2 Now let go of caution, and imagine a story – any story that fits with the text. Add whatever detail you like. Be extravagant. Perhaps imagine you are writing a play or a film based on the text – allow yourself plenty of poetic licence.
3 Next remember you are part of a community of interpreters. See what others have said about this story. If you are working in a group, compare notes. If you are on your own, write several different *aggadah*, each perhaps from a different character's perspective, or with a deliberately different theological spin.
4 Finally reintegrate with the PTR process as a whole. See if you have been writing your experience into the stories. Find out if, through being retold in the story, your experience can be seen in a new light or perspective.

Exercise

Try out this approach for yourself. Take a Bible story – Genesis 22, or some other – and go through the above four stages with it. At stage (1) if you use Genesis 22, you might want to tell it first as the story of Abraham, then the story of Isaac, and then the story of Sarah. At stage (2) imagine you are making a film of this story, full of human drama. List all the features, characters, feelings etc. you would have to add that are *not* described in the text, to make this a convincing and moving film. After working through stages (3) and (4), see if you can make connections between your new look at this passage and any current situation.

When Daniel Blomberg gave the Babylonian Talmud its present form in the sixteenth century, he printed the original Torah in the centre and the various Midrash reaching out from it in two concentric 'circles', as in Figure 6 (reproduced below from Ballard, 2005, p. 66). In PTR a similar technique might be applied: pasting a Bible passage in the centre, with people attaching their own stories around it, then commentaries on those stories around that. This would be best done by a group, but could be done by an individual building up her own 'biblical journal' over a period of time. Ideally one wants a publisher to produce some 'Talmudic Bibles' with the text just in the middle of each page, and maybe a couple of commentaries in the next circle out, and the rest blank for the reader to fill in.

Whether or not you respond positively to the Midrash approach, this way of thinking about the sacred texts can be very liberating and is a model worth keeping in mind for PTR.

Figure 6: Blomberg's Babylonian Talmud

5 Starting from scripture

Although the classic approach in using the pastoral cycle always begins with the situation or praxis (see Chapter 1.3), some approaches, including Midrash and *lectio divina* – begin with the scriptural text and then relate experience to it. In Midrash there is no limit to the imagination or experience that may be brought to bear, so long as there is some connection with the text. When we 'imaginatively perform' a particular text with a view to relating it to a specific experience, the result is more like PTR as we have described it, but from a refreshing angle. For some, starting with a passage of scripture might become the preferred option for regular practice. This can sometimes be particularly appropriate, as illustrated in the example in the box below.

Timothy, whose reflection after a painful church council meeting was described in Chapter 3.4, managed to keep to his resolutions remarkably well, with the help of someone he had asked to act as his mentor. As soon as he felt confident to do so, Timothy shared his disquiet about what happened at church meetings and it was agreed, for a trial period, to include a short reflection on the following Sunday's gospel reading at the start of each meeting. The passage at the next meeting happened to be John 15.9–17 and, before reading it through, he explained that this wasn't a Bible study group, so the aims were different. 'Instead,' he said, 'let's just find ways today's passage might relate to the meeting that we are about to have.' As he finished reading there was a thoughtful silence until gradually first one person, then another, acknowledged how far from the spirit of loving indwelling that resonates throughout this passage, their conduct at meetings seemed to be. The awesome calling to have been chosen by God himself to be 'friends' of Jesus and of one another; and to be ready to love even to the point of death, seemed to be a whole world away from their attitude to one another in their discussions. 'So I suppose it isn't very surprising', said one participant, 'that we end up arguing and getting at each other and each trying to prove that we are right, just like they do in parliament or local council meetings. Wouldn't it be wonderful if the way we talk over things here could be a real reflection of God's love within and among us?'

Of course, the readings set for the following Sunday (or the appropriate passage chosen from the sacred text in another faith community) won't always turn out to be as apposite as this was for the church meeting described. But reflecting in this way, with or without appropriate looking up of notes and exegesis first, always seems to provide something worthwhile to wrestle with, once you open your mind to possible connections between the passage of scripture and current situations in your life, the world and in your community. Try this for yourself, in the following exercise.

Exercise

Read a passage of sacred text that has been set for use today (e.g. in a lectionary). Read it slowly and carefully, and then, whatever it is, find at least three points of connection between what is said in it and today's news stories; and a further three points that connect with current events in your own life. Allow these connections to lead to a kind of dialogue between text and situation, and note significant questions that begin to emerge as a result.

---

6 Imaginatively entering the narrative: Ignatius' Spiritual Exercises

One approach to deepening experience of sacred text which has ancient roots but is increasingly popular in some circles today,[7] is that encouraged in the Spiritual Exercises of Ignatius of Loyola (see Ivens, 1998). Here the participants imaginatively 'inhabit' the text in such a way that they are temporarily taken over by the experience and nourished by the sense of being fully immersed and fully present to the events or situations. Rather than straining to see what relevance the particular passage might have to current or personal events and modern living, those using this approach seek to enter so deeply into what they are reading that, for a time, they 'let go' of their ordinary present-day lives and become, as far as they can, part of the different reality presented in the text. This may be by identifying with one of the main characters in a passage, or, in imagination, being one of a group of people present, and then envisaging how it might feel to be that person: what they might be thinking and experiencing, the sights, sounds and smells and physical sensations, as well as the internal ones. They may even enter into imaginary dialogue with the main characters or others present. In the Exercises they are especially encouraged to enter into a dialogue with Jesus, to hear his personal word to them in their situation. Having done this, they then become ready to respond to the content of the passage being studied.

Such an experience will already be familiar to readers who have shared with a church community in living through of the events of Holy Week (the week before Easter), which many Christians undertake annually. Traditionally, and still for many, this time is accompanied by fasting, avoiding unnecessary talking, prayer through the night for the Maundy Thursday 'watch' (trying not to fall asleep as the disciples did!), walking through the 'Stations of the Cross' – accompanying Jesus on his journey through Jerusalem to Golgotha – and a long service of deep sorrow during the time that Jesus hung on the cross on Good Friday; as well as much rejoicing on Easter morning. Anyone who has participated in such a week will have discovered what it is like to indwell a passage of scripture in this way so as to relive for themselves, at a deep and personal level, the events and experiences described.

The following exercise may help to give you a taste of this approach and begin to assess its value for yourself:

Exercise

Read Matthew 14.13–21 (Mark 6.30–44; Luke 9.10–17): the story of the feeding of the five thousand. Imagine yourself present on that day as one of the crowd. Tired, stressed and hungry as you are, there is something about this itinerant preacher that draws you. So instead of going home to tea you decide to follow the crowd. Someone explains that the preacher and his close disciples have gone ahead by boat, but everyone is following on foot to the landing point because they long to hear his teaching and receive his compassion and healing. Eventually you see the boat for yourself as it approaches, and as the main crowd slows down, you find yourself swept along by a group keen to get close to the teacher, and standing right by the jetty as the boat lands. This is the first time you have seen Jesus, close at hand. What does he look like? What is his expression and what do you see in his face? As he looks round at the gathering crowd, your eyes meet for a few seconds. How do you experience this? A number of sick people are brought to him, for healing. One such person had been standing by you. What is her sickness, and what happens when she comes to Jesus? You notice the disciples anxiously talking with Jesus about the fact that everyone is hungry and there is nothing to eat. What happens next, and how do you respond? What are your feelings as you watch the five loaves and two fish being distributed to this huge crowd – and still there is plenty left over? Who brings you food? What do you eat and what does it taste like? What conversation do you have with your neighbours as you eat, and what are your thoughts and feelings as you do so, and as you walk home, tired, satisfied and amazed?

Spend as long as you can in role, reflecting on what you have seen and heard from a quasi-contemporary perspective. Let your responses lead you where they will. Then, very gradually, come out of your role and return to your own identity and situation. Without labouring or forcing anything, find connections between what you have just experienced and any situation or decision-making process you are currently involved in. Try to do this by feeling rather than analysis at this stage; and note down, uncritically, whatever comes to mind.

Finally, and with someone else if possible, note at least three and not more than eight points for further reflection; anything that seems to suggest a new way of thinking or acting in any current situation. From the perspective of this imaginative experience, how do these events in your life begin to look?

There is no doubt that, according to personality and temperament, some people will find the 'entering the narrative' approach much more congenial and fruitful than others. But encouraging yourself – and others – to operate outside your normal comfort zone can have very interesting results. As always, in reflective practice, however, whatever comes to you as a result of this exercise must be used with caution; remembering that following the dictates of your own feelings, though it may be a new and refreshing experience, cannot be equated with obeying the voice of God! While some of the new thoughts and alternative perspectives may, indeed, be divinely inspired, others may simply be your own set ideas and opinions resurfacing in a new form.

It is here, again, that Ignatius' advice may be helpful: that we attend to which imaginations, though challenging, bring 'consolation' and a sense of peace, and which, while immediately stimulating, in the long term leave us feeling 'desolation' and loss of energy.[8] The Spiritual Exercises were intended for long retreats in which the results would be shared with a spiritual guide. Careful scrutiny of the results of this reflective process with a critical friend who is able to be both honest and affirming is always a wise course of action and, indeed, part of the reflective process itself.

7 Identifying themes and subject areas

One of the blocks to the imaginative use of sacred text in PTR, especially if one begins with the problem or situation and then looks for elements in the Christian tradition that may have some relevance, is that, however familiar one is with scripture, one's power of recall may vary. It is also a facility influenced by personality types and learning styles (see Chapter 7): people who relate more readily to specific and concrete detail are likely to have more natural aptitude for locating texts and pieces of narrative, whereas those whose natural style is more creative and intuitive may have a deep sense of a relevant passage or theme but have great difficulty accessing the phrase, story or commentary that exemplifies it.

One simple way of having the riches of the Bible more immediately accessible is through building up a list of significant biblical themes and experiences they relate to. A fine example can be found in Laurie Green (1990, p. 88), where he develops themes from Jesus' life of incarnation, discipleship, miracles, parables, sending, table fellowship, sacraments, crucifixion, resurrection and ascension, and suggests what we can learn about experience today from them, and how we might apply them in our own actions. An excellent source of readily and intriguingly accessible material for accessing the riches of the Bible in this way is *A Dictionary of Biblical Imagery* (Ryken *et al.*, 1998).[9] Not only can such an approach be of immediate and practical value in discussion groups, study groups and church meetings, but it is also an imaginative and intriguing way in to the appreciation of some of the rich layers of meaning and allusion which are so characteristic of sacred writing, but can easily be lost in a more literalistic modern approach. There are, as it were, glittering seams of wisdom and spiritual depth awaiting rediscovery and prizing for those who have the patience and diligence to find them and the imagination and discernment to see how they relate to current issues and events, and the ordinary circumstances and challenges of everyday life.

Exercise

Peter is a good friend but lives far away, so you keep in touch mainly by phone. He has been ordained ten years and works absurdly long hours, but finds his ministry very fulfilling – or has until recently. His wife Theresa has been under a lot of stress, which has resulted in uncharacteristic behaviour and serious accusations and rumours. They are very much committed to each other, and have been supported by one or two good friends, but at local meetings and church events Peter has felt increasingly shunned and isolated on a number of occasions. He admits he may be a bit paranoid about it, but has felt hurt, lost and lonely and sometimes so bleak he wonders how he can keep going. He knows there are plenty of examples in Christian experience and history of people being unjustly treated – not least Jesus himself. He knows, too, that many of the great saints experienced 'dark nights' of despair – but somehow he is too upset to focus on any of this, and wonders if you can help him get a new perspective.

Write a letter to Peter suggesting stories, commentary and teaching in the Bible relating to the themes of wilderness and exile, injustice mercy and forgiveness. Pinpoint five or six passages from the Bible, or events in Christian tradition which relate to these themes in a variety of ways and suggest pointers which might connect with his situation.

8 Using images and motifs

Lists of images and motifs in the Bible, of which there are a vast number, can be built up, recorded and accessed in much the same way as with themes and subject areas. Any concordance and a variety of Bible handbooks can help you get started in developing your list of biblical themes and building up a reference of images and motifs, but the most useful 'index' to such treasures will undoubtedly be one that you make yourself over a period of time. As you approach your normal pattern of the reading of sacred text, you can develop the habit of noticing and noting such images and thematic links each time they occur. There is probably no substitute for a pocket notebook – whether of the paper or electronic variety – for this purpose, transferring its contents to an indexed ring-back file at regular intervals.

A *Dictionary of Biblical Imagery*, referred to in the previous section, will provide you with all you need to get started, and you are invited to maintain and develop such a list of your own, and have it ready-to-hand when needed. It is important, of course, even as you build your list, to develop sensitivity and lateral thinking in making connections between aspects of modern living and particular themes and images.

Exercise

Over the coming week, keep your mind's eyes and ears peeled for events and issues that might relate to some of the images and motifs recorded. You can approach this creative task from either perspective: by looking out for events that could relate to items in your embryonic list, or by starting with the list and looking out for connections with what is going on around you. At the same time, continue to add references to your list to develop its comprehensiveness and availability.

It is, of course, important to use your list of images and motifs with wisdom and never misuse it as if it has a kind of magic power – like the use of oracles and divination. Rather than assuming that God is giving you a message through the set of images you have identified, let them provide avenues for entering the text and gently reflecting with an open heart and mind on what emerges in such a 'sacred space', so that you may then return, refreshed and revitalized, to reconsider the matter you began with. The last of the three paradigms in Chapter 2 gives an example of using images and motifs in this kind of way.

9 *Lectio divina*

Lectio divina is a very ancient reflective and systematic reading of the Bible by means of a particular approach which has been kept alive through the ages especially in monasteries of the Benedictine tradition, and formalized by the medieval Carthusian Guigo II (1978). It lends itself readily to a contemplative style of TR, relying as it does on the development of a deep spiritual rhythm to all the activities of daily living. It centres on reading scripture very slowly in a carefully focused way, which is understood as a dialogue with God – a 'loving conversation with the One who has invited us into his embrace' – and encourages deep reverential listening with the 'ears of the heart', seeking to encounter and respond to the still small voice of God deep within the text and in the heart.

Although *lectio divina* comes very definitely from within the Christian tradition, it is a method which, we believe, would lend itself readily for use with other sacred texts, and there may well be parallel processes already in use. It is perhaps especially appropriate for approaches to PTR that *begin* with scripture (see below).

As described by Guigo, the process of *lectio divina* has four phases – *lectio* (reading), *meditatio* (meditation), *oratio* (prayer) and *contemplatio* (contemplation).

1 For the *lectio* the reader starts with a short passage of scripture, which might be a reading set for that particular day, or could be a small part of a continuous reading of a particular book of the Bible, or part of any other structured approach to reading scripture. After a period of quiet preparation and silent prayer, the text is read very slowly and gently, while you thoughtfully listen with your inner ears and wait to receive from the passage a particular word or phrase which somehow suggests itself to you as the focus for today.
2 You are then ready to proceed to the next phase of *meditatio*. For this, the selected word or phrase is memorized and slowly repeated over and over

again. This is the phase of rumination or inner pondering in which the word of scripture gently interacts within you with your thoughts, worries, hopes, fears and memories, until it has become internalized in a process of mutual indwelling.

3   This naturally leads on to *oratio*, a time of prayer and offering. At this stage the word or phrase that you have invited into your inner being begins to touch and change you in such a way that you begin to pray, putting into words your offering and longing as your mind and heart become attuned to God's will and being.

4   When you have thus offered up your whole self and being you are ready to move on to the final stage of *contemplatio* when you simply relax in quietness and peace, content to be in God's presence and to rest in his love.

It seems important that, in adapting this method of reading sacred texts for use in PTR, its sense of gentleness and God-centredness should be cherished and retained, along with a sense of unhurried offering of yourself and the situations you are involved in.

Exercise

Find a short passage from the Bible, or other sacred text, as described above. Having selected your passage, allow yourself at least 30 minutes for this exercise. Place a clock where you can easily see it, and, without being rigid about it, work gently through the four stages of the *lectio divina – lectio, meditatio, oratio, contemplatio* – allowing at least five minutes for each stage, preferably more for the two middle stages, so that you have time to relax and take a gentle, peaceful attitude to your reading, meditation, prayer and contemplation. When you have completed the whole process (and not before!) make very brief notes as a reminder of what emerged for you during your time of meditation and of prayer, and only now – not during the time of prayer and meditation – engage your cognitive, reasoning faculties to begin to relate what came up from your *lectio divina* which seems to connect with anything you are currently involved in.

Lectio divina is intended to provide a particular way of allowing God to speak to each person individually. The danger of self-delusion lurks – as with any kind of prayer or communication with 'higher powers' – and therefore self-scrutiny and honesty is essential, and sharing with a critical friend or group advisable. But, even with this warning and proviso, the results of such 'divine reading' can be truly remarkable, and have enriched the lives of many through the ages.

Summary and conclusion

Just as wood needs to be split and prepared in the right way to make good fuel for a fire, so in this chapter we have explored a number of ways of opening up the sacred texts in order to provide fuel for the experience-transforming, action-creating fires of PTR. At the same time, just as throwing a great many chunks of unseasoned timber onto a fire will rarely help it burn, and may even put it out, so we have looked at approaches to scripture that will put the dampers on PTR, namely those that treat it as an undigested collection of proof-texts that can be used with neither analysis nor imagination for scriptural and thematic contexts.

With this in view we have considered

- a range of traditional hermeneutical approaches to set PTR in a long tradition of interpretation;
- ways of using and abusing scriptural texts, and the fundamental ways of viewing scripture, on which our use of scripture will be based;
- one of the oldest methods of interpretation, Midrash;
- the virtues of PTR starting with scripture;
- another way of imaginatively entering text, the Spiritual Exercises of Ignatius;
- the value of identifying themes and subject areas; and
- images and motifs;
- finally, we have examined what PTR can learn from another traditional approach, *lectio divina*.

But throughout this discussion we have presupposed two things that need further investigation:

1 Scripture is capable of 'catching fire'; that there are ways in which it can interilluminate with experience and suggest, through the reflective process, paths of creative action.
2 The use of scripture in PTR needs to be part of an ongoing discipline that is integral to the life of the participant, and rooted in a faith community and preferably within a reflective group.

The next chapter examines how (1) might happen in PTR, and Chapter 6 explores (2) the ongoing contexts necessary for PTR.

Further reading (see also Core Texts at end of the book)

Ballard, D. (2005), *Explorations in Computer Mediated Theological Reflection*, MTh thesis (unpublished), Cardiff University.

Brown, D. and Loades, A. (eds) (1996), *Christ the Sacramental Word*, London: SPCK.

Day, A. C. (1992), *Roget's Thesaurus of the Bible*, London: Marshall Pickering.

Dennis, T. (1991), *Lo and Behold: The Power of Old Testament Storytelling*, London: SPCK.

Dulles, A. (1992), *Models of Revelation*, Maryknoll NY: Orbis Books.

Ford, D. (2007), *Christian Wisdom: Desiring God and Learning in Love*, Cambridge: Cambridge University Press.

Frei, H. (1993), *The Eclipse of Biblical Narrative*, New Haven: Yale University Press.

Green, L. (1990), *Let's Do Theology*, London: Mowbray.

Guigo II (1978), *The Ladder of Monks and Twelve Meditations*, ed. E. College and J. Walsh, New York: Doubleday Image.

Ivens, M. (1998), *Understanding the Spiritual Exercises: Text and Commentary*, Leominster: Gracewing.

McCurry, J. (2007), 'Towards a Poetics of Theological Creativity', *Modern Theology* vol. 23, no. 3, pp 415–33.

Miles, J. (1991), *God: A Biography*, London: Vintage.

Oliver, G. (2006), *Holy Bible, Human Bible*, London: Darton, Longman & Todd.

Parker, D. (1997), *The Living Text of the Gospels*, Cambridge: Cambridge University Press.

Pattison, S. (2000), *A Critique of Pastoral Care*, third edition, London: SCM Press.

Reed, E. (2000), *The Genesis of Ethics: On the Authority of God as the Origin of Christian Ethics*, London: Darton, Longman & Todd.

Ryken, L., Wilhoit, J. and Longman, T. (1998), *Dictionary of Biblical Imagery*, Illinois and Leicester: InterVarsity Press.

Schwartz, H. (1998), *Reimagining the Bible: The Storytelling of the Rabbis*, Oxford and New York: Oxford University Press.

Walton, H. (1993), 'Breaking Open the Bible', in E. Graham and M. Halsey (eds), *Life Cycles: Women and Pastoral Care*, London, SPCK.

Wright, S. (2002), 'The Bible as Sacrament', *Anvil*, vol. 19, no. 2.

5

God, Gaps and Glory – The *Kairos* Moment

The '*kairos* moment' is a concept applied to PTR by Andrew Todd. *Kairos* is the Greek word for time that emphasizes the proper season or the right moment. Such moments often arrive suddenly and unexpectedly and cannot be forced by our own efforts. It contrasts with *chronos*, which is the ongoing measured time of chronometers, watches and clocks, often implying a long hard slog, or the pain of a 'chronic' condition that just has to be endured. Both *kairos* and *chronos* are important to PTR. Chapter 6 considers the *chronos* element which can enable PTR to become a regular part of the routine of our ordinary life and labour. This chapter focuses on how PTR can make room for *kairos* moments of sudden inspiration, in the following stages:

---

1 Dry bones: recognizing the gap between experience, faith and practice, and the genuine difficulty of crossing it.
2 Closing the gap: exploring how it may be crossed in a 'kairos moment'.
3 Negative capability: clearing the mind of certainties, preconceptions and being prepared to wait without expectations.
4 Creating sacred space: preparing the ground to enable these things to happen.
5 New life, transformation … and a caution: the test of a genuine 'kairos moment'.

---

1 Dry Bones

'Theological Reflection is simply the art of making theology connect with life and ministry so that gospel truth comes alive' (Ballard and Pritchard, 2006, p. 118). This clear assertion seems almost to suggest that the process of making such lively and truth-bearing connections is quite straightforward, and would follow as a matter of course. Almost everyone agrees on how vital it is that faith and practice should constantly and rigorously interrogate each other with reference to wider issues in Church and society, so that what people actually do in their lives, the decisions and choices and changes they work for, and how they do these things, may be a practical expression of the faith in which they believe. But how to bring this about?

A variety of models for understanding this process have been considered and explored in Chapter 3; but however perfect a theoretical process may be, the fact remains that what students, tutors and practising believers are looking for to bring it to life is little short of divine intervention. A reflective practitioner may have done everything the methodology requires with meticulous care: she may have identified a specific situation for scrutiny, built a 'thick descriptor' (Chapter 3.1) around it with attention to social issues and the wider context; she may have sought diligently for themes and parallels in sacred text and tradition and have assembled a sparkling array of appropriate material, but how to proceed from here? What is it that will enable her, immersed as she now is in relevant parts of her faith tradition, to take from it life-giving insights that will empower her to let go of previously held assumptions and prejudices, with bits of her own ego mixed up in the process, and see the original issue afresh with a tentative but bold enlightenment and new possibilities of responding that are more fully in harmony with the deep truths of her faith?

The 'gap' between faith and the issues of daily life is often extremely hard to cross. TR, and practical theology more generally, have often been seen as relying on a 'critical correlation' (a term coined by Paul Tillich, and advocated as a basis for practical theology by Tracy (1996)) between Christian texts and common human experience and language. But, as you may find in PTR yourself, this 'correlation' is far from simple. Theology and experience do not always map easily onto each other so that we can relate them together. From Barth onward, many theologians have argued that God's revelation in Christ is in radical discontinuity with experience, which we can never reach by our own unaided efforts, but only by God's grace. The voice of God's Word in Christ and scripture, they argue, is 'wholly other', disrupting rather than confirming the concepts through which we habitually understand the world. Boeve (2007) has argued for an intermediate position, whereby God 'interrupts' experience and history, with elements of continuity and difference. Oliver's analogy of 'hospitality' (Chapter 4.3), where we engage in conversation with a stranger whom we have welcomed as such, perhaps convey a similar balance of familiarity and otherness.

There are connections, too, with the story of Ezekiel's vision of the valley full of dry bones (Ezek. 37.1–11). The bones which the prophet saw strewn across the valley, gradually, as a consequence of obeying the spirit's commands given though the prophet, reformed themselves into bodies with flesh and sinews and skin, 'but there was no life in them'. For this to happen, the prophet was told to command: 'Come from the four winds, O breath, and breathe upon these slain, that they may live', and so the breath of God 'came into them, and they lived'. The 'dry bones' could be likened to the bare facts of the original matter under scrutiny, the valley in which they are found to the context, and the flesh, skin and sinews – the potential for new life – to the new look at themes and elements of the faith tradition that has been carefully undertaken. What then will enable the intervention of the 'wind of the spirit' to bring new life and new vision and an authentic plan of action for the situation under consideration, from this point on?

2 Minding the gap

The following exercise and discussion may help to provide an answer.

Exercise: similarities and differences in PTR approaches

Spend about 40 minutes considering and comparing the different models of PTR described in Chapter 3, noticing particularly ways in which they are similar and different. Note down whatever strike

> you as the two or three most significant differences and most evident similarities. If you are working on this exercise with others, spend a few minutes comparing notes and reflecting on what you have discovered.

One of the similarities which you may have noted in your response to the exercise above is that, however neatly the methods may be expounded, or the flow diagrams drawn, there is an identifiable 'leap of faith', '*kairos* moment', 'emerging insight', or some equivalent recognizable 'event', in a slightly different form in each case, in which the tide turns, as it were, and the process changes from one of exploration and assessment to one of fresh insight leading to new action. It is this 'moment' or 'movement' which seems to be capable of providing the flash of energy and meaning which makes the reflective process sparkle into life, supplying the vision which places the matter under investigation in a new light, generating pointers for change, renewal and action.

The importance of such moments has been recognized in many other disciplines. Arthur Koestler (1970, pp. 35ff.) argued that moments of what he termed 'bisociation' were vital to scientific discovery and artistic creativity, and also to humour. In them elements hitherto seen as unlike are brought together to shed light on each other. He writes:

> I have coined the term 'bisociation' in order to make a distinction between the routine skills of thinking on a single 'plane', as it were, and the creative act, which … always operates on more than one plane. The former may be called 'single minded', the latter a 'double-minded', transitory state of unstable equilibrium where the balance of both emotion and thought is disturbed. (1970, pp. 35–6)

The disturbance, he continues, may reflect itself in laughter, a shiver down the spine, or an ecstatic sense of 'Eureka! Now I have it!'

Thompson (1990) has argued that a similar 'interillumination' is at the root of both scientific models and good poetic metaphor. In theology Laurie Green uses the image of two faces (Figure 7) to provide such illumination – almost literally, as well as metaphorically – in TR. In the illustration, as you can see, one face looks at the situation under scrutiny, the other faces towards the traditions of faith.

Figure 7: 'Interillumination'

Reflection

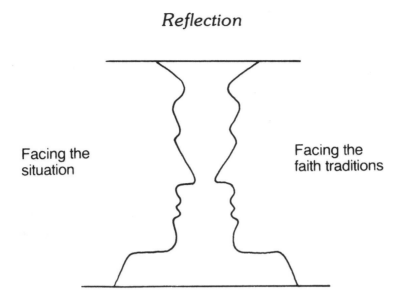

Facing the
situation

Facing the
faith traditions

It does not take long to discover that the two faces we have drawn, when brought together, create a whole new factor – and the image of a candlestick emerges from between the two faces as if to shed new light on the old faces. The intuitive leap is made. The mind has been allowed to move into a new dimension and to look at the meeting of experience and tradition from whole new vantage point … As they meet, we have a new light shining upon both and so this encounter illuminates whole new spheres of understanding. (Green 2001, pp. 80–1)

This is an excellent visual image to explain how in PTR we create an 'interillumination' or bisociation between life and tradition.

Like all things sacred and life-changing, such moments cannot be forced or produced to order, and yet without such an event, the attempt is likely to be lifeless, mere pastiche, and lacking in that sense of reality that gives energy and vitality to the whole PTR process. Of course the 'moment' may not always occur, literally, in a sudden flash of time. For some people, and on occasions for everyone, it is likely be a more gradual process. The reflector may simply find that, returning to the matter under consideration after a time attending to other things, her understanding of the issue has subtly changed; or she may find that, when focused elsewhere, perhaps during a time of prayer, or when listening to the radio or spending time with friends, connecting insights come unbidden, which, cumulatively, begin to bring newness of life into the reflective process. Prayer, of course, is key to this: particularly a deep prayerfulness that wonders, ponders and seeks to hear God's word and discern God's purposes (see Chapter 6.3).

Exercise

Whether the 'moment' of inspiration or new insight comes in an instant or more gradually, it is important to consider what it is that happens in that moment. How can it be prepared for and recognized? And what might help (or hinder) its occurrence? Spend about half an hour reflecting on this, and, if possible, compare your reflections with those of others.

---

3 'Negative Capability'

The 'gap' identifiable in each PTR approach could be likened to a 'sacred space' (cf. Sheldrake, 2000); a space in which certainties and preconceptions are abandoned and in which theological reflectors are open to receive fresh insight from text and tradition. So how may this receptivity be enhanced and cultivated?

Along with sacred space and hospitality, 'cultivation' provides a helpful – and hopefully 'fruitful' – analogy. Anyone who has done a bit of gardening will know that just scattering seeds on the ground is rarely successful. To enable the seeds to germinate, take root and eventually grow to maturity bearing fruit or flowers or edible leaves, attention needs to be given to the conditions that will enable this to happen. The soil needs to have warmed up from the winter's cold, to contain appropriate nutrients, to be smoothed to a fine tilth to enable root hairs to penetrate; rain and sunshine are needed, and protection from strong winds and hungry birds. In the same way, the human spirit, if it is to be alive and receptive to the kind of insight we have in mind, so that the vision may take root and grow into something tangible, also needs careful nurturing. If the would-be faith practitioner is worn out, stressed and weary, allocates very little time to recreation of any kind, or to experiences that delight and stimulate the mind and heart, and rarely, if ever, sits in stillness enjoying landscapes, music, sights, sounds and beauty – or simply the quality of being, and awareness of self in relation to creation, the Creator, and to others – then his cognitive and emotional processes are likely to get stuck in the same tired circles, and, however diligently he may try to apply the pastoral cycle in some form, nothing is likely to happen to bring the process to life (see Introduction 5).

What is advocated here, however, is not some sort of narcissistic reverie, but a proper attention to what is necessary for a human being to flourish, to be at peace within herself, and to have the kind of quiet inner strength that makes 'letting go and letting God' a real possibility. For this to happen, it is important to be able to live comfortably with a state of mind described by Keats as 'Negative Capability' the essence and context of which is provided in the box below.

From a letter of John Keats, written on Sunday 21 December 1817

Brown and Dilke walked with me back from the Christmas pantomime. I had not a dispute, but a disquisition, with Dilke, on various subjects; several things dove-tailed in my mind, and at once it struck me what quality went to form a Man of Achievement, especially in Literature, and which Shakespeare possessed so enormously – I mean Negative Capability, that is, when a man is capable of being in uncertainties, mysteries, doubts, without any irritable reaching after fact and reason – Coleridge, for instance, would let go by a fine isolated verisimilitude, caught from the Penetralium of mystery, from being incapable of remaining content with half-knowledge. This pursued through volumes would perhaps take us no further …

Coleridge, interestingly, whom Keats refers to here with some disparagement, had a comparable concept of the 'willing suspension of disbelief' (2004, ch. 14), with which it was necessary to approach any great work of art or literature, in order to enter into it in its own terms, appreciate its nuances and respond to its dealing with particular circumstances, however differently things might be viewed from one's own perspective.

As far as PTR is concerned, what seems to be necessary is something akin to a combination of both:

- 'negative capability' – a readiness to let go of the security based on long-held opinions and assumptions, and accept for as long as is needful, a state of doubt, uncertainty and mystery; and a
- 'willing suspension of disbelief' when the next step is taken, to look anew at what can be learned from the exploration of text and tradition that has been undertaken.

What is suggested, therefore, in order to be receptive to the kind of fresh vision that makes theological reflection come alive is that one needs both to be able to let go of previous certainties and also to be ready to look afresh at the material considered and the situation as a whole, with open-mindedness akin to the joyous wonder of a child – or the eyes of Miranda in the *Tempest* when she first encounters other people on the island of her shipwreck: 'O brave new world, That has such people in it' (Act V scene i.83). Miranda had never before seen any other human beings apart from Prospero and thus found each one an object of wonder and beauty. To be able to look at each situation under scrutiny, and the people involved, with this kind of freshness and clarity, we are suggesting, one needs first to ensure that one is continually refreshed and renewed so that one's God-given self may flourish, and second to start again in one's assessment from a completely different perspective such as may be assisted by the use of the kind of 'tools' outlined in Part 4 of this book.

4 Creating the sacred space

Some people need to enter a 'sacred space' before they can benefit from such tools to help bring the reflective process to life; for others, making use of the tools helps to create sacred space, but usually both are needed. It is important both to set aside significant amounts of time and space for a peaceful, prayerful openness, and also to find new perspectives through whatever delights and enlivens you or through using some of the creative tools suggested.

Exercise

This needs to be undertaken in a group if possible, or with at least one other person, allowing a minimum of 40 minutes.

Having identified an issue for attention, and decided which of the patterns for PTR suggested in Chapter 3 to follow, go through the earlier steps, including the theological perspective, until you reach the '*kairos* moment' or its equivalent.

- Then, without thinking too much about anything, as far as possible, enjoy using felt-tips, crayons or paints, for 15 minutes or so, without trying to create a picture or achieve anything. Just let the colours, textures and doodles take you where they will, becoming as fully absorbed as possible in the process as an end in itself. Enjoy the space and quiet and absence from pressure.

- After 15 minutes or longer, stop drawing and gradually allow the situation you began with, and everything you have noted from your faith tradition that seems to relate to it, to re-enter your mind as you look at the abstract drawing or painting you have made. Find connections, however tangential (some people will find this much easier than others) between the lines, colours and patterns and what they seem to suggest, and your current issue.

- Note your responses and thoughts and see if connections and fragments of meaning begin to take shape. Don't try to force premature conclusions or action plans, and if you haven't completed the process at the end of the allocated time, that is all to the good.

- Share this process and what has come to you so far as a result with at least with one other person, allowing about ten minutes (more if possible) to focus on each person's contribution in turn.

- Finally write a very brief summary of the process and identify what you have learned and insights gained into the situation you began with, and the actions you will take next.

How well this exercise does or doesn't work for you will depend on a number of factors, such as the context: some people need absolute quiet and space on their own for such creative activity, others prefer plenty of background noise; whether or not the particular 'tool' used here – abstract drawing or painting – is one that has a natural appeal for you; your mood and how far you are feeling pressured and weary or are in a sacred space of your own. You may enjoy seeking to enable the more free-flowing, intuitive feeling processes to emerge and take precedence, for a time, over the logical analytic cognitive processes usually employed in academic work, or you may find it alien and uncomfortable. Hopefully this will have been a worthwhile experience and one which, even if you found it difficult, you will try again using a tool that you enjoy and in other circumstances. What is important is to find an approach that will help you embrace 'negative capability', letting go of preconceptions, long-held assumptions and patterns of thought in order to enter and wait quietly in a 'sacred space' in which new possibilities and connections come alive, making it possible to look again at a situation with insight and vision informed and transformed at a deep level.

This exercise is not remotely intended to suggest that doing doodles is a tried and tested way of enabling you to hear the voice of the Spirit: merely that finding a relaxing and creative way of letting go can enable receptivity to a *kairos* moment. You may find some of the tools in the Toolkit more helpful, or you may already have approaches of your own that enable the kind of peaceful yet expectant waiting that is needful.

5 New life, transformation and a caution

Note: The exercise below belongs to this section but needs to be begun well ahead. (It could be undertaken simply as an agreement with oneself, or between members of a group using this book together, or it could be set as an assignment for an appropriate module.) The conclusions from this exercise will form essential background material for the issues studied in this section.

Exercise

Begin by reading and considering carefully the examples of PTR – all based on real life, though suitably disguised – described in some detail in Chapter 2, and in the box below. Make brief notes on what it is that seems to enable the reflectors to begin to see things in a new light. Then, over the next month or so, as you participate in the life of your local or placement faith community, note at least three events when you find yourself feeling uncomfortable at some slight or serious failure, as it seems to you, to translate the precepts of faith into reality. Identify them briefly, and then for each, build a thick descriptor so that you can appreciate the context and the issues involved more fully. Then, by a similar process to that described in section 4, use one or more of the 'tools' from the Toolkit to assist you in your reflective process. Finally – and this is the most significant part of the exercise – as you look back at the problems you identified, note how far your view of them and what disturbed you has remained essentially the same, and how far you have gained new insight through the reflective process.

So what is it that can bring about this sense of 'newness of life'? How can we receive a fresh perspective on a situation that has become contaminated with pain, stress and misunderstanding and from which there seems to be no way out? Or on a situation that has simply become stuck and stale and devoid of energy or sense of purpose? Or one that – more dangerous perhaps – has become characterized by complacency or fear of change such that those involved have come to resist any kind of reassessment and would rather return to the 'good old days' than give any serious thought to the future? As already noted, 'transformation' is an essential component in theological reflection. Unless there is a sense of change and renewal, fresh insight and a new energy to engage creatively with the problem under scrutiny, the reflector has probably sought to prove that he was right in the first place, rather than been genuinely open to receive new insight and inspiration from his faith tradition and sacred text.

Group exercise

In twos or threes, share with each other the results of your work from the previous exercise. After about twenty minutes sharing in some depth, choose two or three examples which best illustrate the transformative component of reflective practice, to share with the whole group. Identify together the key elements that seem to enable transformation to take place.

Margaret had been churchwarden at St James' Anglican Church ever since her children were at primary school, and had given a huge amount of her time and energy and creativity to working alongside a succession of vicars to sustain and develop the life of the small community of faithful who worshipped there week by week. Now in her late 50s she had supported the present vicar, Tony, in starting up a monthly family service to make the church more accessible for young families with no previous church connection, and had also begun a taster course to train as a Reader. To everyone's surprise, the family service quickly became popular and, as a result, several young adults joined a 'nurture' group and then began to prepare for confirmation.

Gradually, in numbers and liveliness, the newcomers increased. A few had attended other churches in the past and began to suggest innovations in music and worship styles, and in social activities and community serv-ice. While very encouraged that years of hard work and commitment at last seemed to be bearing fruit, Margaret and other longstanding church members gradually began to feel rather threatened. It was as if 'their' church was being taken over and the way things had always been done was no longer assumed to be right. Murmurings increased, and Margaret asked to see Tony to talk things over. She felt very torn between her loy-alty to the older church members whom she had known and loved and cared for over many years on the one hand and, on the other hand, her desire to see the church grow and her genuine delight in the new people who were coming to worship. 'And you see,' she said to Tony, 'the older members are the ones who have kept things going all these years. It has been their faithfulness, Sunday by Sunday, and their money and hard work that has paid the bills and kept the building in good order. These newcomers are happy enough to come along to the family service and the social events, but they aren't the ones who keep it going. It's like they've only been here five minutes, and yet they are acting as if they own the place – not that the older ones "own" it, but, you know what I mean.'

Tony was disappointed that Margaret took this view. He didn't say so, but listened to her carefully, describing the situation as he saw it. St James', like many other churches, had experienced a considerable drop in attendance over the last twenty or thirty years and there was a generation gap in the church, which the unexpected recent influx of younger people had exposed. The younger people's faith was no less real, but it was expressed differently and without the years of nurturing that Margaret herself had experienced. The church was different from a 'club' in that it was always open to all and existed as much as anything for the sake of those who were not its members (as William Temple put it).[10] The difficulties, therefore, were easy to explain but it was harder to work out what to do. At first Margaret couldn't think of anything, but then, remembering an event someone on the Readers' course had told her of, Margaret wondered if a potluck Sunday lunch after the family service to which everyone could be invited might be worth trying. The idea would be not just to share a meal but also to put into a metaphorical melting pot any issues, concerns or ideas that would be helpful for the church community to talk over together.

They agreed to put the idea to the next PCC meeting, and, in the meantime, to make the matter of newcomers and the church community a focus for prayer and reflection. Margaret both prayed regularly on her own and often came to morning prayer said daily in church. She wouldn't have used the words 'theological reflection' to describe what she did but she actively tried to make connections between what she believed and how she lived her life. She was deeply troubled by what was happening at St James' and prayed for guidance, spending longer than usual reflecting on her daily Bible reading notes and the passages they related to. A few days before the PCC meeting, the reading set happened to be Matthew 20.1–16, which, of course, Margaret had read many times before. As she read it this time, parallels began to dawn on her between the workers in the vineyard who had laboured through the heat of the day and the 'old guard' at St James; and between those who had only worked one hour but were given the same wage, and the newcomers to the church. When she read the vineyard owner's question, put to the angry workers who had been hired first, she felt as if God was speaking almost directly to her: 'Are you jealous because I am generous?' She felt very ashamed and afterwards explained to Tony, 'I've been thinking along the kind of lines that members of any club might think – that those who have been members over a long period of time should have greater weight in planning and decision-making. It just didn't seem fair that new comers should come along and change things. But now I see that the calling to follow Jesus through church membership is different. He loves and values everyone equally – it doesn't matter how long or how short the time we have tried to follow him: we are all his brothers and sisters and of equal worth – and that has to be reflected in the way we decide and do things at church.'

Margaret felt so much happier now she could see all this that she looked and felt quite radiant as she explained it to Tony – and happily volunteered to share it both at the forthcoming PCC meeting and at the potluck lunch which might follow.

From the work for this section, and from the examples given in Chapter 2 and in the box above, it is hoped that the reader has a sense of what is meant by 'the *kairos* moment' and the process of transformation in reflective practice and what is likely to help and hinder its occurrence. In order to guard against the dangers of self-delusion and distortion, or even returning to old positions in a new guise, refer back, regularly, to the 'marks of good practice in PTR' in Chapter 1.6. In addition, the value of the checks and balances provided by undertaking such reflection with a group of fellow reflectors, or at least with one other person, cannot be overestimated.

More important still, however, is to keep focused on the fact that the test of whether a *kairos* insight has been genuine is not how wonderful and uplifting it felt, or how clearly everything seemed to come together, but the change of attitude and practice that has resulted, and its validation and acceptance within the wider Church or faith community. This needs to happen both as part of our regular practice of PTR and also as a result of regular corporate reviews of what has been decided and acted upon as a result of such moments of insight. This leads on to the dimension of *chronos*, which is the subject of the next chapter.

Summary

This chapter has:

- noted the gap between scriptural and traditional resources on the one hand, and life today, on the other;
- looked at what we mean by the *kairos* moment and the place of an 'interillumination', or 'bisociation', that makes a momentary imaginative leap across the gap to forge lasting new concepts that shed light on both sides of the gap;
- investigated how we can not force, but must create room and receptivity for such a leap, by a 'negative capability' and a 'willing suspension of disbelief'…
- … and by ensuring that we have adequate time for the kind of rest and recreation and appropriate self-care that makes such receptivity possible;
- urged that the test of whether the insight that comes about in such *kairos* moments is authentic is partly whether we have arrived at a real and ongoing transformative insight, and partly whether it resonates with the truth-seeking visions of others and the collective wisdom of our church or faith community.

This is explored further in the next chapter.

Further reading (see also Core Texts at the end of the book)

Ballard, Paul and Pritchard, John (2006), *Practical Theology in Action: Christian Thinking in the Service of Church and Society*, London: SPCK.

Boeve, L. (2007), *God Interrupts History*, London and New York: Continuum.

Coleridge, S. T. (2004), *Biographia Literaria*, Whitefish MT: Kessinger.

Green, Laurie (2001), *Let's Do Theology*, London and New York: Continuum. Figure 7 on p. 101 is reprinted with permission of the publisher, The Continuum International Publishing Group.

Keats, John (1995), *Selected Poems and Letters*, Portsmouth NH: Heinemann.

Koestler, Arthur (1970), *The Act of Creation*, London: Macmillan.

Pink, Daniel (2006), *A Whole New Mind: How to Thrive in the New Conceptual Age*, London: Cyan.

Sheldrake, Philip (2000), *Spaces for the Sacred: Place, Memory, Identity*, London: SCM Press.

Thompson, Ross (1990), *Holy Ground: The Spirituality of Matter*, London: SPCK.

Tracy, David (1996), *Blessed Rage for Order: The New Pluralism in Theology*, Chicago: University of Chicago Press.

Valdes, M. J. (ed.) (1991), *A Ricoeur Reader: Reflection and Imagination*, Hemel Hempstead: Harvester Wheatsheaf.

6

PTR in the Context of Daily and Community Life – *Chronos*

This chapter explores ways in which the practice of PTR can be integrated into the ongoing *chronos* time of daily life and ministry and its place within existing or growing patterns of prayer and worship and personal and spiritual development. There is also a change of focus in the later parts of this chapter from seeking inspiration, which is generally an individual matter, to the community in which inspiration is tested and worked out into a practice of living – crucial in the process of validating more widely what might otherwise be mere idiosyncratic delusions.

This exploration takes place in seven sections:

1. Identifying your own approach to PTR: finding what works best for you.
2. PTR and the rhythm of life: how it can become part of your ongoing life pattern?
3. PTR and prayer: their connections and mutual enrichment.
4. PTR and personal development: keeping a journal.
5. PTR and supervision: the benefits of support and accountability.
6. PTR and church communities: how individual PTR can be tested and received, and the church enriched.
7. PTR and integration: making it part of a whole life.

1 Identifying your own approach

Like prayer, theological reflection can be approached in a variety of ways, and it certainly cannot be claimed that there is only one right path leading to good practice. Chapter 3 provided a number of models, and Chapters 4 and 5 have examined how scripture and moments of grace contribute essentially to the process. You are now invited to find an approach that feels both comfortable and challenging for you to use, with the potential to enable the kind of transformation you seek.

Answers to the following questions may help in establishing the approach you will use at least for the present:

- Which model from those outlined in Chapter 3, or others you have encountered, will you take as the basis for your approach?
- How will you adapt it to make it your own?
- How will your patterns of prayer and of PTR be related?
- What will you do to enrich your knowledge of and ready access to sacred text and tradition?
- Which four or five tools from among those suggested in the Toolkit, or others you can think of, might assist you in being open and responsive to new understanding and awareness?
- What else will you do to ensure that you remain receptive to whatever insights may be awaiting you?
- How frequently, and on what sort of occasions, will you set aside time for the purpose of PTR?
- How often will you undertake it alone and how often with others?
- Who will those others be, and how will you establish your group? What will be the pattern of its meetings?
- How will you keep a check on your carrying out of the decisions you make to do things differently in future, as a result of your reflection?
- How often will you review your reflective pattern and process, and with whom will you undertake this review?

Whatever approach to PTR you have begun to identify as the one you will work with for the time being, you will very likely discover that, as with patterns of prayer, you may need to vary it from time to time. PTR is, quintessentially, about keeping the practice of faith fresh and alive: it would be a sad irony, therefore, if the approach to PTR itself became stale and lifeless.

2 PTR and the rhythm of life

No amount of knowledge, understanding, theorizing and affirmation about the practice of PTR is at all the same thing as actually doing it. Although that seems obvious, it is surprising how many faith practitioners who are familiar with TR and are committed to it in theory, fail to make the disciplined practice of it a regular part of their pattern of life. In some cases this may be a reaction against having to do TR at college or in training and now wishing to exercise their freedom to choose when and how they do it – but, in reality, rarely doing it at all; or perhaps because with little spare time and so many matters pressing for immediate attention, TR simply fails to make it to the top of the priority list and gets neglected.

The point about integrating the practice of PTR into the regular rhythm and fabric of daily life and work is key here and cannot be emphasized too strongly. Although PTR may be particularly of value in times of crisis, allowing its use in practice to be crisis-led and determined only by such moments, is to miss the point. It is like resorting to prayer only as an act of desperation: better than not doing it at all, but neglecting 95 per cent of the riches of this life-enhancing activity. And, as with prayer, those who pray regularly and thus seek to integrate their lives into the life of God will be in good shape for knowing *how* to pray in times of crisis (rather than imagining it is simply a list of requests or petitions), so those who practise PTR regularly will have habits of structured procedure and critical discipline well in place to enable them to approach their reflection with a degree of objectivity even in difficult times, rather than becoming so overwhelmed by the crisis that they become quite unable to function or retain a sense of perspective. (See section 3 below on PTR and prayer.)

If the practice of theological reflection is already a regular part of your pattern of living, this may be a good moment to re-examine when, where and how you engage with it actively. If, on the other hand, it is something you have so far used only nominally or sporadically, beginning to settle yourself into a pattern for its regular practice in your life is part of the process of making it habitual. The exercise below encourages you to do this. As you prepare for this exercise, it may be helpful to look ahead to Chapter 7.6 which considers the advantages of working in a group. Group work inevitably requires making committed arrangements with others and will need to be allowed for appropriately in your daily/weekly/monthly/annual timetable.

Exercise

Looking at the present rhythm and structure of your life, and your answers to the questions about a future pattern of PTR in Section 1, identify the moments in the course of a week, when you do or will spend time in theological reflection. Use a table like Table 1 provided, or devise your own. Some people may find it more productive to identify specific times, while others may naturally identify regular occasions like 'after lunch' or 'after morning prayer'.

Table 1: PTR and my time.

Days of the week	Times/occasions identified for PTR	Record of times spent in PTR last week/ month/year/ quarter	A PTR pattern for the for the future
Monday			
Tuesday			
Wednesday			
Thursday			
Friday			
Saturday			
Sunday			
Monthly			
Quarterly			
Annually			

When you have completed your table, if possible, compare your results with those of others. List five factors that might help you keep to the pattern you have devised for yourself, and five that might prevent you from doing so. What might help you to ensure that the former take precedence?

Finally, making use of your table, write brief notes under the following headings:

A plan for a regular pattern of TR in daily life
- length of time to be set aside (a) daily, (b) weekly, (c) monthly, (d) annually
- percentage of TR sessions to be undertaken (a) alone, (b) with others (informal), (c) in a more formally arranged group
- tools to be tried (from the Toolkit, or your own ideas):
  - tools that I might use naturally
  - tools that might extend my repertoire
  - tools that would feel uncomfortable but would be worth using as a challenge once or twice a year
- the recording of outcomes and actions
- process for reviewing outcomes against actions undertaken
- frequency of review of reflective activity and process.

3 PTR and prayer

While prayer is likely to be of fundamental importance to all PTR practitioners, the way PTR and prayer are linked, contrasted or integrated will vary for each individual. Prayer and PTR are distinct and not at all substitutes for each other. But deep prayer can feed good PTR and be enriched by it in turn, and you may decide to relate your regular pattern of PTR to an established life-rhythm of prayer and Bible reading.

This introductory book on theological reflection cannot possibly encompass all the rich variety of ways into prayer that have been practised through the ages and today. Restricting the focus instead to one simple and traditional way of understanding different types of prayer, provided by the 'ACTS' mnemonic, is a helpful place to start. 'ACTS' suggests that prayer needs to include all the categories of Adoration, Confession, Thanksgiving and Supplication. These relate well to different aspects of PTR as suggested below:

- **Adoration and contemplation.** Spiritual writers describe seeking God for God's sake (rather than seeing God as a means to our own enrichment) as the beating heart of the spiritual life (as in Davies, 1993; Silf, 2004). This is why most acts of worship begin with an opening to the wonder and mystery of God. Similarly, a readiness to respond to the rich, thick texture of experience, as God-given, and a vibrant yet critical love for the resources of faith, are surely essential if PTR is to be genuinely theological, oriented to the love and service of God.
- **Confession and repentance.** PTR clearly seeks *metanoia*, the transformation of mind and perspective that makes new growth and new life possible. This in turn requires the growth of critical self-awareness, and the acknowledgement and if possible removal of blind spots so that creative responses to situations may flourish.
- **Thanksgiving**, or the blessing of the good things God has made so that God can be seen in them, lies at the heart of Christian liturgical prayer: the Eucharist means 'thanksgiving'. Such thanksgiving, both in prayer and in PTR, opens the eyes and mind to see and reflect on that of God in people and situations, so that practice may be in greater synergy with the work of God.
- **Supplication or intercession** is for many the core of prayer. It is perhaps especially relevant as we move in PTR towards deciding, choosing and willing in the light of our reflection. Action is then a continuation of prayer. Renewed desire, hope and prayer for the coming of the kingdom in a situation are in themselves part of the normal outcome of PTR. When people pray for things they *can* do something about, action must surely be the inevitable result.

Prayer and PTR are not the same. In prayer, the focus is on the knowledge and love of God, and the means to that knowledge and love is life itself, and the understanding of life that scripture and tradition help to shape. In PTR the focus is on understanding our experience, and learning to act in the world more fully, deeply and reflectively in the light of the God we believe to be revealed in creation, scripture and tradition. But these perspectives are complementary. Both in prayer and in PTR, God, the world and the believer are brought closer to one another.

Exercise 1

Write 200 words on what the relationship between prayer and PTR has been for you up to now and what you would like it to become in the future.

Exercise 2

Over the next two weeks write very brief notes in your learning journal (see section 4) on how you find prayer impacting on your PTR process and vice versa. Try to avoid evaluation or judgement. Just notice what happens and record it as gently as possible. At the end of two weeks, spend a short time reading your notes and noticing what pattern seems to emerge. Using your 'right brain' facility,[11] find an image which encapsulates your feelings about it. Let the image lead you to explore different parts of sacred text and enter as fully as you can into some of the narrative and comment that you find. Ponder this gently, and let it help you develop your approach to PTR and prayer in a way that might help to enrich both.

The art of PTR, as in the practice of prayer, is partly the art of balancing active and passive, neither trying to force the process nor just sitting back and waiting for it to happen by itself. And it is about balancing light and dark, conscious and unconscious, valuing both the moments of conscious insight, and the subtle changes that take place in the long term without any definable moment of transformation. In all these ways PTR has a lot to receive from prayer, and a lot to offer it.

4 PTR and personal development

Now that students at all UK universities are expected to evidence 'personal development planning' (PDP), including the use of a learning journal, theological students might find using such a journal as a regular part of reflective practice an excellent place to start. While PDP requires certain details of study, progress, planning and assessment to be included in the journal, there is also considerable freedom as to how it might be used. This offers scope for using PTR not only to reflect on matters as part of module requirements for theology courses, but also on any of the issues or subjects currently under the student's scrutiny for which it might be appropriate.

Journalling has been used very successfully on a number of courses to enable reflective practice (Walton, 2002; 2003; Ward, 2005) and has been a required part of some courses, for example in social work, counselling, teaching and medicine for a number of years. Jennifer Moon (2004) has provided useful ways of analysing and developing the use of journal writing exploring both practical and academic issues, including the areas of personal development and assessment. Using a journal is helpful, first, in that the simple act of writing in it slows down the pace of thinking, and provides a focus and time for reflection in itself. In addition, it requires writers to organize their thoughts and recognize what they have difficulty in understanding, and enables depth and appropriate self-criticality. It captures thoughts and ideas which can be reconsidered and related to other events and reflections in the future; and for some, writing in a journal is in itself a creative and enjoyable process (Moon, 2004, pp. 31 ff.). It is, of course, not just for courses and is equally valuable as a life-skill for practitioners of few or many years experience, and can be used as part of a formal or informal process of continuing professional development (CPD).

Some people take to journal-keeping easily and naturally and find it an essentially refreshing activity; for others it is never easy and can only ever be accomplished as a matter of disciplined commitment. Whichever end of the continuum you are nearer to, you will find journalling an extremely valuable aid to the process of PTR, if only you can persuade yourself to undertake it regularly. If you take the time to complete the following exercise carefully (especially the last part of it, which involves returning to reflect on your reflection in six months' time) you will almost certainly begin to discover its value in the PTR process.

Exercise

Write a 500-word reflection on an issue that is current for you in a way that would make it an appropriate entry for your learning journal. Divide it into four sections: (1) Outlining the matter under scrutiny; (2) identifying wider issues and insights that have a bearing on (1); (3) identifying theological themes and perspectives that relate to it; and (4) discussion of all of these, leading to an appropriate, if provisional, conclusion, including at least one specific and measurable action that you will take as a result of this exercise.

Try to complete 1 and 2 in 200 words or less, and keep 300 words or more for 3 and 4. If you are writing in a book, leave a blank page next to this entry (flexibility is easier with an electronic or looseleaf journal) so that you can return to your reflection in six months' time and make your own assessment and further reflection on your reflective process.

The goal is the establishment of an attractive and manageable pattern of PTR so that it becomes an enjoyable as well as essential part of continuing professional development and practice – without the need for any external pressure from tutors, mentors or faith-community authorities. One way of helping this to happen with appropriate thoughtful assistance, but without coercion, is through the regular practice of supervision.

5 PTR and supervision

So far in this chapter the focus has been on methods and rhythms you can pursue on your own. The remainder explores the benefits of involving others, both to support your commitment and to taste and test its fruits.

Supervision is accepted as a regular and essential part of professional practice in counselling and social work and in other professions. In counselling, for example, for a counsellor to maintain her accredited status with the British Association of Counselling and Psychotherapy (BACP), it is a *requirement* that counsellors should have at least one and a half hours a month of supervision on their work, either with someone who is experienced and qualified in this work, or as part of a peer supervision group.[12]

In the faith communities active in the UK at present, few if any have any such explicit requirement for supervision though some would argue that, for example, regular reflective sessions held between a vicar and curate, or between clergy who work together in a team, amounts to much the same thing. (It certainly can be, though often it probably is not!) The authors of this book urge that whatever the current or future practice in the particular denomination or faith community to which you belong, establishing a regular pattern of individual and/or peer supervision in which PTR forms the pivotal component is easy, enjoyable and even essential, both for ministerial practitioners and for faith-community members who wish to grow in wisdom, maturity, integrity and faithfulness (see Foskett and Lyall, 1988; Ward, 2005).

In practical terms this could be done in a variety of ways:

- One-to-one individual supervision could be made a required part of the process of 'continuing professional development' for clergy of all faith communities, with a list of accredited supervisors for them to chose from.
- If not a requirement, an equivalent arrangement could be facilitated on a voluntary basis, with strong encouragement for all to take part.
- A co-ordinator for peer supervision groups could be appointed in each locality to assist in the setting up and monitoring of such groups for those who wished.
- Such groups could be denominational, ecumenical or even interfaith and, in the latter case, could provide a reality base for interfaith dialogue and understanding.
- In the absence of any official framework for such one-to-one or group supervision, individuals can seek out colleagues who would be willing to work in this way to an agreed pattern and process.

As far as the content and process of such group or one-to-one sessions is concerned, a carefully structured format, adapted and agreed between group members, would help to ensure good use of the time available.

6 PTR in faith communities

Immensely valuable as solitary PTR can be, it is surely even more life-enhancing for the Church as a whole that local church communities should commit to the practice of PTR *together*. When members of a church or faith community, having had the process of PTR explained and demonstrated to them, are able to share together in a communal PTR exercise related to a specific decision or issue of concern, this can not only transform the current discussion and decision-making in relation to the matter in question, but also revitalize the whole community in its commitment to relating their understanding of faith to their daily personal and corporate living.

The classic model for undertaking PTR in this way as a local church community comes, of course, from the 'base communities'[13] in Latin America, where liberation theology had its birth. In this model (Chapter 1.3) participants would start by identifying a current local issue of concern and, together, develop a fuller understanding of its context and then identify theological themes and biblical passages that related to it. After a time of shared and often passionate discussion around the issues raised by this process the community would agree together on what action should be taken and who would undertake it, and how and when they would assess the results of their action.

That said, it seems that this model isn't easily transferred to other countries and cultures. Examples of good use of theological reflection in church communities have proved hard to find.[14] We can only speculate as to why this is, suggesting three possible factors but inviting you to buck the trend:

1 **A tendency to compartmentalize.** For example, a feeling that the main assembly of the church or faith community exists primarily to worship God – which of course it does – rather than reflect on experience or develop world-changing practices and strategies. Likewise church meetings and committees are often – again rightly – seen as having a practical, decision-making job to do, and so (in the authors' experience) resist engaging in theological reflection to relate specific decisions to the broader and deeper issues of faith.
2 **Issues of power and authority.** Traditionally expertise and authority to reflect on the world in the light of scriptural readings and make challenges to people's practice of faith is seen as vested in the priest or minister. The classic Bible study, likewise, often has its leader whose authority the group respects.

To engage as a congregation or a house group in PTR would be to introduce a more democratic process, shifting the centre of gravity from the priest or the venerated leader to the people as a whole. Both the minister and people might resist this redistribution of theological authority.

3 **Practical issues.** Theological reflection, as the term *chronos* suggests, takes time, and is often best done over an extended period. It does not lend itself to the relatively short time slots westerners tend to be prepared to allocate to worship and study groups, nor does it produce the instant rewards that are increasingly expected.

Exercise

Consider examples you have known where PTR has worked in a church community and ask why it has. If you don't know of any, imagine trying to introduce PTR to your local congregation. How would you go about it and what resistances would you expect to find?

In congregations that do manage to make PTR central, the benefits will work in two directions. The congregation will benefit from the insights of not just one but many members. And the individual members will have a place where their inspirations, insights and possible courses of action can be tested against the experience and wisdom of the congregation as a whole, including their understanding of the scriptures and traditions of the faith. This process of testing – of which more is said in Chapter 10.3 – will be nothing new: we see it at work, for example, in the way Peter's reflections were tested by the wider Church in Acts 10 and 11. It may be experienced as new, however, by many congregations; and may, indeed, bring them new life and vision.

7 PTR and integration

While it may be difficult for you to adjust your pattern of life (let alone that of the local church!) on all fronts at once, it is hoped that the patterns of thinking, feeling, praying, living, recording and sharing outlined in this chapter, and commitment to a regular discipline in doing this, will encourage you to take stock and make deliberate choices to allow for the regular practice of PTR both in your personal living and in your church or faith community.

If you are able to achieve this regular practice of PTR, by the means suggested, or by other means, you are likely to be well rewarded. Having a regular pattern and programme of PTR helps to ensure that when particular difficulties arise in the context of your work or ministry, or painful events occur in your personal life, you have a well-tried and tested system for putting these matters in context and reflecting carefully, appropriately and theologically without being blown off course by the problem.

More importantly, your whole pattern of living and – for some – of ministering, instead of being crisis-led, can be constantly refreshed and renewed by subjecting each aspect of it, over time, to the friendly but critical scrutiny that PTR makes possible – especially if you are able to ensure that this is done, at least at regular intervals, in partnership with others. This will both give you confidence – though hopefully not arrogance – that your prioritizing, decision-making, words and deeds are, as far as possible, in harmony with your beliefs and vice versa, and also enable you to keep a careful check on how these decisions work out in practice and keep alive your critical faculties as you do so.

Summary

In this chapter there has been a widening and deepening in the understanding of PTR from the momentary individual experience that lies at its core to something ongoing and corporate. Through sections 1–7 you have been invited to

- identify you own best PTR approaches;
- establish these as an ongoing practice interwoven with your life through time;
- relate PTR to prayer through mutual enrichment;
- relate PTR to your ongoing personal development;
- develop and make good use of a supervision process;

- relate PTR to your local faith community and consider how that community might become open to it; and finally, by combining all these approaches,
- integrate it with your life and that of others.

These are fine ideals; but now it is over to you to put them into practice – while making allowances for the particular person that you are. It is to this more personal ingredient in the PTR process that the focus turns in the next chapter.

Further reading (see also Core Texts at the end of the book)

Bolton, G. (2001), *Reflective Practice: Writing and Professional Development*, London: Chapman.

Burrows, R. (2007) *Guidelines for Mystical Prayer*, London: Burns & Oates.

Davies, J. (1993), *The Mind of God: Science and the Search for Ultimate Meaning*, Harmondsworth: Penguin.

Foskett, J. and Lyall, D. (1988), *Helping the Helpers: Supervision and Pastoral Care*, London: SPCK.

Gerkin, C. (1984), *The Living Human Document: Revisioning Pastoral Counselling in a Hermeneutical Mode*, Nashville TN: Abingdon.

Gutiérrez, G. (1984), *We Drink from our Own Wells: The Spiritual Journey of a People*, London: SCM Press.

Hawkins, P. and Sholet, R. (2002), *Supervision in the Helping Professions: An Individual, Group and Organizational Approach*, Buckingham: Open University Press.

John of the Cross (1990), *The Dark Night of the Soul*, tr. E. Allison Peers, New York: Bantam Doubleday Dell.

Moon, J. (2004), *Reflection in Learning and Professional Development*, Abingdon: Routledge Falmer.

Mudge, L. and Poling, J. N. (eds) (1987), *Formation and Reflection: The Promise of Practical Theology*, Philadelphia: Fortress Press.

Silf, Margaret (2004), *On Prayer*, Oxford: Lion Hudson.

Suchocki, Marjorie (1996), *In God's Presence: Theological Reflections on Prayer*, St Louis: Chalice Press.

Walton, H. (2002), 'Speaking in Signs: Narrative and Trauma in Practical Theology', *Scottish Journal of Healthcare Chaplaincy*, 5(2).

Walton, H. (2003), 'Women Writing the Divine', in P. Anderson and B. Clack (eds), *Feminist Theology of Religion: Critical Readings*, London: Routledge.

Ward, Frances (2005), *Lifelong Learning: Theological Education and Supervision*, London: SCM Press.

7

PTR and Personality: Differences in Thinking, Feeling, Learning and Doing

Having looked at some basic elements of the PTR process – the Bible in Chapter 4, moments of insight in Chapter 5, and the ongoing discipline of practice in Chapter 6 – this chapter considers that other indispensable element: you, the PTR practitioner. So far we have kept 'you' out of the picture, discounting the huge impact the emotions and personality of the practitioner will inevitably have on the process. This is rather like considering the process of driving without thinking of how different cars perform, or writing about winemaking without any consideration of the properties of different strains of yeast. It can be done, but better results will follow if allowances are made for different kinds of yeast and car, and if you don't try to drive a mini as if it were an articulated lorry. In the case of PTR the subjective factor is equally crucial, since the influence of your personality, emotions and preferred learning style will be present anyway, and, without any awareness of this, there is a danger that what is asserted as objective truth may be the result of unacknowledged personal bias or distortion.

This chapter therefore investigates:

1 PTR and the emotions
2 PTR and personality: introduction
3 PTR and personality: the MBTI
4 PTR and personality: The Enneagram
5 Learning style theory
6. Alone or in a group: pluses and minuses.

1 PTR and the emotions

Much has been written recently (e.g. Goleman, 1996; Sharp, 2003) about 'emotional intelligence' and how we need to learn to harness and use our feelings to discern what is happening around us and how to respond. In PTR, correspondingly, emotion is important at two points: as a (fallible) cognitive indicator, important at the stage of reflection on experience; and as a discerner and motivator of possible responses at the action stage.

To regard emotions as fallible cognitive indicators[15] is to recognize that emotions often alert us to realities and possibilities in a situation, but can get things wrong. Fear can alert us to real dangers: we may see a tiger and then feel fear, but sometimes it is the onrush of fear that makes a person focus sharply on the tiger hidden in the jungle, before she has consciously registered it, as well as filling her with the adrenaline she needs to escape! Anger, likewise, can signal real injustice in a situation. Joy and delight can open us up to genuine creative opportunities. On the other hand, the onrush of fear may merely relate, on closer inspection, to the tiger-coloured jacket someone left on a branch, and running away turn out to be hopelessly inappropriate. The anger may have more to do with my own frustrated agenda than any objective injustice. The joy may have more to do with the pint I have just sunk, making me 'merry' and imparting a rose-tinted glow to life, than anything real 'out there'.

A problem with emotions is that they tend to get 'stuck on' to people and things. Instead of seeing someone as a person I have bad feelings about, I tend to see the person himself as bad. The emotion he evokes in me has become seen as part of him rather than part of me. In such situations the observer tends to see and feel neither the person nor the emotion clearly. One great benefit of PTR done well is that the 'thick descriptor' and reflection stages provide the opportunity to peel the emotions away from the person or situation and look at them more objectively.

So, for example, I can begin to move from describing that person as having said stupid and harmful things, to describing them as having said things that made me feel angry or upset. Only then can I reflect appropriately, namely on what the anger or upset relates to. It may relate to a real injustice or malevolence in what the person was saying. Or it may have triggered feelings in me that have nothing to do with any injustice, but with my own emotional life. Or there may have been elements of both. For example, the person may have said my article in the magazine was rubbish. This may have been very unjust, because the article was excellent. Or it may be that the article was not very good, and I half knew that, but my ego was personally overinvested in it, and my pride has been wounded. Only after this 'peeling away' will my emotions be able to guide me to appropriate action; in the one case, perhaps, challenging the injustice by asking the person to spell out what he means in greater detail; in the other, recognizing I am not as good a writer as I clearly want to be, and going on a creative writing course to improve my skills.

Exercise

Revisit the two examples for the exercise in Chapter 1.4. List the emotions involved in each case, and the people to whom they might be attached. Consider how you might help the people involved to 'unpeel' the emotion from its object, and attend to what, other than the object, might lie behind the emotional response. How might this 'unpeeling' be helpful, and what might prevent it from happening?

One important point to note here is that emotions are never 'wrong', but we may be 'wrong' in the way we handle them. Of course, as Pattison notes (2007, pp.

185–92) there is much in Christian tradition from Jesus onwards that encourages us to think of many emotions as sinful.

> By teaching that appears to emphasize the inseparability of desires and actual actions such as the saying that a man who looks lustfully at a woman has already committed adultery with her in his heart (Matt. 5.28), Jesus, or the tradition that emanates from him, creates a link between feeling and deed that cathects desire with enormous danger. (p. 186)

This tradition also looks at the matter from the point of view of the male and the perpetrator rather than the woman or the victim; the latter would surely feel there was a difference between being desired and being sexually molested. Yet Christian tradition soon took on from classical culture the notion that all emotions or impulses need firm control by reason. If they take control of us, they become dangerous 'passions':

> If reason should let go of the reins and like some charioteer entangled in the chariot should be dragged behind it, wherever the irrational motion of the yoke-animals carries it, then the impulses are turned into passions, as indeed we can see in the irrational animals. (Gregory of Nyssa, 1993, p. 57, quoted by Pattison, 2007, p. 187)

Even this statement, however, unlike that ascribed to Jesus, suggests that an emotion is not 'wrong' to have, but it may be 'wrong' in where it – like the uncontrolled horses of the chariot – might lead us if we are not careful and self-aware. After all, 'irrational animals' seem on the whole to be well directed by their impulses, otherwise they would not survive.

So in the cases cited earlier, the fear was not wrong, but if it was only a jacket and not a tiger I was wrong to run away. The anger and upset were not wrong, but if the article was really poor, I would have been wrong to launch into an angry tirade against the injustice of the speaker, or go away and sulk. Desire for a good-looking man or woman is not bad in itself; what matters is whether we respond by attempting inappropriately and perhaps immorally to seduce that person, or by, say, thanking God for that person's beauty and moving on.[16]

One important thing in PTR, therefore, is to let ourselves experience our wonderful emotions of delight, fear, dread, awe, anger, rage, sorrow, desire and so forth as the emotions they are, and stay with them rather than be impelled by them. *Apatheia* – the tranquil freedom from passion sought by the Desert Fathers – is sometimes wrongly understood as not having emotions, but really it means not letting *them* have *us*; not being passive to our emotions, not letting them distort our perspective and drive our decision-making, but harnessing their energies to the goals we as whole people want. PTR requires that we attend to our emotions as the emotions they are, not attaching labels 'good' or 'bad' to them or feeling guilty about them, or disowning or repressing them, but treating them as facts that we can use well or badly. This is roughly what Sharp describes as 'emotional literacy', which he defines as 'the ability to recognize, understand, and appropriately express emotions … using your emotions to help yourself and others succeed' (2001, p. 1).

For as well as influencing our perceptions, emotions are what direct our actions and movements, as the word 'e-motion' implies. It is probably mostly the case with most people most of the time that we act not on the basis of what we think we ought to do, but what we want or desire or even yearn to do. Most of us will have had the experience of resolving in our heads, whether through PTR or more generally, to do something – be more generous with our money, say, or read the Bible or pray more, or be kind to someone we dislike, or drink less beer. When we review the situation – and one benefit of disciplined PTR is that it requires us to do so – we find we have done nothing of the kind, and if we are reflective and honest with ourselves, we have to admit that this has simply been because we have not really wanted to do it.

The art involved in the decision phase of PTR, which will often require hard work and determination to master, is to bring ourselves to a point of really wanting to do emotionally what we have decided intellectually is best. Only then will it get done. How is this achieved? There is no automatic recipe, of course, but the more you have engaged your emotions in the rest of the process, the more likely it is that they will be still be with you in the outcome. If in PTR you have, as just advised, explored your emotions and discerned what you really wanted in the situation, and what really made you joyful or sad or fearful or whatever; and if you have also engaged passionately with scripture and tradition and allowed them to fire you and inspire you, culminating in a *kairos* moment, or equivalent, of interillumination, then it is far more likely that the decisions you then make will be underwritten with a genuine emotional wanting that will ensure they are carried through into action. As with so much else in PTR, however, you are much more likely to remain true to what you have decided, if the whole process, and the action that follows, are undertaken as part of a group to which you are accountable. If you are on your own, a greater degree of self-discipline will be needed.

2 PTR and personality: introduction

As implied in the previous section, a significant part of good reflective practice is the ability to be 'reflexive', that is, the ability to understand oneself and one's own personal processes, emotions, feelings wounds, 'buttons' and personality, sufficiently to make appropriate allowance for these things when engaging in reflection. Without such awareness there is a danger of reacting and responding to events without realizing that what has caused that reaction may, for example, be a knee-jerk response to similar experiences in the past. (This, of course, is even more serious when such gut reactions are dressed up in apparently respectable theological arguments.) Appropriate self-awareness is quite different from self-indulgent navel-gazing, but care may need to be taken to ensure that the one does not degenerate into the other.

Having established in earlier chapters a framework for PTR and identified its main ingredients, and acknowledged the influence of emotions, the rest of this chapter aims to encourage you in a practice of PTR that goes with the grain of who you are. This will mean that instead of a burden, it can become a natural, enjoyable way of enriching and energizing your life and ministry (lay or ordained). Sometimes it may be valuable to try different approaches – even one which may feel quite alien and uncongenial – to stimulate, if at cost, new thoughts, perceptions and possibilities for action. Each person is unique, but different personality 'types' and preferred learning styles have been identified and there is a considerable body of literature – some more research-based than others – relating to these distinctive patterns of personality and preference (Briggs, Myers and Myers, 1995; Bayne, 1997; Beesing *et al.*, 1984; Rohr and Ebert, 1994; Reed, 2005). It may be helpful to begin by making your own mini audit of some of your preferences for yourself, in the following exercise.

Exercise

In Table 2, on a scale of 1–5 (1 for least and 5 for most), circle your preferences, when thinking, reflecting and learning:

Table 2: What I find useful.

Thinking, reflecting and learning process:	Personal preference
Listening while others teach or discuss	1 2 3 4 5
Active sharing in the process of teaching/discussion	1 2 3 4 5
Writing things down in lists and bullet points	1 2 3 4 5
Continuous writing, eg description or reasoned argument	1 2 3 4 5
Abstract drawing or doodles	1 2 3 4 5
Flowcharts, diagrams, schematic drawings	1 2 3 4 5
Reflecting for a long time before responding	1 2 3 4 5
Responding immediately and actively to each part of the learning experience	1 2 3 4 5

When you have filled in the table, consider what else helps or hinders your thinking, learning and reflecting processes, and how you learn new knowledge and skills in pursuit of a new interest. Record these learning traits in whatever way is easiest for you. Compare your scores on the table, and the other preferences you have recorded with those of friends, colleagues, fellow learners, or whoever may be willing to undertake this simple exercise.

The following sections consider two well-known theories which are worth examining if you are not already familiar with them: the Myers-Briggs Type Indicator (MBTI) and the Enneagram. Both of these theories are widely used in industry and other fields, as a brief search on Google will reveal.

3 PTR and personality: the MBTI

The Myers-Briggs Type Indicator, which is loosely derived from Jungian theory about personality, identifies 16 different personality types based on 4 different dichotomies:

- **E**xtroversion/**I**ntroversion: whether in terms of giving and receiving energy one is naturally oriented towards the outside world and other people and objects; or towards one's own inner world of thoughts and feelings.
- **S**ensing/i**N**tuition: concerns how one *perceives* situations; whether one focuses mainly on the five senses, and on present reality; or is more engaged by patterns, future possibilities and interrelationships.
- **T**hinking/**F**eeling: concerns how one *judges* and decides matters, whether one relies more on factual, systematic logic based on objective principles; or more on the felt needs of, and the effect on, all involved, and what feels best in that particular situation.
- **P**erceiving/**J**udging. 'Perceivers' prefer an open-ended, flexible approach to a task allowing it to evolve along the way, with a focus on the 'whole' rather than the parts, and a resistance to final closure. 'Judgers' like to set about a task to be done with a clear stage-by-stage blueprint, attending to rules and procedure, leading to quick decisions and completion.

By taking the first letter – the second letter in the case of iNtuition – of each pair of preferences, each person, according to the results of their MBTI test, will find the four-letter combination that identifies and describes their 'type'. The 16 resultant possibilities, and some of the characteristics typical of each, are indicated in Table 3, but this should be viewed with caution. This provides a taster only, since each 'type' is much more complex and varied than such a chart suggests, and needs to be understood in the context of a fuller reading of material suggested for further reading.

Table 3: Myers-Briggs types.

ENTP	Inventive, likes to instigate change, challenging, innovator
ENTJ	Controlling, task-oriented, organizer, likes to improve things
ENFP	People-oriented, likes variety, experimentation and new possibilities
ENFJ	Committed to personal growth and relationships, enabling others
ESTP	Problem-solver, organizer, action-orientated
ESTJ	Discerning, likes logic and structure and dealing with what is, managing
ESFJ	Encourager, team player, likes harmony in relationships,
ESFP	Likes working with others and getting things done quickly, trouble-shooter, but sensitive to inner spirituality
INTP	Likes to grasp complexity and structured thinking, theoretically inventive, responds to mysticism, prefers thought to action
INTJ	Imaginative, likes plans and strategies, and logical development
INFP	Oriented towards meanings, patterns and possibilities, committed, focused on growth and healing
INFJ	Imaginative, insightful, reflective, intuitive
ISTP	Individualistic, creative, analytical, likes to build on experience
ISTJ	Likes order and rationality, clarity, values experience and structure
ISFP	Caring and sensitive, focused on the here and now, and the personal
ISFJ	Loyal and conscientious, observant, people-oriented, likes clarity

Since PTR involves perception of situations, reflection and judgement, different MBTI profiles indicate considerable differences about what comes naturally and what has to be worked on. For example, do you find yourself rushing towards decisions (J) or wanting to linger long in perceiving and reflecting (P)? When reflecting do you rely more on obvious facts (S) or intuitive insights (N)?

And when making decisions, do rational logic (T) or gut and compassionate feelings (F) count for more?

Of course, in all four 'dichotomies' the different preferences or orientations are not as clear-cut as the word implies. The distinctions are helpful in understanding the opposite ends of a continuum between the different 'orientations', but, in reality, everyone has a bit of each, and, as MBTI theory makes clear, individuals may change in their preferences according to life events and stages. Some of these changes occur spontaneously but others may come about deliberately (at cost) if you decide that you want to work hard to suppress or enhance different elements of your personality.

MBTI theory and the 'Indicator' (a carefully worked out questionnaire the answers to which reveal your 'type') have been in widespread use over the last sixty years in both social and business institutions and have been found to be helpful in finding the right-fit person for a particular job and in enabling groups of people to work together more effectively. Until recently, for example, the Church in Wales required all of its clergy-in-training to undergo an MBTI programme. Much research has been undertaken in relation to this theory and its use, but it has never had a firmly established scientific basis, and some remain sceptical about it. We are not remotely suggesting that you use this or any other personality or learning theory as if it were proven fact; still less would we want to encourage you to pigeonhole yourself or anyone else in a restrictive way. But it can be of value if you use it simply as one tool among others that may help you to know and understand yourself and your reflective processes a little better without thinking of it as something fixed and determinative.

With that caveat, there are a number of ways in which MBTI theory may be of service in PTR. It may help you both to find a reflective style to suit your own 'orientation' and also enable you to understand and allow for difference in other people more generously when approaching any task as well as the task of reflection itself. In addition, it makes possible the tough option, on occasion, of deliberately choosing to work against your naturally preferred style – or, in MBTI terms, in 'working with your shadow' – to provoke, enliven and alter perspectives, particularly at times when the PTR approach used may have become somewhat stuck.

It emerges that an important aspect of personality theory in the process of developing and evolving a regular practice of PTR is the recognition that 'thinking' or analytical cognition is one factor which, among others, will be more naturally a part of one person's repertoire than another's. In the academy, cognitive and analytical processes are generally accorded pride of place in establishing good practice in nearly all disciplines and activities, and certainly for PTR these processes remain of high importance. However, in terms of interpreting, integrating, understanding and responding to a range of events and experiences, the dimensions of feeling, perceiving and intuition are sometimes of equal or greater importance.

Exercise

You need to begin by establishing what the four letters of your MBTI type are likely to be. A full MBTI indicator test is the best way to do this. (If instead you use one from the Internet, such as www.personalitypathways.com/type_inventory.html, you should be aware that MBTI has a strict programme of training and accreditation for those qualified to use its official indicator questionnaire, and short-cut quick-fix approaches are not recommended.) Having ascertained your 'type' (see Table 3), look back at the approaches to PTR outlined in Chapter 3 and identify which are likely to be more or less congenial for you to use.

---

4 PTR and personality: the Enneagram

The Enneagram, though only regularly (and increasingly) used in modern times over the last thirty-five years, has much more ancient origins than the MBTI, and can be traced back as far as Sufi mystics in the tenth century. Connections have also been made with the teaching of the Desert Fathers, of Evagrius of Pontus and Gregory of Nyssa, and within other faith communities including Judaism and Buddhism as well as Christianity and Islam (cf. Beesing *et al.*, 1984, pp. 1–3; Riso and Hudson, 1999, p. 9). George Gurdjieff, a Georgian Armenian, in the early twentieth century, promoted the Enneagram, though suspicions about his esotericism generated some hostility in church circles. Oscar Ichazo set up

Enneagram workshops in Chile, and then in North America, and in time the ideas began to be adopted as a tool for Christian, and especially Roman Catholic, spirituality. It is also used in New Age and other religious groups as well as in many secular contexts, as, again, a search on Google will reveal.

'Enneagram' means 'nine points' and consists of a crownlike figure (Figure 8) identifying nine basic personality types, whose typical characteristics are indicated in Table 4. As the figure suggests, three of these types function primarily at a feeling and relationship, 'heart' level, three at rational, head or 'mind' level, and three at a gut level of desire and 'will'.

Figure 8: The Enneagram.

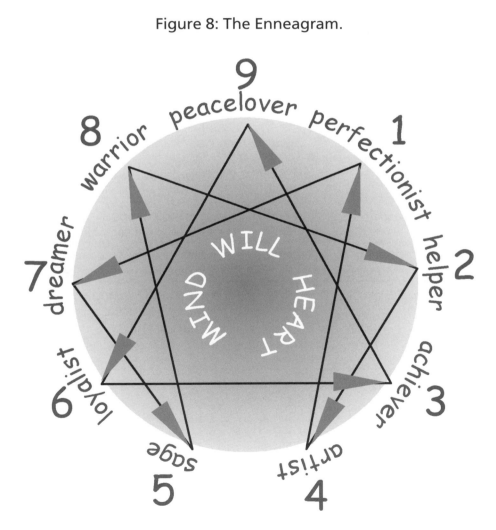

Table 4: The Enneagram.

No.	Typical characteristics	Compulsons	Distinctive gifts
1	Perfectionism, integrity	Perfectionism	Hard-working, orderly, reliable, independent, practical
2	Helping, generous	Pride	Warm, sensitive, aware of others' feelings, ingenious, appreciative
3	Ambitious, performer	Deceit	Energetic, efficient, makes things happen, entertaining, encourager
4	Individualistic, 'special'	Envy	Imaginative, creative, stylish, intuitive, clear-thinking
5	Observer, perceptive, original	Avarice	Non-judgemental, able to see the big picture, insightful
6	Likeable, loyal, responsible	Fear	Conscientious, persevering, lively, balanced outlook
7	Accomplished, enthusiastic	Self-indulgence	Multi-tasker, optimist, sparkling, positive, philosophical, accepting
8	Self-confident, decisive, 'the boss'	Lust for power	Self-sacrificial, idealistic, strong sense of justice
9	Receptive, reassuring	Sloth	Mediator, reconciler, compassionate, tolerant, resourceful

Exercise

From the Enneagram characteristics described in Table 4, and preferably after attending an Enneagram workshop or at least after further reading of your own, make a provisional assessment of the numbered 'point' which best fits you. If possible, do this in a group and discuss results with each other. Having done this, identify which aspects of PTR are likely to be easy or more difficult for you if your judgements on this are accurate, and if the theory has some validity.

The most useful aspect of personality-type theory, as far as PTR is concerned, is that it enables theological reflectors to recognize and value differences in approach and practice; and also to recognize that these characteristics are not set in stone, and sometimes particularly valuable insights may emerge when you deliberately work against the flow of what feels comfortable and natural. In Enneagram theory, for example, Fives are natural observers, Ones are critics and reformers, Fours are creative, intuitive and individualistic: yet sometimes every one of those 'types' – and all the others – will be in a situation that needs rigorous attention and radical change. A One might find such a task congenial, but might be over-perfectionist in carrying it out; a Five might work out a wonderful solution for the problem on paper, table it, file it, perhaps show it to others, but do absolutely nothing about implementing it; whereas a Four, finding the whole business tedious, cramping of style, and a complete waste of real giftedness might just produce a sketchy diagram at the last minute, which no one else could understand!

Exercise

The noticeboard at your church, mosque, synagogue or gurdwara is a mess. Notices are stuck one on top of the other, old ones left up and important ones about current events often obscured. It is unclear who has responsibility for it and for a long time nothing is done. Finally it is raised at a leaders' meeting and the task of ensuring that the noticeboard is kept well ordered in the future is assigned to you.

Your tasks for this exercise are:

- Identify which personality types according to MBTI and Ennea-gram theory respectively would be likely to find this a congenial task, and how this does or does not fit with your own.

- In the light of this awareness outline two (or more) different approaches to getting this task done: one that accords with your personality and one (or more) that would work well for someone of a very different 'type'.
- Identify two or three theological themes and two or three passages from sacred text which seem to have a bearing on this matter and write very brief notes for a theological reflection on the issues involved and how your reflection may help to reframe this task and the actions it suggests.

5 Learning-style theory

Learning-style theory, is, if anything, even more complex than personality theory, though not unrelated to it. Gavin Reid (2005, pp. 54ff.) lists 13 different major models of learning styles. Rather than attempt any kind of summary of all of them, the focus here is on one of the earliest, that developed by Honey and Mumford (1986) from the work of Kolb.

Kolb noticed that when using his learning cycle (Chapter 1.2) students evidenced different preferences about different parts of the cycle. Some were keen to try new experiences straight away and were less keen to think through the experience afterwards; others enjoyed the abstract conceptualization of an experience but were reluctant to try it out in reality. From such observations, Kolb identified four types of learning preference, which he characterized as converger, diverger, accommodator and assimilator. Honey and Mumford (1986) studied these different approaches to learning further and developed a diagnostic test consisting of 80 statements for agreement/disagreement, resulting in the identification of 4 types of learner: activist, reflector, theorist and pragmatist, each with particular likes and dislikes. Activists, for example, prefer to learn by doing and don't much enjoy having to analyse the process; while reflectors need plenty of time to assimilate and ponder what they are being asked to do, to understand clearly what is required, and to try out different approaches in their mind before feeling able to take action. These and other characteristics are outlined in Table 5.

Table 5: Learning styles.

Learning preferences	Likes	Dislikes
Activists	Getting involved, brainstorming, new ideas, games and tasks, working with others, leading, being challenged	Demonstration, detailed preparation, detailed reflection, repetition, following instructions
Theorists	Patterns, structure, clarity, logical theory, sequence and rationality, detached analysis, the opportunity to question, closure	Open-ended, evolving situations, emphasis on feelings and emotions, vague instructions
Pragmatists	Techniques with clear applications, models, guidelines, clear relevance to the job in hand, efficiency, trying things out	Lengthy explanations or discussions, theory without obvious practical benefit, abstract concepts
Reflectors	Observing, time to take stock, careful preparation, listening to others, thorough exploration, analysing, writing carefully thought-out reports	Having to act or speak with insufficient preparation, being rushed, leading without being absolutely clear about task and approach

Exercise

Identify the description in Table 5 that seems to suit you best. If possible, working with a partner or a group, identify the learning preferences of your colleague/s and compare notes. Recall occasions when what was required of you felt very comfortable/uncomfortable and the different responses of others. In similar situations in the future, what might you do to maximize your effectiveness?

As has already been said, Honey and Mumford's learning-preferences theory is only one among many, and you may already be familiar with it, or know of others. People encountering such theories for the first time often find them quite liberating (as with personality theory). Having such differences described and identified somehow gives permission for each person to be as they are in this respect. Once again, differences can be valued and prized and tasks can be allocated according to each person's particular gifts and approach. But this cannot always be the case. Sometimes the new material that has to be worked with by a particular person is a perfect fit in terms of their natural learning style, and sometimes it is a complete mismatch.[17] Recognizing this and understanding the reasons for it and managing your work approach in the light of this knowledge is infinitely preferable to a pattern of tackling the more congenial tasks straight away and avoiding or neglecting the difficult ones with endless excuses. Obviously the (for you) cross-grain tasks will be more demanding, and allowances need to be made for this – such as doing them when you feel at your best, rather than when your energy levels and motivation are at a low ebb.

A good piece of PTR will often include elements which accord with each of the four learning preferences identified, and can, potentially, work well in a mixed group. Theorists will enjoy adducing different arguments and concepts from a variety of disciplines and developing ideas that may contribute to the thick descriptor; reflectors will particularly enjoy finding possible connections with theological themes and ideas, and weighing up the applicability or otherwise of each; pragmatists will help to sift out what has immediate practical application to the situation in hand (as opposed to interesting theory!); and activists will be keen to get from the original event to the new action as fast as possible, and thus help to keep the whole process moving. Someone engaging in PTR on her own can structure the process to suit her own learning style, while being aware of the need to put extra energy into the aspects of it that come less easily.

Exercises

(1) Imagine you have a team of four people: Andy the activist, Tessa the theorist, Peter the pragmatist and Rachel the reflector. Ideally do this exercise in a group of four people assigning the different roles appropriately. (Of course, you will be lucky to have exactly

one of each type so you'll have to make compromises.) Now imagine the task of preparing for the coming AGM of an organization – the local church or some other. List the tasks that need to be done, for example:

- publicity for the meeting
- encouraging people and organizations to attend
- inviting local dignitaries etc.
- reports on the church events – spoken and written
- planning the agenda
- chairing the meeting
- keeping the records
- finding people to stand for the key posts in the coming year,
- and others you think of ...

Now assign the tasks to the different imaginary characters or members of your actual group of four. Are some easier than others to allocate? At the end, are there some people with few or no jobs and what might this indicate?

(2) Pick one of Jesus' disciples (including the female ones) for each of the four learning styles and give your reasons. Now look at what Jesus said to those disciples and/or the tasks he gave them. What does this reveal?

6 Alone or in a group?

Everyone would probably benefit from doing PTR in a group at least from time to time. If you are reading this book as part of a course, you will have a ready-made group to work with. If you are – or will later be – on your own, you will probably derive great benefit from setting up a group of like-minded people who will meet with you regularly for this purpose. However, to allow the Spirit to be alive and at work in a theological reflection group of this kind it is suggested that the members consider using an approach to sharing ideas quite different from that often used in academic debate in which each contributor tries to prove their point.

A 'creative listening' approach (Pinney, 1992) or something similar provides a helpful alternative. Typically, in creative listening, having agreed on the matter for attentive reflection – which might be a particular issue or event or passage of text – a group starts by inviting responses from each member who wishes to make one, without interruption or comment, followed by a time of shared silent reflection. After an agreed period, the group begins to interact more freely, making connections and teasing out themes and lateral insights, perhaps using drawing or flowcharts or brainstorming, or even – from the Toolkit – group 'Sculpting' or 'Music Making'. The exercise is then brought to a close as members wish. In the case of a PTR group this would be by identifying new approaches and actions to be taken.

'Creative listening' might require further adaptation for use in PTR, and would not be appropriate for use with all of the exercises provided in this book. But whenever PTR is undertaken in a group, it is suggested that a more 'appreciative' *modus operandi*, such as that outlined above, should sometimes be used, rather than the more 'oppositional' proof-point style. It is important to find a way that encourages openness, pondering and even uncertainty, rather than clinching an argument too quickly. However, it needs to be remembered that – as noted above – whereas some personality types enjoy leaving things open-ended and provisional, for others, completion and closure are essential if the task is to feel worthwhile at all.

In a group it is important to recognize and note different personality and learning styles, and to choose a specific approach at one meeting and another at the next so that the preferences of each member can be accommodated. It is helpful for members to articulate what they hope to gain from their group membership and the results they are seeking. If this is done, and if differences are openly acknowledged and allowed for, the group process is likely to be more fruitful as a learning experience, and in its impact on daily life and practice. These issues are addressed in Exercise 1 below.

Learning resulting from working in a group can also enhance the reflective process for each person when reflecting on their own. While personal reflective practice has the advantage of much greater flexibility about when and where it can be done, it lacks the greater objectivity, and commitment to task, that sharing with others makes possible. The committed use of a learning journal (see Chapter 6.4) both provides valuable material for sharing and working on in a group, and also, on occasions when being part of a group is not possible, can provide a more objective record and kind of accountability to oneself than simply relying on mood and memory.

Group exercises

(1) Using the material in this chapter, and other additional material as appropriate, group members are invited to:

- record their probable MBTI and Enneagram type, and their learning-style preferences;
- discuss what they like and dislike about group work;
- identify between three and six outcomes that they would wish to result from their membership of this particular group;
- share the results of this exercise together; and then
- agree on an appropriate way of working for the group;
- record and keep a copy each of what has been shared and agreed;
- decide how modifications may be made.

(2) Over the next few weeks:

- identify a specific matter for reflection which is important to you and likely also to be important to members of your group;
- complete a PTR on this matter on your own;
- write a brief account of it in your journal;
- invite members of your group to share together in a group reflection on the same issue;
- record this process and the conclusions and actions it leads to;
- compare the two experiences based on your recordings in your journal;
- identify at least three plusses and minuses, respectively, in relation to group and individual reflection.

Summary

This chapter has provided pointers to ways in which personality traits and particularities can have a bearing on each person's reflective process and how this might affect approaches to PTR and methodological choices, through.

- looking at how emotions can be employed well in PTR;
- considering the influence of our personalities on PTR, and the usefulness (and dangers) of personality indicators like the MBTI, the Enneagram and learning-style theory;
- noticing the way personalities function in groups, and the benefits and risks of group PTR.

These may be areas which you decide to explore and evaluate further. A brief experience of living readily indicates that personality differences exist, and it is hoped that this chapter has provided basic tools for a rudimentary appreciation of such differences which can then be included in making decisions about using and developing PTR for different people and contexts.

Hopefully the material discussed here will also encourage you to be gentle with yourself in relation to aspects of the PTR process and putting it into practice which you find particularly uncongenial or difficult, and in making allowances for others whose areas of sensitivity or discomfort may be different. 'One-size-fits-all' rarely works very well in practice in terms of bicycles, car seats, hats or women's tights. Personality differences may be less obvious and more malleable than physical ones, but they are no less real, and taking them into account as fully as possible in the vital matter of reflecting on how we relate our faith to daily life and work is as important as ensuring that a crash helmet or walking pole is the right size for its user and thus fit for purpose.

Further reading (see also Core Texts at the end of the book)

Bayne, R. (1997), *The Myers-Briggs Type Indicator: A Critical Review and Practical Guide*, Kingston upon Thames: Nelson Thornes.

Beesing, N., Nogosek, R. and O'Leary, P. (1984), *The Enneagram: A Journey of Self-Discovery*, Denville NJ: Dimension Books.

Bergin, E. and Fitzgerald, E. (1993), *An Enneagram Guide: A Spirituality of Love and Brokenness*, Dublin: SDB Media.

Briggs Myers, I. and Myers, P. (1995), *Gifts Differing: Understanding Personality Type*, Mountain View CA: Davies-Black Publishing.

Duncan, B. (1993), *Pray your Way: Your Personality and God*, London: Darton, Longman & Todd.

Goleman, D. (1996), *Emotional Intelligence,* London: Bloomsbury.

Gorringe, T. (2001), *The Education of Desire: Towards a Theology of the Senses*, London: SCM Press.

Gregory of Nyssa (1993), *The Soul and the Resurrection*, tr. C. Roth, New York: St Vladimir's Seminary Press.

Hirsh, S. (2006), *Soultypes: Matching your Personality and Spiritual Path*, Minneapolis: Augsburg Fortress Press.

Honey, P. and Mumford, A. (1986), *Using your Learning Styles,* Maidenhead: Peter Honey Publications.

Pattison, S. (2007), 'Mend the Gap: Christianity and the Emotions', in *The Challenge of Practical Theology: Selected Essays,* London and Philadelphia: Jessica Kingsley, pp. 185–92.

Pinney, R. (1992), *Creative Listening,* London: Children's Hours Trust.

Reid, G. (2005), *Learning Styles and Inclusion*, London: Paul Chapman Publishing.

Riso, D. and Hudson, R. (1999), *The Wisdom of the Enneagram*, New York and London: Bantam Books.

Rohr, R. and Ebert, A. (1994), *Discovering the Enneagram: An Ancient Tool for a New Spiritual Journey,* North Blackburn, Australia: CollinsDove.

Sharp, P. (2001), *Nurturing Emotional Literacy,* London: David Fulton.

Sheldrake, P. (1994), *Befriending our Desires,* London: Darton, Longman & Todd.

Stead, C. (1994), *Ministry after Freud*, New York: Pilgrim Press.

Watts, F. (2002), *Theology and Psychology*, Aldershot and Burlington VT: Ashgate.

Part 3

The Wider Perspective

Having looked in Part 1 at the heart of how PTR works, and narrowed the focus in Part 2 to examine key elements of the process, we turn in this third part to the wider perspective, setting PTR in its theological, socio-political, cosmological and everyday context.

- Chapter 8 explores the place of TR within practical and other theology, arguing that PTR uses the *method* of critical practical theology, and – potentially – the *content* of every kind of theology. The question addressed is: How does PTR relate to the search for divine wisdom?
- Chapter 9 considers how PTR may be used to evaluate and challenge institutions and political structures and our part in them, and so contribute to issues and events in the wider world. The question here is: what can PTR contribute to institutional, global and personal liberation?
- Chapter 10 affirms and explores the role and mission of PTR in Church and society, addressing the question: how is it appropriate to use PTR, for myself, in my local church and community, and further afield?

8

PTR and Theology

Theology, so long as it is not confined either to an academic or an ecclesiastical ghetto, but allowed to roam freely and attain its natural glory, is and always has been a practical pursuit. It is 'thinking about life in the light of our faith in God' (Wilson, 1988, p. 53), leading to real change in people's lives. Or as Luther put it (quoted by Wilson, 1988, p.53), 'not reading books or speculating but living, dying and being damned make a theologian'. Heitink argues that 'Theology is based on experiential knowledge and is aimed at faith and action. From its very beginning, theology had a practical purpose' (1993, p. 105). And finally, according to David Ford, 'describing reality in the light of God is a basic theological discipline … Theology hopes in and seeks God's purposes while immersed in the contingencies, complexities and ambiguities of creation and history' (2007, p. 4).

PTR is arguably one of the main ways in which theologies, learning from experience and tradition, are directed to the task of changing life. This means that, as Todd emphasized (Chapter 3.1.d), in engaging in PTR you are not just applying theology, you are making or doing it. This chapter will seek to establish these bold contentions in the following sections:

1 PTR and practical theology: investigates the relationship between PTR and the different kinds of practical theology, and its key role within it.
2 PTR and theological context: considers the 'publics' addressed by theology and PTR, and argues that wider society, not merely the Church, must be seen as the ultimate context of PTR.

> 3 PTR and theological mood: explores how different 'grammatical moods' in theology necessarily engage different phases in PTR and different kinds of theological discourse.
> 4 PTR and theological wisdom: considers where theology learns and grows its wisdom, or fails to, and how PTR draws the fruits of its wisdom together in practical theology.
> 5 PTR and interfaith reflection: broadens the enquiry from mainly Christian theology to suggest how PTR could work in inter-faith groups.

1 PTR and practical theology

As has already been noted (Chapter 1.1) theological reflection is central to, and perhaps the defining element of, practical theology, but it is not synonymous with it. It provides the means for making connections with other aspects of theological discipline (Thompson, 2008, provides a worked example of this in relation to Christian spirituality); and between theology and pastoral practice (as in Pattison, 1997b). It also enables a fruitful interchange between theology and the events of daily life and ministerial practice so that both are enriched and transformed.

Practical or pastoral?

Believe it or not, the question of whether *practical theology* and *pastoral theology* are one and the same thing, or whether they refer to two different areas of theological discipline, is a matter that has exercised some passion and vexation among those who concern themselves with such matters in academic institutions. While the aspiring theological reflector need not worry unduly about this, clarity about what practical theology really is and how PTR relates to it in practice is a useful starting point.

Pattison and Woodward (2000, pp. 1–19) provide a helpful summary of the history and different nuances in meaning of the two words, and their evolution. 'Pastoral' theology derives from 'pastor' (shepherd) suggesting that as a shepherd looks after his sheep, so the pastor cherishes and provides for those in his care: a concept based on imagery from the Old Testament used by Jesus when he described himself as 'the good shepherd', on whom pastors through the ages have sought to model their practice. *Pastoral theology* is the theological underpinning of such activity.

Practical theology, on the other hand, is a term deliberately created in the late eighteenth century among German theologians, who were seeking to apply theological principles both to pastoral practice and to all other areas of church government and activity including education: the term, therefore, was understood as including pastoral theology but much else besides. Today the concept of *practical theology* has a more extensive brief relating theological principles to almost any area of academic or social activity and public life. The two terms, therefore, have different historical roots, and in Germany and the USA are still used to indicate distinctive fields of theological application. In the UK, however, the two terms are often used as if they are interchangeable, with *practical theology* tending to have the cutting edge when used as a title for a particular theological discipline. In this book, partly, perhaps, through the influence of the British and Irish Association of Practical Theology (BIAPT) and because of its authors' experience in teaching on practical theological courses, *practical theology* is the preferred generic term for the whole magnificent enterprise of making firm links between belief and practice – of which *pastoral theology*, in the sense outlined above, is a very significant part and for which PTR provides the key.

Varieties of practical theology

However, there are other approaches to this enterprise. Heitink (1993) distinguishes five 'currents' in practical theology, whose titles are here simplified as follows:

- **Deductive.** Starting from the Bible as the revealed Word of God, practical theology *applies* this to experience and practice today. Theology 'in a deductive way, starting from the theological mystery, integrates the contributions of the auxiliary disciplines in a meaningful, comprehensive unity' (Jonker, cited in Heitink, 1993, p. 172). There is no cycle here: the direction is one way, from Word to life.

- **Hermeneutical.** More emphasis is placed on the need to interpret or understand the Word by correlating it with our life and experience, and vice versa. A two-part cycle appears: understanding the text changes our life, but our changed life comes back and sees the text in a new light.
- **Empirical.** Great emphasis is placed on gathering data about religion and belief, which theology then interprets. The emphasis is on experience and reflection, and the move is an inductive one, from experience to theology; one way, but in the opposite direction from that of the deductive variety.
- **Critical.** The classical 'liberation theology' cycle on which PTR is based, and which has been extensively discussed. Theology develops 'a liberating practice through a process of seeing (observation, experience, analysis); judging (evaluation according to established criteria); and acting (development and execution of projects) in a constant reciprocity' (Höfte, cited in Heitink, 1993, p. 175). Praxis and the critique of institutions have a decisive role, relatively absent in the other varieties of theology.
- **Pastoral.** As just described, the emphasis is on enabling pastors and ministers to relate their beliefs to good professional practice and vice versa. This Studyguide has been designed primarily for a 'pastoral theology' context, and for that reason the core of this book has necessarily and explicitly focused on PTR, a method of theological reflection which is particularly suited to pastoral theology.

In terms of these varieties of practical theology, we could broadly say that PTR is pastoral in goal and critical in method. But it is important to be aware of the other approaches and methods of theological reflection, such as those outlined in Chapter 1.1, and to begin to identify which of the approaches, respectively, are likely to be more appropriate in the various currents of practical theology.

But what of our contention that the goal of all theology is practical? And how might PTR relate to theology in all its rich but rather jungle-like variety? To explore this we need to find some ways of seeing pathways and villages in the theological jungle, so that we can trace the places PTR might lead to, and where it might offer hospitality to, or receive it from, the various kinds of theology on the way.

In the following three sections, three ways of mapping the theological jungle will be offered, each of which indicates, in a different way, the place of PTR within theology as a whole. The three different mappings arise in response to three questions, which could be asked about any kind of written or spoken discourse, but here apply to theology and PTR:

- **Context**: to what 'public' is theology – and PTR – addressed, and in what community does it take place?
- **Mood**: in what grammatical mood(s) does theology – and PTR – speak?
- **Wisdom**: where and how does theology – and PTR – listen and learn?

2 PTR and theological context

David Tracy (1981) distinguishes three broad categories of theology according to whether the 'public' it addresses is the academy, the Church, or society at large. His arguments are summarized in Table 6.

Table 6: Varieties of theology, based on Tracy.

Kind of theology:	Philosophical	Systematic	Practical
Public:	Academy	Church	Wider society
Aim of argument:	Rational demonstration	Significance for the faithful	Leading to liberating praxis
Ethical standard:	Honest critical enquiry	Creative fidelity to tradition	Solidarity in the struggle
Stance:	Non-confessional	Confessional	Identity with oppressed group
Criteria:	*Validity* of argument in philosophical terms	New *meaning* for accepted truth	*Ethical* action, leading to liberation

The appropriate theologies to these publics are, he suggests, philosophical, systematic and practical theologies respectively. Each has its own style of discourse and ways of assessing truth. To gain credence in the *academy*, he contends, theological arguments must be philosophically sound (though here it seems that the academy has moved on since Tracy wrote in the 1980s, as universal stand-ards of reason have been called into question with the advance of postmodern-ist deconstruction). To gain credence in the *Church*, theology must be firmly based in Christian scripture and tradition, and also generate lively and relevant meanings for life in today's world. And to be a force to be reckoned with in *wider society*, people must find theology personally and corporately meaningful, chal-lenging and liberating, leading to a richer life.

The focus of this book so far has been practical and pastoral: designed to enable ministers and other faith practitioners to respond to the challenges they face with a better understanding of themselves and their situation, and a greater ability to relate these to their faith in the way they respond. But while PTR is certainly an activity *of* the Church or faith community and its members, it exists *for* people in general and society as a whole, for two reasons:

- First, the roots of the pastoral cycle in liberation theology and the critical model (see above) commit PTR to the task of challenging and changing the wider world. The whole point of PTR is to harness tradition, scripture and other faith resources to the task of personal, institutional and ultimately glo-bal transformation. If the immediate goal of PTR is to enable the lives of its practitioners to resonate more fully with the wisdom of the tradition, the ultimate goal is that through that greater resonance the wisdom of the tra-dition will be freed to engage more fully with the wider world. Hypocrisy – a dissonance between belief and practice, examples of which were cited in the Introduction.3, and explored in Chapter 1.4 and elsewhere – is arguably more damaging than acknowledged to the effectiveness of Christian faith in a community. By focusing awareness on this dissonance, and bringing the traditions of belief into practical focus, PTR can liberate theology from its self-serving ghetto (Pattison, 2007, pp. 197ff.) to become a force for spiritual and institutional change in society at large. So if the immediate 'public' of PTR is the Church or faith community, the ultimate 'pubic' addressed is soci-ety as a whole.
- But as Chapter 9 makes clear, to change institutions and the world, we need first to understand them. And that means PTR has to involve art and sci-ence, though not of course as an academic exercise. Its goal is not to produce dissertations that increase the body of human knowledge, or to present fine arguments to convince academics. But it will need to make discerning use of

all the academic resources – sociology, psychology, cultural studies, philosophy and so forth – that enable people to understand their world better. If it does not 'address' the academic public, it certainly needs to listen to it. (This is explored further in Chapter 9.) At the same time, the teaching of theology can be enriched by PTR at every point. Students studying to prepare for ministry sometimes see theology as the production of essays simply to satisfy 'academics', when what they really want to do is go and serve the Church and the wider world. PTR can keep alive the links between theology and practice, and so convince students that, while their immediate goal might be the production of essays on theological topics, these do in fact serve their deeper purpose in the end.

The idea of three 'publics' for theology can help us understand why theologians can often seem at odds with one another, when actually they are writing for different audiences, each of which is looking for something different. In the same way, a politician would write differently if producing a paper for an academic seminar, an address to the party faithful, or a speech for the general public. However, the differences Tracy highlights seem to go rather deeper than a matter of 'spinning' the same content in different ways depending on the audience. Which is why we need to look at two other approaches that take the question of theological variety a little deeper.

3 PTR and theological mood

In discussing the Bible, David Ford argues (2007, pp. 45–9) that it is important to discern what is the grammatical mood of the particular text being considered. He also urges that this can be applied to theology as a whole. This gives us another, subtle angle on the way theologies vary. Most theologies will include a variety of the moods outlined below, but it is always worth asking which mood predominates, and then to see where PTR sits in relation to it.

Grammatical mood refers to these five different forms a verb can take:

a Indicative – statements like 'It is raining'.
b Subjunctive – suggestions like 'It might rain'.
c Interrogative – questions like 'Is it raining?'

d Optative – wishes like 'If only it would rain!'

e Imperative – commands like 'Rain!'

And this is how these voices are involved in theology and PTR.

a Indicative

This theology is primarily concerned with the nature of reality, including the divine reality, aiming to describe the world, set forth the truths about God, and develop a systematic theological vision. Aquinas' *Summa Theologiae* and Calvin's *Institutes* are classic examples. PTR will clearly need the indicative most when it is striving to describe an experience or situation and produce its thick descriptor. It will not engage in the system-building of Aquinas and Calvin, or strive for a total world-view. Nevertheless when those great systems collide with current world-views and assumptions PTR provides a means of processing the resulting connections and challenges, as in the box below.

Dante's world and sexual sin

Despite Freud, and the 'sexual revolution' of the 60s, there remains a widespread assumption in the media and culture of today that sexual sins are the most shameful and scandalous there are, especially if committed by a vicar or other 'respectable' person. Now you may know from your reading that Dante placed sexual offenders at the highest (least punitive) level of hell; their eternal destiny was to be blown about, in each other's arms, not unpleasantly by a continual wind! You may also know that this reflects the ethics of Aquinas and others, according to which the sins of excessive desire (greed, lust and avarice) are less serious than those of deficient desire (sloth) and those less bad than the sins of desire's negation (malice, envy and pride). It is unlikely that PTR would gain much from a wholesale adoption of Dante's world-view with his nine-tiered celestial spheres of heaven, his mount of purgatory and subterranean hell! But the radical difference between that world-view and our own could be very instructive in a PTR exercise based on an experience of sexual shaming or scandal. It might suggest a hypothetical or 'subjunctive' world in which we asked, 'What if … church leaders and politicians were shamed and ridiculed in the press, and forced to resign, not because of sexual impropriety, but on a Dante-cum-Aquinas basis, if they ever showed evidence of envy, malice or pride? Would we have any of them left?' Such considerations might well result in kairos turning-arounds of perspective on situations being scrutinized in a PTR process.

b Subjunctive

This expresses imagination, a 'what if' mood, conjuring up different worlds from our own. Such unrealized worlds cascade out of the Bible: what if … Adam and Eve had not eaten the fruit … Cain had not killed Abel … Abraham had sacrificed Isaac … Moses had perished unfound among the bulrushes … Mary had said no … Jesus had retreated to Galilee to avoid crucifixion … Paul had ignored that confusing light and gone on persecuting the Christians! But Christian theology has tended to harden its subjunctives into indicatives – a real purgatory and hell, real angels and so forth – thus polarizing over questions of whether they are real or not, or how many can stand on a pin, instead of, as Tibetan Buddhists and others do, resting in the dread and delight of the imaginary. Such resting can surely be a wonderfully helpful thing to do in PTR. Again, the box above suggests how such a 'what if' might effect a kairos moment. Finally, if we cannot first imagine alternative worlds, and how things might have been other than they are, we surely cannot begin to hope for anything better. Without subjunctives, our optatives will be stifled and our praxis cramped. Indeed, perhaps at the core of today's malaise (as contrasted with say the dreams of the 1960s) is that we are so stuffed full of indicative 'facts' and imperative regulations that we are unable to imagine difference or deep change at all.

c Interrogative

This is the theology of question, search and inquiry, asking questions of God, and puzzling over things: 'faith seeking understanding'. Augustine, Anselm and many modern theologians fall mainly into this category. In PTR, the appropriate interrogatives emerge from getting the indicatives and subjunctives right. Once we have said, 'This is how things are' and 'This is how they might have been or might yet be' we inevitably start asking, 'Why are they as they are?' 'Why did the meeting go the way it did?' 'Why did I respond in this way and not that way?' 'Do things have to be like this?' Quite clearly this is something that happens at the reflective phase, where we allow the tradition to ask questions of our experience, opening up possibilities we might not before have seen (as in the boxed example). At the same time, the experience questions the tradition, asking, 'Why does the Bible say that?' 'What is the doctrine of the Trinity really saying in this situation?', and so forth. Conversely, experience often throws tradition and doctrine into question. For example, suffering can invite questions about the love and omnipotence of God. Working through bereavement may provoke questions about the resurrection. Experiences of shame at one's body may invite questions about the embodiment of God in Christ and perhaps the shame of the cross. A deep understanding of the theological tradition will enable better, many-angled interrogation at this point, being more robust and less brittle than a shallow understanding which might want to ward off questions altogether.

d Optative

This expresses wish, hope and desire. Many mystical theologians major on this, their work pulsating with yearning for, and eager anticipation of, God. This is something they share with liberation theologians, whose main task in theology is seen as the development of inspiring yet realistic hopes for the oppressed. It is, incidentally, Ford's own favourite theological mood. PTR may sometimes arrive at imperatives, as just described, but probably it more often leaves the practitioner with optatives – new hopes, desires, choices, yearnings and prayers. Only gradually will these be untangled into imperatives for action. That is why for PTR the scripture and traditions of faith are less like rule books, more like a school of desire, leaving us to tease the imperatives out of our optatives as we live our lives.

e Imperative

This is the theology of authority and command, whose main point is to articulate the summons of God and what our ethical response should be. Martin Luther and Karl Barth are classic examples. Some love, and others hate, the robust – and sometimes rude – commanding voice with which they speak theology. Quite clearly as PTR moves from reflection to decision and action, the voice of scripture and tradition will shift from posing questions to offering commands. But note carefully what has had to happen first. The Bible is not a rule book uttering commands for every situation. There are a whole host of issues – from child abuse through IVF to nuclear warfare – about which the Bible has no direct command to offer, but of course this does not mean the Christian is free in those areas to do as he pleases. It is the careful pondering of a situation in the light of tradition – the PTR process – that enables the Bible sometimes to offer us clear commands: 'in this situation, in the light of all those texts and traditions, and in consultation with my friends and the Holy Spirit, it has become clear to me that I am bidden to do this'.

Exercise

Table 7 represents a worked example in which the example of the box on pages 54–6 is examined according to the moods that prevail at each of its five stages. You'll notice that one of the moods is in italics and bracketed because in the course of reflecting on the exercise in this way, a hidden optative was detected, a yearning for equality which was never explicitly expressed but seemed to be informing the whole argument.

Choose one of the three worked-out paradigms of PTR in Chapter 2. Make a similar table and note the moods that occur at the different stages of the process. Note whether you find an even spread, or whether different moods predominate at certain stages. If the latter, why might this be?

Table 7: The progress of mood in a PTR exercise.

Stage of exercise	Indicative **descriptions**	Subjunctive **hypotheses**	Interrogative **questions**	Optative **wishes**	Imperative **commands**
1	Staff currently sit apart from students.		Is positioning of tutors right? What is aim of college?		
2	Society is changing, becoming less formal. Approaches to discipline are changing.	Power may be being abused.			
3	Sayings of Jesus. St Francis and Russian fool. No hierarchy in Trinity. But Church has always been hierarchical.	Church might become more egalitarian.			
4			Should Church be egalitarian? Is there a mismatch between practice described at stage 1 and tradition described at stage 3?	[*If only we could be more equal like Jesus and the disciples!*]	
5					Abandon staff pew. Note the results carefully.

4 PTR and theological wisdom

Theological wisdom does not spring full grown from the heads of theologians like Athene from the head of Zeus, all ready to start addressing publics and expressing herself in different moods! Theology has first to learn and grow the wisdom it seeks to impart. So there is a question prior to our other two, about where theology learns from. And there are at least three kinds of answer – though you are invited to suggest others. These can be justified in three different understandings of what theologians call 'revelation', though perhaps the notion of different places where wisdom can be learnt is a little less daunting, and less exclusive of other faiths. As we shall see, PTR draws on each of these places of revelation or wisdom:

a God's wisdom in creation

Theology learns many things from exactly the same places as the secular world. For theology, God is the Creator, revealed in all things, like an artist in his work. Or in terms of specifically Christian tradition, the Word of God is the universal *logos* or intelligible order of everything, the light of reason which shines in everyone (John 1.1–14). Though this source of wisdom was of vital importance to patristic and medieval thinkers, modern theologians have tended to turn away from it, with Kant and Barth undermining 'natural theology' from their philosophical and theological points of view respectively. However, indications are that for the ordinary believer it remains hugely important, perhaps becoming even more so as theology begins to become, under green and feminist influence, less androcentric and more cosmocentric (Primavesi, 2000; Ruether, 1989). As for our culture generally, TV viewing and church attendance figures suggest that people at large may find the world of natural science even more inspiring of awe and wisdom than the average church service!

Philosophical theology is one name for the theology that investigates the possibility of an ultimate explanation of the world, and explores the relationship between God and ordinary experience. It asks whether the ultimate can be said to act or suffer in the world, whether miracles are possible, what the relationship is between religion and science, and between grace and nature. It explores the nature of sin and evil, free will and predestination, and indeed whether religious language can be meaningful at all. PTR needs to embrace such questions. Since the raw material for PTR in the initial stage of the pastoral cycle is ordinary experience, questions of whether and when it is appropriate to speak of God as revealed in, acting in, suffering in or working through experience are crucially important matters which the theological reflector must ponder for himself. The box below offers some reflections which may help such pondering.

Warnings: God at work?

If Wilson (1988, p. 147) is right when he says 'Christian hope lies in God, present and at work in the situation, and in responding to God's will', the reflector will always be trying to discern God's presence and how she may work with him in each situation. But she must be wary of four common mistakes:

- Assuming that God is at work only in the gaps where other explanations fail, for example in miracles or special interventions that override natural laws and human freedom. Opinions differ over the possibility of miracles, but those who do believe in them would concede that they are by definition exceptional, and that looking for God *only* in the miraculous would be perverse.
- Wanting to leap too quickly to seeing divine involvement, as if this rendered other levels of explanation superfluous. The temptation to resist psychological or sociological explanations of human behaviour because they are 'not Christian', or because they imply a restriction on human freedom and dignity, is misplaced. It is normally the case that the divine work only becomes clear once we have painstakingly explored the natural and human levels; just as we can only discern the mind of a poet once we have painstakingly examined the poem's structure, metre, rhythm, rhyme and all its other literary qualities. Chapter 9 returns to this point.
- Speaking too easily and fluently about the experience of God in events. Though 'classical theism' affirms all things as manifesting God, the God they manifest remains a mystery, beyond understanding. Nothing can literally be known about God, and created things are only analogies

---

for God. In them we see God 'through a glass, darkly' (1 Cor. 13.12). Perhaps the term *inscendence* is appropriate to denote the idea that God is *immanent* in everything, but in a way that *transcends* our understanding. God is in events but elusively, and language about God's presence, in PTR as elsewhere, must have a provisional, tentative quality, and what theologians have aptly termed 'reserve'.[18]

- Thinking we infer the mind of God from examination of the material and human world. Cosmologists these days often come remarkably close to this notion:

> If we discover a complete theory [of the universe] … we shall all … be able to take part in the discussion of the question of why it is that we and the universe exist. If we find the answer to that, it would be the ultimate triumph of human reason – for then we should know the mind of God. (Hawking, 1988, p. 193)

In the old days of 'natural theology' and the argument from design,[19] this kind of approach was common; we saw the cosmic watch ticking away, and inferred God must have made it. However, classic theism as expressed, for example, in Psalms 19, 139 or 148, and the entire tradition up to the medieval times when theologians started 'proving' the existence of God, did not infer God from the world; rather, it saw God at work in the world. For those with eyes to see, it is God who is there ticking away, God 'godding' in God's world, God creating, without any need for the logical inference from watch to watchmaker.

So PTR has things to learn – unexpectedly perhaps – from the often remote-seeming academic discipline of philosophical theology. But it can contribute to it too. Very often philosophical theology discusses the issues mentioned above in a highly abstract way. Discussion of sin and evil may, for example, be based on discussions of colossal events like Auschwitz or the tsunami. But it is in many ways easier to see where God might be active, and where perhaps frustrated or suffering, and where there might be evil systems at work, in major events, than in say a train conversation I had yesterday, or in something that unnerved me at last week's cricket match. PTR can assist philosophical theology by requiring it to address the fine texture of ordinary life.

b God's wisdom in scripture and tradition

Most faith traditions give special authority to certain texts, traditions and liturgies, and in Christianity it is biblical, systematic and liturgical theologies that study these and strive to unpack their meaning. Of course, the emphasis differs: for traditional Protestants the Bible is the key revelation, while Catholics give more weight to tradition and doctrine, and for the Orthodox the divine liturgy is in many ways the decisive source of wisdom. With Barth and his neo-orthodoxy, and in recent years in English theology with Milbank's radical orthodoxy, Christian scripture and tradition have become crucially important, sometimes being identified with revelation itself, though as Pattison also points out (2007, pp. 212ff.) this has had the sad consequence that theologians often now only make sense to fellow theologians.

Wilson, with whose definition of theology this chapter opened, goes on to distinguish (1988, pp. 54–5) between the activity of 'theologizing life' – effectively what we call theological reflection – and 'the study of theology' which codifies this reflection in formulae and practices of faith that can be passed on and evaluated by others and later tradition. This is certainly a valid way of understanding sacred texts, doctrines and liturgies and the theologies that express and explore them.

If that is so, then in learning as best she can from such traditions and theology, the reflector is simply learning the codified results of the reflections of previous generations. To be sure, as remarked in Chapter 4, a deep knowledge of biblical criticism is not essential for PTR. Nevertheless, by learning as much as possible about how the Bible came to be written, in what kind of culture, and under the impact of what events, you will see how it embodies the reflections and emotions of the generations living when it was written. In Oliver's terms, the 'holy Bible' will become for you a 'human Bible' which you can use in your own reflections some two to three millennia later.

Likewise systematic theology can be regarded as a big name for reflections on scripture in the light of experience and philosophy conducted by theologians since biblical times. The great 'themes' of creation, slavery, exodus, exile, incarnation, deliverance, salvation and so forth are not labels with which the Bible comes to us fully furnished; they have emerged as succeeding generations have tried to make sense of their own experience of creation, slavery and so forth in the light of the biblical story. It is therefore important that PTR is also able to draw on the amazingly rich stock of themes, artwork, imagery and doctrine – relating to incarnation, atonement, Trinity, judgment and so forth – which the Church has developed over the years, as well as the sacred texts themselves.

Conversely, employing PTR in the teaching and learning of biblical, systematic and liturgical theology can only enhance it. For the Bible, doctrine and liturgy, which were created as reflections on experience in the light of past traditions with a view to future action, surely come alive again most fully in the context of similarly focused reflection today.

Exercise

Identify a doctrine of the Church or your faith community which is important to you and consider why this is so. Write down (a) experiences of your own which it relates to and (b) actions in the past or future it has or might inspire. Suggest (c) experiences that may have given rise to this doctrine and (d) the ethics or life practice that flowed from that doctrine at the time. Compare your personal list with your 'historical' list. What similarities and differences do you note, and what do you think they indicate?

---

c God's wisdom in human fulfilment

As Irenaeus said long ago, 'the glory of God is a human being fully alive'.[20] Liberation theology has called attention to the human experience of freedom as revelatory. Certainly all theology worth the name has tried to address the issues it describes in terms of human liberation, flourishing, transformation, healing, salvation and divinization (an understanding still current in Eastern Orthodoxy). These concepts all point to the process by which human beings become able to share in 'life in full abundance' (John 10.10). Theologically this source of wisdom can be understood as the work of the Holy Spirit who births or incarnates Christ afresh through history, complementing and elucidating Jesus' incarnation as witnessed in Christian texts.

The unique contribution of practical theology has been to show that theology needs to relate both to the Church and its important verbal message, and also to wider society in the task of transforming the world and its institutions for the better. The focus shifts from the indicative to the optative – the 'cry of the poor' that is the recurrent refrain of much liberation theology – and the imperative. These moods describe the things we desire or long for, which it becomes imperative to accomplish. They move and direct people to act.

Interestingly, a cycle emerges. Different notions of liberation abound. The liberation theologians were not talking about the kind of 'liberation' the allies achieved by bombing Iraq and killing its citizens. So the search for good praxis returns to the cycle to discover what experience illuminated by scripture and tradition has to teach about what liberation, freedom, justice and human flourishing are, and are not. Otherwise we could simply soak up uncritically the many dangerous, ideological accounts that abound. (The liberation theologians were accused of uncritically soaking up Marxist accounts, but today perhaps the most dangerous accounts come from the neo-conservative right (Northcott, 2007).)

The answer to the question of what PTR can glean from and offer to practical theology is made evident in section 1. What this chapter has introduced is an understanding of how PTR, whose core method is that of practical theology, draws on and contributes to the other varieties of theology, such that the content of PTR includes them also, as well as wider resources from the traditions of human science, art and wisdom.

Finally, note that the method of PTR and of practical theology requires this comprehensive content, since PTR works towards its practical, transformative goal from understanding ordinary experience through reflection in the light of – among other things – faith tradition. It therefore has to draw on the theologies that explore experience and tradition and how God's wisdom may be found in them.

Exercise

Allow plenty of time for this.

Choose a work of theology with which you are reasonably familiar (Pattison, 1997, is a useful example). Draw three big circles and write in them, respectively, headings for its exploration of:

- scientific analysis of the cosmos and human society
- scripture and tradition
- action to improve the world.

Draw arrows to show connecting arguments. What balance and flow emerges between the sections? How far could the book be thought of as a giant PTR exercise progressing from experience through analysis and reflection to action? Finally, you might like to write a short critical review of the book based on this exercise.

5 Interfaith reflection?

This chapter has focused in the main on Christian theology, and hence the decisive resource has been the Bible and the traditions of the Church. Muslims here would obviously focus rather on the Qur'an and Muslim tradition, Buddhists on the Pali Canon and Buddhist tradition, and so forth. But Christians, Muslims and Buddhists operate within the same world (albeit perhaps with a different understanding of it) and are equally concerned with human flourishing (albeit, again, understanding this a little differently). So two out of the three 'areas of wisdom' are common to the different faiths. This fact poses the question of whether PTR might be carried out in interfaith groups, where each brings to the same issues resources from their own traditions with a view to action together in wider society. Informally this IFR – interfaith reflection – has no doubt happened a great deal already, with interfaith groups responding together to crises like 9/11 and the tsunami.

There are of course advantages in single-faith TR groups operating with a defined 'canon' of texts. This enables the group to share a common basis for evaluating one another's reflections, and for contributing, in a small way, to the development of their particular faith tradition. Nevertheless a confidence that one's own sacred texts contain 'all things necessary to salvation' (Anglican Article 6) does not mean that no other texts contain anything relevant to it, and many would want to affirm that they do.

Most people practising PTR will operate with three categories of resources:

- canonical texts, which will carry a special authority for those in the same faith group;
- a wider range of texts – including spiritual and theological writings, hymns and other liturgy – which have been honoured and found useful within their faith tradition;
- texts and other works, including perhaps art, which have rung true for an individual and upon which she will naturally draw in PTR, though here the authority such resources have for the group will depend on the reflection it inspires.

This last category will, for many, include texts from other faith traditions, and it is a small step further to suggest IFR groups which draw on a variety of faith – and perhaps even non-faith – traditions. The fact that different individuals will regard different texts as 'canonical' or otherwise need not be an insuperable barrier, so long as this difference is acknowledged, and the participants avoid promoting their own 'canon' as authoritative for the whole group. That would mean not diluting the authority sacred texts have for one's own reflection, but extending this to a generous sense of the authority other texts have for others.

IFR would have at least three advantages over traditional 'interfaith dialogue' (IFD).

- The goal would be smaller – restricted to definite experiences and definite outcomes, rather than attempting a global confrontation or fusion of faiths – and hence much more achievable.
- Instead of struggling with differences, IFR offers a win–win situation, in which there is a common goal of offering new possibilities of transformation in a particular instance.
- This shared goal roots IFR in what we manifestly have in common – a shared world and a shared humanity – rather than focusing, as IFD can do, on what separates us, namely ideas and ideologies.

Exercise

Examine setting up an IFR group to reflect on a local issue that is affecting members of all the faith communities – for example, the shortage of affordable housing for first-time buyers, or the restrictions being placed by local schools on children wearing signs of their faith identity, such as crosses, turbans and headscarves. Identify the obstacles that might need to be overcome, and suggest a remit and parameters for the group, in order to make the reflection effective.

Summary

This chapter has considered the ways in which PTR:

- is at the heart of practical theology, especially its critical and pastoral variants;
- addresses not only the Church but the wider public, and needs to use some academic methods;
- has a rich range of moods relating it to all hues of theology;
- engages with the wisdom of God shown in creation, scripture and tradition;
- binds the different theologies together in promoting practically their common goal of human flourishing;
- might profitably be extended beyond Christian and other faith-specific theologies to 'interfaith reflection'.

Further reading (see also Core Texts at the end of the book)

Bordieu, P. (1998), *Practical Reason, or the Theory of Action*, Cambridge: Polity Press.

Bevans, S. (2002), *Models of Contextual Theology*, New York: Orbis Books.

Dulles, A. (1992), *Models of Revelation*, Maryknoll NY: Orbis Books.

Elford, R. (1999), *The Pastoral Nature of Theology*, London: Cassell.

Ford, D. (2007), *Christian Wisdom: Desiring God and Learning in Love*, Cambridge and New York: Cambridge University Press.

Frei, H. (1992), *Types of Christian Theology,* New Haven and London: Yale University Press.

Hawking, S. (1988), *A Brief History of Time,* London: Bantam Books.

Heitink, G. (1993), *Practical Theology: History, Theory, Action Domains,* Grand Rapids MI: Eerdmans.

Kaufman, Gordon (1995), *An Essay on Theological Method,* New York: Oxford University Press.

Lindbeck, G. (1984), *The Nature of Doctrine: Religion and Theology in a Postliberal Age,* Philadelphia: Westminster Press.

Loughlin, G. (1999), *Telling God's Story,* Cambridge: Cambridge University Press.

Mudge, L. and Poling, J. (eds) (1987), *Formation and Reflection: The Promise of Practical Theology,* Philadelphia: Fortress Press.

Mueller, J. (1984), *What are they Saying about Theological Method?* New York: Paulist Press.

Northcott, M. (2007), *An Angel Directs the Storm: Apocalyptic Religion and American Empire,* London: SCM Press.

Pattison, S. (1997b), *Pastoral Care and Liberation Theology,* London: SPCK.

Pattison, S. (2007), *The Challenge of Practical Theology: Selected Essays,* London and Philadelphia: Jessica Kingsley.

Pattison, S. and Woodward, J. (2000), *The Blackwell Reader in Pastoral and Practical Theology,* Oxford: Blackwell.

Paver, J. (2006), *Theological Reflection and Education for Ministry: The Search for Integration in Theology,* Aldershot and Burlington VT: Ashgate.

Primavesi, A. (2000), *Sacred Gaia,* London and New York: Routledge.

Ruether, R. Radford (1989), *Gaia and God: An Ecofeminist Theology of Earth Healing,* London: SCM Press.

Thompson, R. (1990), *Holy Ground: The Spirituality of Matter,* London: SPCK.

Thompson, R. (2008), *SCM Studyguide to Christian Spirituality,* London: SCM Press.

Tracy, D. (1975), *Blessed Rage for Order: The New Pluralism in Theology,* New York: Seabury Press.

Tracy, D. (1981), *The Analogical Imagination: Christian Theology and the Culture of Pluralism,* New York: Crossroad.

Wilson, M. (1988), *A Coat of Many Colours: Pastoral Studies of the Christian Way of Life,* London: Epworth Press.

9

PTR, Ethics, Institutions and the Wider World

(Sections 1–3 of this chapter, including the two case studies, are written by Stephen Pattison.)

Chapter 8 urged that, while PTR is a practice engaged in by members of faith communities, it can also enable faith traditions to address the wider public and contribute to ethical and institutional change in the secular world. This chapter provides pointers for this task. It focuses in considerable detail on the use of PTR to criticize and influence the institutions that surround us, then moves on to the question of how ethical values work through this process:

1 Why institutions? How to influence institutions, and why it matters.
2 Developing an 'etic' or 'outsider' perspective on an institution.
3 Institutional spirituality: looking at institutions from an 'emic', 'insider' perspective.
4 Ethics in PTR: how such analysis, and PTR generally, engages a variety of ethical approaches in a single process.
5 PTR and the 'big issues': how this process can be widened to offer a valuable approach to wider ethical issues.

1 Why institutions? How to influence institutions, and why it matters

As has already been shown (Chapter 1.3), one of the roots of PTR lies in liberation theology which is a political theology primarily concerned with institutions, structures and power. Even if you are not yourself called to work for the liberation of the poor and oppressed it is still crucial to understand how institutions and power structures can affect the lives of individuals and groups for good and ill, and how they may be changed. Such institutions include churches and religious organizations, but most of us have our lives extensively shaped by all manner of institutions – hospitals, schools, prisons, businesses, companies[21] – all of which are legitimate subjects for PTR.

Any complex situation or institution demands appropriately complex understandings. You will probably have had the experience of going to a meeting where people opine on issues without having much depth of knowledge or understanding. This is frustrating. But the alternative is demanding. Much time, effort and extensive research may be needed to establish valid reflection and analysis. This will involve listening to the voices of the social and human sciences (like sociology, psychology and history) and consulting their findings, as well as attending to those from theological tradition. The world is God's world but we may need to explore it largely by secular methods.

Only when we know what sort of world we are in – when we understand how it is descriptively – is it appropriate to go on and ask normative, more prescriptive questions about how it ought to be. In this model consulting and using theological resources and questions comes after analysis. We need to know the 'what?' and the 'why?' before we begin to speculate upon whether this is the way things ought to be from a theological perspective.

Case study 1

As a chaplain in a psychiatric hospital in the late 1970s, I wanted to discover how liberation theology might inform my work in the hospital. Using as a starting point insights and methods from liberation theology, and its preferential option for the poor, I was forced to ask the question, How does this institution liberate and oppress people? To answer this, I conducted a far-ranging exploration of the founding ideas, structures, social context and ideologies underpinning the institution in which I worked. I read books about psychiatry, sociology, politics and organizational theory, as well as talking to people in the institution and observing its ways. This was an extended theological reflection using conventional research methods which resulted in an academic thesis (Pattison, 1997b). However, at all points the thesis was an attempt at a theological reflection, and my aim was to gain theological understanding and insight and change the way I worked. One of the things that I learned was just how much research and knowledge you need to understand fully the social and political context of ministry. To find out who is oppressed and how and why, so you can think of ways of working in a truly liberative fashion, is hard, interdisciplinary work. The first two stages of Segundo's hermeneutic circle, becoming aware of one's social and ideological context, took me three years to complete! I hardly got to the final two stages. This suggests that some kinds of PTR may need to involve enormous amounts of time, energy, persistence, research and systematic intellectual commitment.

2 Developing an 'etic' or 'outsider' perspective on an institution: the art of asking good questions

The words *emic* and *etic* are used in anthropology to denote, respectively, an insider, subjective, and outsider, objective perspective. In this part of the chapter, questions are suggested that might be asked to develop an etic, or outside, objective perspective on any institution or organization. Later on, we will explore questions that might allow a more emic, reflective perspective to emerge.

In the three 'steps' set out below some critical questions are suggested that could be asked of any organization or institution. They might help you develop what the liberation theologians would call a 'hermeneutic of suspicion', whereby you can get beneath the skin of the formal and taken-for-granted. The focus at each step is understanding:

- Step 1: the *'what'* of the institution and providing a descriptive framework.
- Step 2: *why* things are as they are.
- Step 3: *how* theological questions which are more normative or prescriptive can help to suggest changes to structures or practices that might modify attitudes and practices within the institution.

The questions themselves may sound quite simple – getting answers is more complicated. At one level, you may be able to answer the questions yourself from knowledge you already have. However, to gain answers that better reflect the complexity of the instituion you may need to consult the Internet, or undertake some formal or informal empirical research, asking a range of people around you a systematic set of questions or observe closely what goes on (remember, you may need ethical permission or to ask for people's consent if you wish to do this).[22]

Step 1: Describing institutions

These questions fall into five categories:

1 **Identity and purpose.** What does this institution formally exist to do? What is its mission statement? Does the organization do what it says it does, or does it do other things instead/as well? For example, a school might formally say that it exists to develop every aspect of children's lives, but you might find that it is mainly oriented toward producing good exam or sporting results, or that it really just contains children during daylight hours and does not develop them at all. Does everyone within and outside the organization tell the same story about what it exists to do and does? Grateful patients may feel that a hospital is a wonderful healing place with great staff, but the cleaning

staff may feel exploited. You may have to weigh different stories and perspectives against each other.

2 **Structure, authority and power.** What is the formal decision-making structure for the institution and how does this relate to the informal structure and how decisions are actually taken? Often these differ. For example, a church might formally be run by an elected council while the people who actually make the decisions that count are not council members at all. In universities, departmental administrators may be able to exercise a lot of power over what teachers and researchers do. As satirized in *Yes Minister*, government ministers may be severely limited by the civil servants supposedly there to implement their decisions.

3 **Values, beliefs and motivations.** What are the formal, theoretical beliefs, values and motives of the institution and how do these relate to reality? For example, a hospital might maintain that it is there to help people back to health and its professional staff would probably agree with this. Meanwhile in practice you might discover that a hospital made many of its clients sicker, and that its staff were more motivated by the need to economize on resources than by the need to do the best by patients.

4 **Stakeholders and interest groups.** For whose benefit does the institution formally exist? Most institutions like to believe that they exist for a good, benevolent purpose. So, for example, many churches would argue that they exist to glorify God and to serve all people in the name of bringing them closer to God and God's kingdom. However, you may discover that some churches benefit their employees and members providing social and educational facilities for them while non-members may feel that the church is not really interested in them and perhaps not even in God. Again, many institutions pride themselves on involving their members and valuing them, but often institutions are driven by external imperatives such as meeting targets, which mean that they cannot attend to dissenting voices and opinions, let alone those of deprived and inarticulate people.

5 **Context and history.** How, when, and why did the institution come into existence? And how does it interact with its context? A prison, for example, reflects the social context and values of the society that created it. It can also affect the nature of the neighbourhood in which it is placed in various ways.

Step 2: Why are things the way they are?

Having found answers to the questions in Step 1, you should now have a 'thick description' (see Chapter 3.1.b) of the institution you are reflecting on. In the process you will have found yourself asking why things are as they are, and especially in relation to any contradictions or conflicts. Why, for example, does this organization that seeks to help homeless people spend so much time worrying about its own survival? At this stage you need to ask questions that will fill out your discoveries and try to find some explanations for why things are the way they are.

Step 3: What can theology add to this analysis?

According to liberation theology, it is only when we have described and understood institutions and their power structures using the 'first voice' of the social and human sciences that we can venture theological discussion and interpretation. These questions are intertwined, but for clarity they are placed under four broad headings:

1 The question of what we are here for, relating to the theology of creation and anthropology (in the theological sense, which concerns issues of what it means to be in God's image, yet sinful).
   • What fundamental understandings of life and its purpose are embodied and fostered in this institution?
   • What sort of life and view of the world does this institution foster? What sort of human flourishing does it promote?
   • What is regarded as ultimately real and important by this institution?

2 Questions of Christology, soteriology (the nature of salvation) and ecclesiology – what is the community of salvation and who is in it?
   • What sort of character and virtues does this institution value in its members and clients?
   • How does this institution label and deal with good and evil within and outside itself?

- How does the institution deal with 'strangers' and powerless people?
- Does this institution act as servant or master to its members? And its clients?

3 Questions about the nature and object of faith, belief and doxology, worship.
- In what ideas, ideologies and practices are members and clients encouraged to put their trust and faith by this institution?
- What 'gods' are 'worshipped' by the institution and its members? Are they worthy of worship and respect?

4 Questions of the Holy Spirit and the kingdom of God, which also involve soteriology and ecclesiology.
- Does the institution foster creative and loving relationships within its members and stakeholders?
- Is this institution justice-seeking and promoting in its structures and in its dealings with its members and the outside world?
- Does this institution have a rich vision of its context and future, or is it only concerned about its own immediate best interests and survival?

Having begun by making a proper analysis of the institution, from an 'etic' perspective, you can use questions like those listed above to begin to create a valid theological critique. Here PTR proper can begin as you think about which bits of the institution should be affirmed or questioned from a theological perspective.

Case study 2

In the 1990s I became concerned that management ideas and practices were percolating into all kinds of organizations (including churches). I was suspicious that some such ideas and practices were probably incompatible with the gospel so I decided to analyse the 'faith of the managers', the working assumptions, practices, beliefs and values that seemed to be dominant in popular management theory. After reading a lot of management literature, I concluded that in some ways management was itself like a religion, a total way of understanding reality. I concluded that the modern, managed, aims-and-objectives-focused organization can often be myopic, hierarchical, centralized, inegalitarian, self-centred and self-determined, aggressive, competitive, suspicious, dualistic, conformist, slightly paranoid and, despite the rhetoric of enterprise, creativity and innovation, surprisingly conservative. Its narrow, instrumental view of people and of reality excludes much that is of value in human experience, while it is wildly over optimistic in its view of controlling the future. This way of thinking about and living life is challenged by the gospel's much broader view of people and society living within divine grace and providence. This suggested that Christians need to be critical of much that seems life-denying in the culture of modern organizations and should avoid some things entirely, for example the assumption that everyone outside the organization is either a competitor or a customer. Within the Church, particularly, we need to remember that God is not a manager and we are not God's customers, nor are our relations with our human brothers and sisters to be thought of as defined by contracts between buyers and sellers. (See further Pattison, 1997a.)

Exercise

Think of an institution or organization that you belong to, or use extensively. Work through the steps and questions outlined above and see what answers you come up with. You should give yourself plenty of time to do this kind of PTR, and if possible, do it with others from your institution. Even if you are only able to answer some of the questions superficially, you should find that this kind of exercise deepens your understanding and knowledge of the institution and gives you some ideas for thinking differently about it. In addition it should give you a fuller understanding of how PTR can work in practice in relation to the wider world.

3 Institutional spirituality: 'emic' understanding

To balance the 'etic' analysis, PTR needs to form a complex 'emic' analysis (see box opposite). This provides for a more informal, subjective, 'snapshot' way of reflecting on institutional life, here considered from four different perspectives.

If liberation theologians start with the objectivity of social and institutional structures, another theologian, Walter Wink, a New Testament scholar, advances the idea that all organizations and institutions have both an external, material, and an internal, spiritual aspect to them. For Wink, 'spiritual' denotes 'the inner dimension of the material, the "within" of things, the subjectivity of objective entities in the world' (1984, p.187). Just as people have a complex withinness, their personality or character, organizations also have a kind of character or spirit.

Taking a cue from Wink it is then possible to think about the nature of the spirit or character of institutions (Pattison, 2007, pp. 110ff.) which influences the structures, behaviours and experiences of people in them. People often think spontaneously of institutions as being 'happy' or 'depressed'. But it is difficult enough to get to know the withinness of a person: how is it possible to begin to get a grasp of the spirit or character of an organization in reflection? Below are some methods that might be tried either on their own or together:

Visualizing the organization

One way of attempting to gain a sense of the spirit of an organization is to try and find a visual image for it. You might like to pause for a moment and think about what image comes to mind if you think of an organization you know. If it were to be drawn or visualized as a person what would your organization's character look like? When I tried to think about the personality of a teaching hospital that I used to know well, I came up with a picture of a wizened old man in a white coat sitting on his own, high in a tower and counting money with an avaricious expression on his worried face! My picture is only one person's view of this institution's character. A group might come up with a different picture.

If all the members of a particular hospital or trust were to create a corporate image that might look different again.

The point of this kind of simple exercise, employed to great effect by political cartoonists, is to try and become aware of organizational character or 'withinness' at a more conscious level than is normal. We carry these images of the character and spirituality of our organizations around with us all the time and probably act it out in the way we work. If we are aware of this, we may be able to address or challenge such qualities. We might even be able to change them. (It sounds like my isolated, wizened man needs to have more resources and to establish more trust with the rest of the human race!) Awareness of the character of an organization can help us to decide how we might work with or against this position or character.

Reality-shaping myths

All institutions and organizations have myths that guide their behaviour. So another way of trying to understand the withinness of an organization is to become aware of the myths by which they live. Often, myths are unconsidered, unanalysed and unarticulated because they are taken to be incontrovertibly true, so not worth noting.

For example, a main guiding myth that determines the lives of many secular organizations is that of the 'bottom line'. The 'bottom line' is a financial term that denotes whether an organization is solvent or not. This judgement is made by a qualified accountant when an organization's accounts are audited. Depending upon the way in which the accounting has been carried out, for example 'creatively', the judgement of solvency or non-solvency may be right or wrong. There is no objective standard against which the 'bottom line' can be measured. Yet the 'bottom line' readily attains omnipotent realism as a guiding myth within 'business-like' organizations.

All sorts of practices are predicated on the need to meet a 'bottom line' that few people within the organization are aware of. Sacrifices, cuts and changes can all be demanded in the name of meeting the 'bottom line' which, whatever its financial reality, serves in the organization as a mythical image of absolute reality to which people orient themselves. Whether myths such as these are beneficial or harmful in their effects is of less importance than recognizing that mythology is seldom entirely evidence-based and is invariably reality-shaping. Those who question foundational organizational myths are likely to be regarded as mad or bad.

Ritual activities

Organizational spirituality is manifested in, and maintained by, ritual. Ritual activity is symbolic action that sustains social meanings and values but does not of itself affect reality. An example of ritual activity within contemporary organizations is that of strategic planning. Many organizations spend much time concocting detailed plans about future developments. However, strategic plans have a habit of being dated and useless almost as soon as they have been constructed. The future is elusive and unpredictable and the best laid plans often go wrong. This does not prevent planners from writing new strategic plans, even as old ones are discarded, thus demonstrating the ritual nature of this activity.

Planning can be seen as a ritual of organizational control, an attempt to predict and manipulate spirits within and outside the organization. The attempt to control spirits and chaos has, of course, always been a fundamental aspect of human religious activity. The attempt to plan the future is a way of trying to ward off and control anxiety in the face of that which cannot be controlled. It is prominent in the contemporary NHS today in the face of rapid and unpredictable change both without and within. Rituals such as planning are part of the way in which organizations and individuals orient themselves to what they take to be reality.

Foundational narratives

Finally it is possible to look at the stories that give meaning and purpose to the organization and its members. People do not just come to work for money, but for a variety of motives, one of which is to acquire a meaningful role in the world. In this connection, the stories that organizations tell about what they do and their guiding foundational myths are enormously important for providing orientation and direction.

So, for example, for a long time, the National Health Service was guided by the myths and narratives of the post-war Welfare State. The story (or at least one version of it) ran something like this. When Britain had won the war, the spirit of concern and co-operation that had characterized the war effort still persisted, bringing people from all classes in society together in a sense of mutual concern and responsibility. Instead of fighting the Germans, the British people declared war on the evils of poverty, homelessness, disease, ignorance and unemployment and so the Welfare State was founded. The institutions and individuals that comprised the Welfare State were in the front line in the fight against evil. Their work was therefore worthy of respect and support from all in society.

Like many foundational myths and narratives, this one was pitched at a high level of generality, and was in many ways untrue. So, for example, it was never the case that all the people had all their needs met free and at the point of need: health-care professionals in the NHS informally rationed resources and evaluated the needs of those in their care and some of the most needy got less health-care resources than those whose needs were less. However, this narrative myth served an important communal purpose in helping health workers and people in society generally to value and support the NHS.

This mythic narrative of the foundations of the NHS now looks faded and tired. It no longer provides a rationale for health-care work as it used to. The absence of a coherent narrative about what the NHS is for and where it is going has left a vacuum where the Welfare State myth once held sway. Somehow, the myth of being in a care business or a health-care 'industry' does not provide the kind of symbolic richness that motivates and inspires workers. This lack of an undergirding mythic narrative has resulted in a kind of corporate spiritual crisis and malaise that unerringly reflects contemporary social and economic uncertainty. It remains to be seen whether a compelling new mythic narrative will arise in this postmodern era of fragmentation.

Exercise

Again, take an organization or institution that you have some involvement in and try, either on your own or with a group of people, to reflect upon its nature by visualizing it, identifying its reality-shaping myths, describing its rituals and articulating the undergirding narratives that support its functioning. Compare these with the theologically derived questions that were included at step 3 in the 'etic' method of theological reflection. What sort of institution or organization do you feel you are working in? How should it change? How might you change the way in which you interact with it in the light of your PTR? How might you exercise some kind of 'spiritual care' for the institution that you have been reflecting upon?

4 PTR and ethics

In the discussion of *etic* and *emic* analysis of institutions, and throughout this book, we have been suggesting that PTR is a fundamentally ethical process, both in the ethical insights it generates and in the enhanced spiritual and ethical awareness of the practitioner. We are suggesting not just that it can enable us to criticize institutions, but that through asking good questions and exercising the imagination in a creative and insightful way, it can suggest ways of organizing them and behaving in them that are ethically better. These are bold claims that you may, as you read this book, have begun to believe, but perhaps at this point, before we move on to glance at the wider ethical issues, a little more needs to be said about this ethical dimension of PTR.

Without going into great detail, the following hypothesis is offered for your evaluation: that PTR works not by applying a particular theoretical ethical approach, but by combining a variety of approaches in a single practice.[23] Of the concepts on which philosophers have tried to base ethics, the following four are perhaps the most significant, and certainly the most relevant to PTR. After sketching each approach, a suggestion is made as to how PTR incorporates it. Table 8 summarizes the same points, but uses the technical terms so that those with an interest in philosophy can cross-refer. As you read, you might like to ponder how far the questions asked about our institutions covered these same four aspects, namely:

a What rules governed it?
b What was the context or situation in which it was set?

c What were its official and unofficial aims?

d What virtues (and vices) did it encourage?

Table 8: PTR and Ethics.

	How is this ethic involved in PTR?	How does PTR influence this ethic?
a Deontology: the ethics of rules	Reflection: PTR involves disciplined obedience to faith tradition	PTR invites neither blind submission nor rational deduction but reason, imagination and emotion together
b Situationism: the ethics of love in a situation	Experience: PTR starts with specific situation not theory	PTR analyses situation carefully and uses theory and tradition to shed light on it
c Teleology: the ethics of purpose	Decision: PTR identifies what is worth striving for and works for that	PTR not based on abstract 'greatest happiness of greatest number' but worked out in piecemeal interilluminations between situations and the broad sweep of tradition
d Virtue ethics: the ethic of what makes a good person	Ongoing use of PTR to instil good responses and educate desire in ways that lead to virtue	Virtues not predefined but learnt through the interaction between life and faith tradition in PTR

a **Rules and Laws.** Ethics is about doing what is right and necessary according to a moral law. This law may be seen as given by God, as in the Jewish understanding of the Torah. Or it may be something we humans have to work out rationally for our human society, as Kant in particular argued. PTR requires both faith and reason such that through disciplined interaction between reflection on experience and the faith's texts and traditions, a good decision can be reached. PTR requires and nourishes an ethic that is obedient to tradition without being slavish or legalistic; and which engages our reason, without leaving emotion behind.

b **Situations.** Joseph Fletcher promoted 'situationism' in the 1960s. He argued (1997) that Jesus consistently advocated a life of love, over against the legalistic ethic of the Pharisees. So Christian ethics must involve not the application of rigid rules, but doing the most loving thing possible in a situation. However, Fletcher failed to make it clear how a situation could be defined or analysed, particularly when the most loving thing for one person may conflict with the interests of another or the wider community. PTR in its focus on specific situations and its provision of a process for analysing a situation from different aspects which go beyond the individual level can help to make good this defect, as can its bringing to bear the resources of tradition, not as a set of absolute commands, but as a means of illuminating the situation and setting it in a wider context. Indeed, for many faith traditions, including the Christian, the ultimate situation in which actions have to be considered is the entire history and future of salvation or liberation. This brings us to the next point.

c **Goals.** Ethics is also concerned with the future purposes and consequences of our actions. Philosophers like Jeremy Bentham and John Stuart Mill who have advocated such an ethic have found it hard to define a universally agreed goal and settled on 'the greatest happiness of the greatest number'. However it is hard to work out – at say a meeting where a decision is to be made about the church drainpipes or a new musical setting for the Gloria – what will actually produce this! PTR requires the practitioner to focus on the specific present reality (the pros and cons of the new setting for the Gloria) rather than the abstract, recognizing her own and others' personal desires, but in dialogue with what the tradition has to say about such things and about people's ultimate goal. In this perspective personal preferences can begin to shift towards what really matters in the present, so that the decision reached becomes really wanted, rather than an 'ought'. This is important because people mostly in the end do what they want to do in preference to what they feel they should do (see Chapter 7.1). This brings us to the next question: whether we can really learn to want what is ultimately good …

d **Virtues.** Plato and Aristotle based their ethic not on individual decision-making but on consideration of what makes people virtuous, and so likely to make the best decisions. In general, 'virtue ethics' were important for patristic and medieval theologians, and have recently regained momentum largely through the work of Alistair MacIntyre (1981). The notion is that goodness is a habit that needs to be learnt and cultivated in an ongoing discipline. Whereas many ethics work from theoretical principles to action, 'thinking your way into acting rightly', virtue ethics more often works the other way, 'acting your way into thinking rightly'. When we have learned good habits by repeated training in right ways of living we will want to go on acting well. Theologian Stanley Hauerwas (1981) sees the Church as a school of Christian virtue based on the Gospels, while Timothy Gorringe (2001) speaks of the 'education of desire'. Whereas the *kairos* element in PTR enables situation and tradition to come together to spark enlightened action, the ongoing training in virtue grows from the *chronos* dimension. The regular ongoing discipline of tradition-obedient reflection, and good goal-inspired action, will develop in us that practical quality of living steeped in careful observation and deep vision which we name wisdom.

There is nothing specially wonderful in the way PTR holds together the four ethical factors described above. Many, perhaps most, skills do. Driving, for example, involves observation of the highway code (rules), responsiveness to traffic situations (situations), knowing where one is going and the best route to take (goals), and the etiquette of good driving – efficiency, courtesy and so forth (virtues). However, if PTR can in reality enable practitioners to hold together and use in its process the different strands of traditional ethics, perhaps it can be a powerful tool both for challenging and changing institutions for the better, and, in a humble and realistic way, approaching the wider ethical issues, to which the final section turns.

Exercise

Identify a controversial moral issue about which you have a strong view. What arguments do you or would you use to support your view, and what arguments are offered by those who take a different view? Which of the categories a–d (see pp. 187–9), or which other categories, do these arguments fall into, and are the categories the same for opposing views? How are the moral arguments distributed among the different categories and why do you think this is?

5 PTR and the 'big issues'

In the first part of this chapter, the main focus in using PTR has been first on evaluating and questioning institutions. One cannot hope to 'change the world' without challenging institutions. The detailed painstaking work necessary is essential if theological reflectors are to acquire the ability and credibility to pose questions in relation to major world issues. There are many such issues and dilemmas that we might like PTR to help us resolve: should there be war, stem-cell research, patenting of DNA, special legal measures for terrorists, the right of freedom for the mentally afflicted, investment in airports, restrictions to curb global warming ...? The question is, can PTR which is always specific and practical in its focus, be of help in the crucial area of relating one's faith to these and other major matters ?

It certainly can, provided these four factors are taken into account:

1 PTR starts from lived situations and therefore needs to be focused not on theory but on your own direct or indirect experience in relation to these issues. Once you have become well informed about the treatment of particular people suspected of terrorist offences, or a specific group of displaced Iraqi civilians, or someone with a psychological disorder whose liberty has been restricted, you can then, by entering imaginatively into their experience, apply PTR from that particular standpoint. Empathy of this kind is a prerequisite of any ethical enquiry, but is essential for PTR because it is always rooted in praxis.

2 All such issues involve institutions. Wars involve governments, armies and so forth. Stem-cell research involves the medical profession, hospitals, research centres. The treatment of terrorist suspects involves the whole legal system. So reflecting on such issues cannot be any less painstaking than the matter of reflecting on institutions as considered earlier. To reflect on any issue, before introducing the faith tradition, we will need to ask what institutions have an interest in the matter, what is their stake, and how it looks from the inside and from the outside. We will need to be informed about such specifics before we leap to conclusions.

3 Then when one introduces the faith tradition and its resources, it will have to be acknowledged that this presents a subjective standpoint on the matter. You will be reflecting on war or stem cells as a Christian, or Buddhist, or

whatever, and indeed, as the particular Christian or Buddhist you are, while drawing as widely as possible on relevant faith resources.

4 Finally when it comes to the decision/action phase, the result of PTR will not be something like the statement 'war is wrong' but 'my faith understanding of the matter I have considered persuades me that I must write to this minister, or join this march or undertake humanitarian work in a war zone'. That is not to say that PTR cannot criticize institutions or decisions made concerning major issues, but that institutions or decisions will only get criticized if particular individuals decide to criticize them.

The upshot of all this is that PTR has a particular role to play in public discussions of such issues. PTR moves from particular situations through analysis of particular institutions, the application of a particular faith tradition, as interpreted by a particular group or individual, resulting in particular decisions to do particular things.

Exercise

Take a 'global issue' you feel strongly about and focus it on a relevant institution, or specific situation. Do the PTR as described earlier or as described in this chapter, bringing in sociological and theological analysis, visualization and so forth, as appropriate. At the end of this exercise list ways in which you can now approach the issue differently, and at least one action that you will take.

The 'particularity' of PTR could be interpreted as a weakness, or a sign that we should, after all, 'keep God out of morality' (Holloway, 1999) and not make the effort to use PTR in relation to global issues. However, the many different abstract arguments people have posed about war and so forth down the centuries seem to have made very little difference to people's practice. The fact that Christian theologians have declared that war is only 'just' if it meets certain very stringent standards has not prevented Christian nations fighting endless wars that do not get anywhere near qualifying as just.[24] Because it is so much more focused on the particular, PTR gives us a way of reflecting from the standpoint of a faith on very specific situations with a view to very definite outcomes. Used more, it might actually make a difference to the practice; and it may be that what society needs is not the keeping of God out of the moral debate, but the careful reflection on issues from a multiplicity of faith and non-faith standpoints. If there were then found to be convergence of outcome in certain ethical areas, that would have the ring of truth and persuasiveness that might change matters more in the long term than abstract argument on supposedly universal principles.

Summary

This chapter has examined:

- institutions – as the first port of call if we are to widen PTR and the challenge and critique it can offer;
- the way in which PTR can be used to provide through painstaking analysis and good questions an *etic* outsider critique of institutions;
- how the *etic* critique is complemented by an *emic*, insider understanding of the spirituality of institutions;
- how, by encouraging the right kind of obedience, focusing on particular situations, clarifying worthy ends and developing virtue, PTR can be a powerful practical means to ethical insight and change;
- how the PTR approach can be widened still further, to engage with global as well as institutional issues, but always in the specifically targeted way that is the genius of PTR, and which, together with its theological perspective, offers a special contribution to the wider world.

Further reading (see also Core Texts at the end of the book)

Ballard, P. and Pritchard, J. (2006), *Practical Theology in Action: Christian Thinking in the Service of Church and Society*, London: SPCK.

Browning, D. (1996) *A Fundamental Practical Theology*, Minneapolis: Augsburg Fortress.

Fletcher, J. (1997), *Situation Ethics: The New Morality*, Louisville KY: Westminster John Knox Press.

Freire, P. (2005), *Education for Critical Consciousness*, London and New York: Continuum.

Gerkin, C. (1991), *Prophetic Pastoral Care: A Christian Vision of Life Together*, Nashville TN: Abingdon.

Gorringe, T. (2001), *The Education of Desire: Towards a Theology of the Senses*, London: SCM Press.

Hauerwas, S. (1981), *A Community of Character*, Notre Dame IN: University of Notre Dame Press.

Holloway, R. (1999), *Godless Morality: Keeping Religion out of Ethics*, Edinburgh: Canongate.

Hunter, R. (2007), *Ministry in Depth: Three Critical Questions in the Teaching and Practice of Pastoral Care*, IAPT Conference, Berlin, Working Group Presentation.

MacIntyre, A. (1981), *After Virtue: A Study in Moral Theory*, London: Duckworth.

Messer, N. (2006), *The SCM Studyguide to Christian Ethics*, London: SCM Press.

Mill, J. S.(2002), *Utilitarianism*, Indianapolis: Hackett.

Pattison, S. (1997a), *The Faith of the Managers*, London: Cassell.

Pattison, S. (1997b), *Pastoral Care and Liberation Theology*, London: SPCK

Pattison, S. (2007), *The Challenge of Practical Theology: Selected Essays*, London and Philadelphia: Jessica Kingsley.

Singer, P. (1993), *A Companion to Ethics*, Oxford: Blackwell.

Tracy, D. (1981), *The Analogical Imagination: Christian Theology and the Culture of Pluralism*, New York: Crossroad.

Vardy, P. and Grosch, P. (1999), *The Puzzle of Ethics*, London: Fount.

Wink, W. (1984), *Naming the Powers*. Philadelphia: Fortress Press.

Wogaman, J. (1988), *Christian Perspectives on Politics*, London: SCM Press.

Yoder, J. (1994), *The Politics of Jesus*, Grand Rapids IN: Eerdmans.

10

PTR for Life – Not Just for Courses

Part 3 of this book has broadened the focus of PTR from its use by individuals and groups in church and faith communities as described in Parts 1 and 2, to much wider contexts. Chapter 8 explored PTR in relation to practical and other strands of theology and Chapter 9 its relation to institutional, ethical and global issues. This broadening of focus needs to be accompanied by a sharpening, if we are to avoid placing PTR at the service of sweeping, unsubstantiated theological and ethical generalizations. We need to ask precisely how we get from the momentary insights into particular situations leading to appropriate action, which PTR aims to generate, to broad shifts in ethics and theology. This final chapter shows, first, how individual exercises in PTR can build up over the years into a growth in theological and personal understanding and practice, and, second, how insights gained in PTR can be tested and received by faith communities so as to contribute to the ongoing critique and renewal of the theological traditions and practice of those communities. The book then draws to a close with a concluding summary and challenge.

This chapter will cover this agenda as follows:

1 From courses to lifelong learning: a discussion of the move from PTR as a course requirement to its becoming a 'life requirement'.
2 From lifelong learning to ongoing commitment: refining one's own definition of PTR and how it will relate to, support and be supported by your local faith community.

3 From ongoing commitment to reflective traditions: a suggestion of how PTR might be received and tested by the local faith community and feed back into the development of theological traditions based on reflection.

4 From reflective traditions to sharing in wisdom: showing how PTR provides one way in which the faith traditions can be 'released' into wider society, offering a much needed third alternative between fundamentalism and secular rationalism.

5 Overview of the book: looking back over the book in order to carry forward all of the above into the regular practice of PTR 'for life – not just for courses'.

1 From courses to lifelong learning

While a satisfactory demonstration of PTR in relation to placement and other experiences is an appropriate component of courses evaluating aspects of ministerial practice, it is even more important that students should acquire this skill for its own sake, resulting in a lively interaction between faith and practice throughout life (Cf. Ward, 2005). Whether or not you hope to become a leader in your faith community or whether you are simply a practising believer with a desire for integrity, the regular, habitual exercise of PTR is fundamental. It is also a renewing and life-enhancing activity which can enable growth and development in a faith-and-practice journey throughout life. One might perhaps think of PTR as a kind of spiritual 'roughage' – though the analogy of vitamins is rather more appealing: if it ceases to be a regular part of someone's faith diet they are in danger of becoming sluggish in their correlation of faith with life, or worse, of allowing what they believe and how they act and what they do to become compartmentalized and disconnected.

The results of PTR practised with integrity can, of course, be costly. It is likely to lead you to notice contradictions that you might prefer to ignore, between what is taught in church, mosque, synagogue, temple or gurdwara, and what is done in practice. For example: however carefully one might contextualize and reinterpret the constellation of Jesus' sayings about our attitude to wealth, they are seriously counter-cultural in the western world in the twenty-first century, yet even in church communities attitudes tend to be closer to the secular world than Jesus' teaching. Or, to take a simpler example, while public expressions of grief are more acceptable now than they were a generation ago, we are a long way from considering those who mourn to be 'blessed' as Jesus taught; and learning to love one's neighbour as one's self takes a lifetime of determined dedication and rigorous self-scrutiny such as is not always evident in churches or communities! And while concern for one's global neighbours may lead to a consistent insistence on buying fairly traded goods only, and care for the stewardship of creation may lead to a policy of reuse and recycling, what about the vexed question of air travel? And what about two faith-based beliefs which come into conflict with each other? Then, of course, there is the matter of loving one's enemy and doing good to those who 'despitefully use you'; and the injunction not only not to kill, but not even to harbour hatred in your heart: easy enough, perhaps, if no one has harmed you significantly or directly. But what if they have?

Even in the smaller details and decisions of life, regular PTR practitioners will find themselves frequently faced with dilemmas that they might prefer to avoid. Reflection on the parable of the good Samaritan, for example, suggests that 'passing by on the other side' is not really an option for those who wish to practise their faith in their daily lives; yet passing by on the other side, or keeping firmly within the safety of one's car is as much normal practice for most Christians as it is for the rest of the public, when avoiding a brawl outside a pub in which someone has been injured.

So PTR comes with a spiritual health warning: this practice could seriously affect your whole attitude to life. And it is not just in the details of specific moral and ethical practice that it will influence what is done, but also in an ongoing reappraisal of ethical principles in politics, economics and every aspect of social and global interaction (see Chapter 9). While precisely what this might mean for groups and individuals is outside the scope of this book, it is clearly within the scope of this book to indicate that there are really no limits to where PTR may lead, if practised regularly and with integrity.

2. From lifelong learning to ongoing commitment

If practitioners are to develop PTR into an ongoing discipline for life, they will need to be certain about what PTR is for them and how it functions in their life as a whole. You are therefore encouraged to re-examine your earlier definition and approach to PTR in the following exercise.

Exercise

In Chapter 1.5 you were invited to write your definition of PTR as you then understood it, keeping a copy of it, to see how your understanding of it evolved. In the light of what you have experienced working through this book, you are now invited to write a new definition of PTR in the following steps:

- list the key elements of the reflective process;
- note the significance of sequence of these elements;
- write a brief comment on each;
- write your own new definition in about 200 words;
- compare this with your earlier definition, and with those of others, and notice and comment on similarities and differences.

You are also invited to re-examine the pattern for the regular practice of PTR that you considered in Chapter 6.2 and its relation to the regular undertaking of PTR in a group with others (Chapter 7.6) and to supervision (Chapter 6.5).

Working with others in this way not only helps you to hold to the commitment you have made through mutual accountability, but also, in microcosm, provides a model for the practice of linking personal insights to those of the wider community and allowing a process of mutual critique and reassessment. This accountability both helps to ensure that you remain part of your faith community rather than invent a new tradition of your own and also enables you to contribute to the growth of theological understanding within your tradition. How this might be done is explored in the next section.

3 From ongoing commitment to reflective traditions

As this book has repeatedly stressed, PTR is not only a process that applies scripture and tradition to experience. It also works the other way, applying one's experience to the reading of scripture. For as passages from scripture and parts of tradition become harnessed into the PTR process, the practitioner's understanding of scripture and tradition will change and grow. Parts of them that seemed dead and irrelevant may come to life, in the manner in which the Exodus stories, for example, have become pivotal to the base communities of liberation theology.[25] A collision between habitual interpretations and experienced reality may force a new interpretation that brings new ethical insight, as for example when passages traditionally used to condemn homosexual practice are seen as dissonant with one's own experience of one's sexuality or that of others, forcing the subtle reinterpretation of those passages as illustrated, for example, in the works of James Alison (e.g. 2001).

Again, PTR may release passages from their habitual interpretation within a particular tradition and enable a richer understanding. A practitioner in one tradition may read the words about being 'born again of water and the spirit' (John 3.5) as referring only to the need for baptism, while someone in another tradition might equate it, equally simply, with the need for a conversion experience. But either practitioner may find themselves repeatedly returning to this image of rebirth in their efforts to describe a variety of situations in PTR. As they do so they may find themselves gradually developing a much richer and more complex image of what 'spiritual rebirth' means and its significance. And that in turn may influence their understanding of what baptism and conversion mean.

It is of course vital that you are not simply adapting scripture and tradition to fit the lifestyle you want or injustices from which you profit – as seems to be the case, for example, in the 'prosperity gospel',[26] or the use of references to the three sons of Noah to justify the slavery of the black races.[27] The test is whether the new reading of scripture effects a rediscovery of riches that have been there all along or whether it involves merely the replacement of one one-dimensional reading with another; a matter already explored in terms of the use and abuse of the Bible (Chapter 4.3). In the end, only the wider faith community can decide, and it is in that context that new insights must be tested.

So we move to largely unexplored territory, namely the process whereby insights drawn from theological reflection can feed back, not just into the individual or group's understanding of the tradition, but into the remaking of the tradition itself. Currently, it appears that practical theology develops in much the same way as any academic discipline, through books and articles written in the light of individual authors' reflections, which are then critically received and evaluated within the academy. By contrast, it was the aim of liberation theologians that ordinary people in their base communities should, through their own deep experience and reflection, contribute to the development of theology, and thereby liberate theology itself from its captivity to western academic standards and procedures (see also Chapter 3.1.d).

However, there are precedents for alternative, non-academic models of theological development. In Chapter 4 we saw how Midrash built up a tradition of alternative readings around the sacred text. And Acts 10 supplies a very significant model of the process of reception of theological reflection by the wider Church. In this instance, Peter had been praying on a roof top at about midday while waiting for food to be prepared. According to the writer, he then 'fell into a trance', which might just be a polite way of saying that he dozed off into a hungry kind of sleep. Whatever it was, it enabled him to engage in a kind of passive PTR. Presumably partly because of his hunger the dream or vision that he had was of food, or, rather, potential but forbidden food: for a great cloth appeared in front of him, full of many different birds, animals and reptiles – all of which were kinds that law-abiding Jews were forbidden to eat. On hearing a voice saying, 'Rise, Peter; kill and eat', he replied, 'No, Lord; for I have never eaten anything common or unclean.' The whole sequence was repeated three times, and as Peter was reflecting on it, messengers arrived, asking him to come to Caesarea to see a Roman Centurion (therefore a Gentile) named Cornelius, a devout God-fearing man who had also had a vision of an angel telling him to send for Peter. It would be fascinating to know how much poetic or theological licence may have been exercised in the telling of this tale. Did the messengers really arrive at the very moment when Peter was having his vision? In any case, Peter was immediately able to connect his dream with the pastoral situation, and, without any further hesitation, recognized that the good news of the gospel was intended for Gentiles as much as for Jews. This insight was then put to the test at a council of the church, at which

Peter described his experience. As a result the council decided to include the Gentiles without imposing circumcision or Jewish food restrictions: a decision which then changed the whole focus of the life and ministry of the early Christians, and eventually led to the establishment of Christendom as we have known it.

Currently most churches accept the need to reinterpret scripture and tradition for each new generation, but a process whereby insights about faith, life and tradition generated by PTR can be formally received and allowed to shape new traditions for future generations does not yet exist. Quite how this is to be achieved, and the part to be played by supervision groups, local faith communities, synods, councils and other structures of the wider churches, and by the academies where theology is developed, researched and taught is not yet clear. This needs further enquiry beyond the scope of this book. Meanwhile genuine new insights will surely be informally received and are likely to contribute to future theological reflections.

One place where new insight is received, grounded and tested will of course be in the Church's corporate liturgy, where Christ is re-membered and re-encountered in the regular office and Eucharist. Here the results of PTR will time and again be offered and received back, and perhaps integrated into the life of the church community. Thompson (2008, ch. 8) has made close connections between the study of spirituality and a practical theology centred on PTR and the pastoral cycle.

But this continued rebaptism of PTR in corporate liturgy and personal spiritual practice needs to be balanced by a more verbal, propositional process of mutual critique. The results of PTR may well involve critique of aspects of church life, which will need to be carefully and caringly offered to the community, and to bishops and other leaders. Conversely, theological reflectors will need to open themselves humbly to the critique of their fellow Christians, if they are not to become arrogant, solipsistic, elitist or otherwise deluded. Safe structures for such caring mutual critique need to be developed, not least for the benefit of bishops and other church leaders. This is surely an important agenda for the Church if it is to harness PTR as a means of aligning its life more fully with the gospel in ongoing exploration (cf. Schreiter, 1985; Hopewell, 1988; Boff, 1997; and Ward, 2005).

4 From reflective traditions to sharing in wisdom

So PTR is not just for courses but for life, and not just for an individual's life and learning and growth but for ongoing discipline in the context of a faith community and its enrichment through the continual development of its traditions. In Chapter 9 a further step was suggested: that PTR can challenge and enrich the wider world. And of course, none of the faith traditions see themselves as existing for their own sake; all of them exist to witness to something vital to the world. This 'something' goes by different names – like salvation, the kingdom, divinization, nirvana and liberation – and these are not necessarily exactly the same 'something', but in all cases it is something the wider world is felt to need. The suggestion this book makes now is quite a bold one, which you will need to think about carefully: namely, that by relating tradition to specific experience and experience to tradition in a reflective and rational yet imaginative way, PTR may enable the traditions of faith communities to develop in a way that resonates with contemporary experience and enables a new 'third alternative' in the way society handles faith traditions.

A broad swathe of scholarship these days divides the world into three 'periods'. This way of looking at history is perhaps one of those grand 'metanarratives' we ought not to accept uncritically, but with a dose of sceptical salt this story will help us make an important suggestion.

In the pre-modern world societies lived by and large by tradition. Laws and institutions were justified by appeal to the founding 'fathers', and beyond them by appeal to the gods who had instructed the fathers – to write that book, found that institution, and so forth. These pre-modern societies were not 'primitive' or irrational: in many cases valuable experience was codified into folklore that served society's needs very well. And plenty of reasoning was allowed: the great conceptual edifices of Plato and Aquinas were built in such societies with a subtlety in the use of reason that has seldom been matched. But reason was in the service of tradition, designed to elucidate what had been revealed to the fathers, not to challenge it. The main problem such traditional societies faced was that believing the status quo was divinely ordained, they were reluctant to adapt to new realities like the growth of capitalism and Europe's 'discovery' of the Americas.

In the 'modern' world – which people date variously from the late Middle Ages, the Renaissance, the Reformation or the Enlightenment, but which is more of a gradual shift in perspective than something that can be precisely dated – societies gave up on their traditions and began to assess their institutions by means of reason. The question was no longer, 'Are kings … schools … parliaments … hospitals etc., divinely ordained and working as sacred tradition states they should?' but, 'Do they follow from the rational principles we have established as being those that serve people's best interests?' So, society was 'detraditionalized' (Heelas *et al.*, 1996) or 'secularized'. The process was very gradual, and pockets of pre-modern society remain, like the monarchy and the churches. But society has taken steps to ensure that these 'irrational' superstitions survive as quaint and interesting relics rather than forces to be reckoned with. And by and large the churches and other faith communities have accepted this role. They had invested heavily in justifying their traditions on pre-modern grounds, relying on sacred texts and hierarchical structures believed to have been ordained by God. So it seemed easiest – except to a few liberation theologians and the like – to settle for being sub-societies governed by special traditions within a wider society that ignored, if not despised, those traditions. Sometimes these faith communities hardened yet further into that typically modern phenomenon, fundamentalism, opting to live rigidly according to the revealed precepts of the fathers, however irrational that might seem to others.

In what is now often called the 'postmodern' world people began to suspect all 'grand metanarratives' which defined 'reality'. This included both the pre-modern traditions, and the modern supposition that there is such a thing as a universal reason to which all societies should conform. At the same time traditions began to be reassessed. Where they claimed absolute validity deriving from the gods, they continued to be unacceptable, as concealing the 'will to power' (Nietzsche) of a particular group to dominate all others in the name of its gods. But humbler traditions of localized peoples began to be valued even as they were beginning to disappear under the onslaught of a mechanistic and rationalistic global capitalism. People began to wonder if, as these societies disappeared from the earth, they might take with them bodies of wisdom that would vanish for ever, just as we know that the disappearance of particular species has deprived the world of certain irreplaceable medicines. So faith communities have begun to be reappraised, not as anachronisms that would inevitably and justly disappear as people became ever more rational and enlightened, but as precious precisely for their difference from standard secular society, and the distinctive wisdom their traditions might embody.

This process is at very early stages, and by and large contemporary critics (Dawkins *et al.*) seem to want to see the Church simultaneously as the power-wielding, anti-rational, anti-progress pre-modern hierarchy it in some ways once was, and as a vestige of the primitive, wandering its dodo-like way to inevitable extinction! But PTR, as described in this book, might have something important to offer both church and world, precisely because of the way it ties together tradition, reason and experience. It is, in essence, a way of seeing experience in the light of tradition, and tradition in the light of experience, and subjecting both to a process of reflection that is imaginatively rational without being domineeringly or narrowly rationalistic.

PTR affirms the sacred traditions and scriptures beloved of pre-modern societies, but not in quite the way those societies do. It affirms them not because they are unquestionable but because they raise questions; not because, or only because, they were revealed to the 'fathers', but primarily because, and in so far as, they can make our daily experience catch fire with a new light, and suggest newer and wiser ways of responding to it.

PTR equally affirms a modern, critical and rational approach. It sees faith not as a way of preventing change in our world and ourselves, but as a way of enabling the kinds of change that will work. But it is not rationalistic, and the 'liberal' attempt to produce a faith that is more rational than that of the rationalists and reductionists is not part of its programme. For it rejects the modern suspicion of tradition and ritual, noting that what has sometimes made religions vicious is not their traditionalism and love of ritual, but their readiness uncritically to adopt and own ideas – slavery, crusades, persecution, war – that a modicum of reflection would have shown to be incompatible with sacred tradition. Often the traditional ritual – like the Eucharist – goes on proclaiming a bloodless, non-violent way (Cavanaugh, 1998), the implications of which unreflective practice and ideology have ignored. PTR, we have seen, involves the use of reason, but in a manner that is reverent, critical and imaginative in its use of tradition, producing that amalgam of tradition, experience and reason we call wisdom.

And this is precisely what enables it to give something that postmodern society, as it develops, might be able to receive: traditions made relevant to experience and tested by reason and imagination in the light of life. Chapter 8 suggested the possibility of interfaith reflection, but there is no reason why we could not go further, and invite those who do not accept religious tradition of any kind to join in the PTR process. For one does not have to accept the whole faith to believe that the parables and teachings and art and ceremony of the Church, and other faith communities, might nourish a reflective and liberating response to experience. In a world of tightening boundaries PTR can facilitate an open approach to the traditions and create a reflective Church that is permeable, 'emergent' (Brewin, 2004) and even perhaps 'liquid' (Ward, 2002) and ready to travel with very different kinds of people.

Exercise

List three things you and your local church could do to become a 'reflective church' of the kind just described; and three things – positive or negative – that might prevent this or render it inappropriate.

5 A concluding overview of the book

Let us see how this challenging point has been arrived at through the process of reflection about PTR itself in the chapters of this book.

- The Introduction established the concept of theological reflection, as a reflective linking of tradition and experience, and set out the strategy of the book, as a moving out to ever-wider circles of something that was, at the centre, very carefully defined and practised.

The first three chapters were about establishing this definite centre in your own practice.

- Chapter 1 introduced various concepts of theological reflection, and the 'pastoral cycles' on which many of them were based, and defined 'Progressing Theological Reflection', or PTR, in this context.
- Chapter 2 illustrated how to do PTR specifically through worked examples.
- Chapter 3 looked at a range of alternative models for PTR which you might find useful.

The next four chapters investigated various crucial elements of PTR.

- Chapter 4 looked at ways of using the Bible or other sacred text.
- Chapter 5 explored *kairos*, the 'momentary' interillumination involved, and how you can prepare for it.
- Chapter 6 examined *chronos*: the business of establishing long-term rhythms of PTR and relating it to wider groups including the local faith community.
- Chapter 7 looked at the crucial factor in PTR which is you, and how both to gain a critical self-awareness of your own limits and to use aspects of your personality positively.

The final three chapters investigated the relation of PTR to the wider world.

- Chapter 8 looked at the part PTR plays in theology: the way it is based on a sound practical theological method, and how it can learn from and contribute to all kinds of theology.

- Chapter 9 considered how PTR might be used to critique and change institutions and the wider world more generally, as well as changing the agent ethically in the process.
- In this final chapter we have considered PTR as something that enhances life as a whole, not just a course requirement. We invited you to refine your understanding and practice of PTR, with a view to establishing it as a discipline within the life of your faith community. We touched on how the results of PTR might be received by and enrich the faith community as a whole, imparting its humble insights to the ongoing development of the theological tradition, and finally suggested that by offering those traditions as bodies of lived and reflective wisdom, PTR can free them up as something the postmodern world is beginning to be ready to share in and receive.

From a clearly defined core process, this book has broadened its scope to bold assertions with wide implications. If the assertions are right, PTR is a very precious thing, worthy of being used with careful discipline and reflective imagination. It is now over to you, the reader, to put these bold assertions to the test, with discipline and imagination, in your own life, your church or faith community, and in the contexts in which you live and work.

Further reading (see also Core Texts at the end of the book)

Alison, J. (2001), *Faith Beyond Resentment*, New York: Crossroad.
Boff, L. (1997), *Ecclesiogenesis: The Base Communities Reinvent the Church*, Maryknoll NY: Orbis Books.
Bonhoeffer, D. (1954), *Life Together*, London: SCM Press.
Brewin, K. (2004), *The Complex Christ: Signs of Emergence in the Urban Church*, London: SPCK.
Cavanaugh, W. (1998), *Torture and Eucharist*, Oxford: Blackwell.
Heelas P. *et al.* (eds) (1996), *Detraditionalisation*, Oxford: Blackwell.
Hopewell, J. (1988), *Congregation: Stories and Structures*, London: SCM Press.
Schreiter, R. (1985), *Constructing Local Theologies*, Maryknoll NY: Orbis Books.
Thompson, R. (2008), *SCM Studyguide to Christian Spirituality*, London: SCM Press.

Ward, F. (2005), *Lifelong Learning: Theological Education and Supervision*, London: SCM Press.

Ward, P. (2002), *Liquid Church*, Carlisle: Paternoster Press.

Part 4

A Toolkit for PTR

No matter how committed you are to the regular practice of PTR as an integral and ongoing element of your pattern of life and discipleship, you will be unusual if you don't have difficulty, sometimes, or often, in getting down to doing it. As has already been suggested (Chapter 7.6) this is one reason why belonging to a mutually accountable group who meet regularly for this purpose can be so helpful – as well as all the other benefits of differing perspectives and insights; discerning one another's blind spots; and the enjoyment and stimulation of each other's companionship. However, on occasion, groups as well as individuals can become stuck or jaded and in need of a kick start at various points in the PTR process.

This Toolkit is provided precisely for that purpose. The 'tools' described here are absolutely *not* intended to be thought of as alternative methods of PTR: rather, they are simply aids or resources to energize or provoke you into different ways of thinking. Looking at things 'slant' can sometimes be much more fruitful than head-on, especially if similar issues have been the focus of your attention many times before. By using one or more of these or other 'tools', you may find a new angle, connection or significant lacuna that helps to liberate your thinking and feeling processes and generate new possibilities. Or it may shift you into unfamiliar territory or raise questions that help you let go and begin to embrace the state of 'negative capability' referred to in Chapter 5.5, thus becoming more open to the promptings of the spirit. Or it may simply be more fun, which is no bad thing in itself.

Some of the tools suggested will link in with familiar conceptual ideas; others may seem alien or outside your usual frame of reference. As Chapter 7.4 on learning styles demonstrates, what feels comfortable and engaging for some may be experienced as strange and inappropriate for others. It is often worth trying out a tool that has little initial appeal; but sometimes you will need to select one which feels easy to use. A number of tools are included that encourage non-linear, visual and playful imaginative thinking, as a balance to the verbal and analytical hegemony of most of this book and of much that is taken for granted in accepted methods of critical thinking.

As with any other toolkit, part of the skill lies in choosing the right tool for the job. However, in this case, some tools which appear inappropriate to the current task may turn out to be just right. You need to find a balance between honing your skills in using a particular tool, and being ready to try out new ones. When using a tool it is best to include all the steps described: glancing at the suggestions and relating them superficially to the issues you are considering isn't at all the same as putting the tool to work as suggested.

Important notes for using these tools

1 In every single instance of the use of any one of these tools, please use it only as *part* of your reflective process. When you have completed the suggested procedure, you will need to stand back and evaluate what has emerged and how it may illuminate the current issue, and then continue with the rest of your theological reflection. This essential point is not made at the end of each tool's description because the repetition would be tedious; but please consider it made in every instance.

2 Most of these tools are theologically neutral. They can certainly be used to assist you in the explicitly theological aspects of your reflection but are no substitute for your own theological thinking and assessment. The tools offer assistance in the process of reflection: but you yourself provide the 'content', theological and otherwise.

3 You may already be familiar with some of these tools or similar ones from other contexts. Feel free to substitute or invent others at any point. The tools presented are only to get you started – they are not in the least intended to be thought of as prescriptive.

4 Take care with the interim 'products' generated by the use of these tools. You yourself may understand how important it is to be as uncensored and uninhibited as you like in drawing, describing or recording your thoughts and feelings about your current issue and the people involved in it. Letting go in this way may help deepen your understanding and trigger theological connections and reassessments – but most of what you record at this stage will be much better kept for your own eyes and ears alone (or those of your reflection group members with whom you have a confidentiality agreement).

The tools – in alphabetical order

Animals

This can be fun and can help you recognize and work with some of your less rational reactions to the matter under consideration. It's a tool to use when the personalities of some of the main protagonists in the situation are particularly significant in the way it is, or isn't, developing, and you need to see how this is influencing things and what might help. All you do is identify a number – say 5–10 – of the key people involved, and then, without thinking too much, assign each person, including yourself, an animal identity. If possible draw (however inexpertly) each of the animals, and name them appropriately. Then ask yourself why you have assigned each, respectively, the animal identity you have given them. In particular, what do the characteristics of the animal you have assigned to yourself suggest about you in relation to the other animals? What do these respective identities teach you about your perceptions of the various relationships, and what influence might such perceptions have?

Applying parables

Parables exist in all religious traditions, and for good reason: they are an engaging and simple but richly effective way of helping us to see a situation in another perspective. You are encouraged to build up your own collection of parables whenever you come across one which seems worth keeping. Here are three to start off your collection, all derived from the versions found in Anthony de Mello's *Song of a Bird* (1983):

- **Nasreddin's Key** Nasreddin, always more renowned for his simple faith than his wit or wisdom, had lost the key to his house, and his neighbour found him searching for it with increasing frustration. His response to his neighbour's enquiry revealed that Nasreddin had been in his shed when he lost it and led to the question: 'So why are you looking for it in the yard ?' 'Because it's dark in the shed and I would never see it there' replied Nasreddin. 'Out here in the yard, at least I can see what I'm looking for – if only I could find it.'
- **The fish in search of the ocean** The little fish was out of sorts and feeling very frustrated. He had heard of this marvellous thing called 'The Ocean' which was vast and exciting and life-giving and full of wonder and beauty – but, through he searched and searched, he couldn't find it anywhere. At last he plucked up courage and approached a much larger and older fish and asked for help. The older fish responded, in some surprise, 'Why, little fish, The Ocean is where you and I are, and what you are swimming in right now; it is all around you.' 'Oh no,' said the little fish, deeply disappointed, 'This is only the sea. There's nothing special about it at all. What I am looking for is The Ocean!'
- **The Golden Eagle** This parable is almost the reverse of the previous one. History doesn't relate how it came about, but a golden eagle's egg came to be in a nest of eggs being carefully incubated by a farmyard hen. In due time it hatched out, along with the little chicks, and grew up among them, imagining that it was one of them. As it grew older it scratched about the farmyard, looking for worms, occasionally flapping its wings, like the rest of the chickens. One day it happened to look up into the sky and there, far above, was a golden eagle, floating majestically on the wind currents with its great

Figure 9: The Golden eagle.

wings outstreched. In fear and awe the subject of our story asked his fellow chickens, 'Who is that?' 'Oh that', replied his friend, 'is a golden eagle – but don't worry your head thinking about him. You and I are quite different. We could never learn to fly like that.' So he went on scrabbling about in the yard like the other chickens, and never gave the golden eagle another thought – until, eventually, he died.

Points to note with parables in relation to the current matter for attention:
- similarities
- differences
- the key point of the parable
- connections between the key point and the matter being considered
- changes this might suggest need to be made: in perception; in communication; in action.

Association

Free association is a well-known technique in psychoanalysis which can also be useful in PTR. You can do this on your own, but it is more fun and often results in more interesting connections in a small group. All you do is start off with a word – any word will do, but you may like to begin with something that encapsulates a particular aspect of the matter under consideration – and the next person (or it could be you), as fast as possible and without thinking about it, simply says whatever word comes to mind; and so with the next, and the next, and the next. You can do this for, say, three minutes, or a specific length of time, and see where it leads you; or you can record the words to look at again later. Each one of the words could probably yield a rich harvest of ways of producing a thick descriptor for a situation or clues for interesting links.

Compass points

This notion is a suggestion of David Runcorn (2006, p. 117). It can be used to help discern your feelings about a situation, or to direct you to resources, thoughts and feelings relevant at reflection and action stages. You simply draw two intersecting lines and label them with the four compass points, north, south, east and west; or, if you prefer, winter and summer, spring and autumn.

- **North** is for placing the fixed points and values in your life, or the situation: that which your conscience orients itself towards as a compass points north. It also represents winter, the time when plants die away and animals suffer; so it represents the things you want to suffer and endure for, and not let go of.
- **East** is for what is new and fresh, like the rising sun and the spring, what takes you by surprise and gives you new hope or challenge.
- **South** is for what is warm, pleasant, rich and exotic: like summer, it is for recreation and enjoyment.
- **West** is for what is in decline, like the setting sun and the autumn; things you need to cherish – like the glory of the sunset and the autumn trees – and then allow to blow away on the wind of change.

There can be variations: north-west for something or someone you are deeply committed to even as they recede from you; north-east for new ideas or people currently entering the centre of your life; south-east for new challenges you are beginning to meet and enjoy; and south-west for pleasures tinged with a sense of transience though you are reluctant to let them go. As you draw all this, some things will be very close to the centre, others far away at the edge of your life.

This tool helps in journalling too, especially as 'Compass points' becomes familiar and you add your own associations appropriately: people in your life, biblical themes and images, and key experiences, events and places (see 'Map' on p. 222).

Computer games

If you're a computer games buff you could design one that corresponds with the situation you are focusing on. First you'll need to decide the genre. If it's adventure quest you'll need to decide what you're seeking, and whether it might be found in a maze, a dungeon, a far-off land, or maybe in your own living-room. You need to identify: the obstacles, traps and dangers in your quest; the main figures who are obstructing you; and your team members and who or what is likely to help you. Other genres like combat and puzzles have different roles to assign. Computer games contain elements of other 'tools' like maps and fantasy fiction. You can be very goal-directed in computer games, or simply wander round exploring mysteries on the way; which is why Duncan Ballard sees computer games as a metaphor for theological reflection (2005, p.8) (see also Pink, 2006, pp. 180–8 and 204–5).

Fantasy fiction

Whereas in a journal you write down the ongoing true story of your life as far as you can, here you simply write a short story – or the basic outline of one – that is completely fictional, fantasy-ridden and totally unrelated to any reality you know of. The trick is that when you have completed your little story – and only then – you reflect on it to see what in it corresponds with things going on in your life. Nearly always things in 'real life' will have impacted on your fantasy, as they do in dreams. Understanding how you have fantasized your reality may help you reframe it radically. Relevant here is the closely related tool, 're-plotting'.

Figure and background

The concept of 'figure/ground', or foreground and background, will already be familiar to some. We tend to appreciate pictures that have something to focus on but also a background landscape where the eye can wander. However, in order to make progress you need to focus on particular aspects rather than everything at once. Often at a meeting with difficult issues to discuss, there will be a collective readiness to focus on easier issues – how to organize the refreshments at an event being planned – rather than the uncomfortable imponderables such as who is going to be in overall charge or what the input should be. In PTR it can be very releasing to view a situation from a previously ignored perspective and to make matters which, at first sight, seemed trivial take centre stage (and vice versa).

Flow chart

Think of a word or a symbol to represent each aspect of the matter under consideration and write or draw each well spaced out on a page or flip chart, with a circle around each one in a neutral colour. Then, using different colours, draw labelled arrows to express the links you see between the circles. Add new ideas in circles or branches from the arrows till you have a veritable thicket or maze of interconnections. This frees you from the linearity of verbal descriptions, and may lead to re-envisioning. Images from the Bible and tradition can also be explored in this way, making connections between them and with experience. Don't try to be too analytical and objective, just express the relationships between the ideas whether they are right or not, so as to produce a 'fuzzy cognitive map' (Kosko, 1994, pp. 222–35; see figure on p. 226).

Fly on the wall

Almost everyone expresses the wish, on occasion, to be 'a fly on the wall', unnoticed but present and able to observe from an elevated distance exactly what is going on. This tool is a very simple one: so simple and easy to use that it is easily overlooked. Just imagine yourself to be that fly – or invite someone else to do so – and then describe exactly what you can see from the vantage point of a very clear view but with absolutely no involvement. To make this tool work well you need to be careful to remain the objective fly and not start taking a view on things – especially not your own issues – until after you have completed the objective description.

Force-field analysis

This is a useful tool to use when a group or an individual has become stuck, and action agreed on doesn't seem to be carried out. Reasons given – lack of time, illness, difficulty in finding materials etc. – may be true, but only part of the truth, and the real inhibiting factors may never be mentioned. For force-field analysis, you need a diagram like the one shown in Figure 10. Above the centre line with arrows pointing downwards, list all the forces at work which *hinder* the goal from being reached. Below the line, with arrows pointing upwards, indicate all the forces which could *facilitate* the reaching of the goal. Having done that, focus on what might be done to decrease the hindering forces and strengthen the facilitating ones.

Figure 10: Force-field analysis.

(from F. Inksipp, *A Manual for Trainers*, London: Alexia Publications, n.d.)

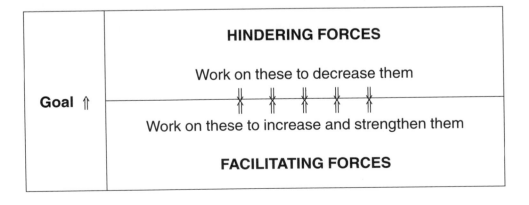

Grown up godly play

'Godly play', now well established in many parts of the UK as well as in North America where it originated, is a method of inviting children to reflect on parables and other teaching in their own way, readily accepting whatever responses they may have. Its gentle and engaging, Montessori-based approach can work well with children of all ages, and with adults too, and offers a particular tool which can transform parts of the PTR process for anyone who is able to draw on its style and insights and improvise appropriate materials for the simple presentation of events and stories. Its approach gives children – and surely adults too – 'a way to confront the existential questions common to all people; the questions we all struggle with … about the meaning of life, death, freedom and aloneness' (Berryman, vol. 5, 2003, p. 12). The better acquainted you are with these volumes the more possibilities you are likely to find from the wide range of material provided. A few examples are given here to whet your appetite. The 'Exile and Return' session (Berryman, 2002, vol. 2, p. 93) or 'Parable Synthesis 2: I Am Statements' (Berryman, 2002, vol. 2, p. 114) could be used exactly as they are with a group of adults – or even on your own. 'The part that hasn't been written yet' (Berryman, vol. 4, 2003, p. 143) or 'The Good Shepherd and World Communion' (Berryman, vol. 4, 2003, p. 91) could also work well. In response to the various 'I wonder' questions, connections may be made between the narrative as presented and the particular matter under consideration for PTR. The method could also be used more freely while remaining in keeping with its mood and style. The suggestion (Berryman, vol. 5, 2003) of relating two stories side by side, one biblical and one from your own life, and making connections between the two, can be very fruitful, as can inventing your own parable, responding to it and feeding your responses back into your current reflection.

Human figure

This involves use of a human shape like Figure 11, in which you inscribe:

1 what you are thinking about the situation but not wanting to say;
2 what you are saying or wanting to say to others;
3 what you are feeling;

4 what is in your 'right hand' – visible to all and ready for use;
5 what is in your left hand – concealed, perhaps weaker and more vulnerable;
6 where have you come from;
7 where are you going or wanting to go.

This is a simple way of ensuring all these factors are included in your PTR process.

Figure 11: Human figure.

Hypertext

Duncan Ballard (2005) has explored the possibilities of groups developing websites, or using his own website (www.etheology.com) to engage in virtual dialogue and comment on issues. He argues (2005, pp. 53ff.) that the non-linearity of hypertext, whereby pages can contain multiple links to other pages, can be liberating for TR as compared with journalling and other written description, in which the pages form a linear progression. There are, quite literally, no bounds to where your reflections may lead you and the connections and possibilities that can link in with the matter you began with: a stimulating method to help you think creatively 'outside the box'.

Imaginary dialogue

Choose a mentor or wise guide. This could be someone you know or know of, or a historical figure. It could be a saint or a prophet such as St Francis or St Teresa, a biblical figure like Lady Wisdom or Jeremiah, or a well-known contemporary such as Desmond Tutu or the Dalai Lama, or it could, of course, be Jesus. Your guide should be someone you can talk to easily. Following an imaginary discussion with them about the issue, write them a letter about a particular aspect of it. Then write the reply from your wise guide to you commenting on yours, and suggesting how your reflections could further be made wise.

Inspiration board

This is a tool that can be used in all sorts of ways and can be maintained so it is always available, or can be put away after each use and brought out whenever needed. All you require is a cork board or empty noticeboard, a supply of drawing pins and a deliberately heightened alertness. Whenever you see or hear about an event or an enterprise or a way of doing things that strikes you as original or exciting, record it on your 'inspiration board'. It might be in the form of a picture, or a newspaper cutting, or even an advert, or your own brief description of something you have experienced or heard about. When you have a good collection of items on your board, see what connections you can find between them. This is the challenging part of the exercise – much better undertaken in a relaxed frame of mind.

This tool is one which can work well in groups, including colleagues, families or existing church groups – such as the choir or the women's meeting – and can provide a creative way forward when discussions in meetings reach an impasse.

It can, as in that instance, be focused on a particular issue or area of interest or concern, or it can be much more widely focused and open to spontaneous thoughts and responses. (It can be particularly helpful in enabling those who find discussions inhibiting to make their own input.)

Journalling

Journalling is considered in some detail in Chapter 3. This is just a reminder.

Limerick or rhyming couplets

This may sound impossible if you don't rate your literary skills very highly, but if you can ignore such negative thoughts and have a go, you may be agreeably surprised by the results. They may not excel as pieces of literature, but they don't need to. By forcing yourself to find particular rhymes or rhythms, surprising new perspectives may begin to emerge, as in the following examples:

a There once was an enterprising vicar
   Who wanted everything to happen much quicker,
      He listened to some
      But attended to none
   And labelled everyone else as a sticker.

b There once was a busy young dandy
   Who liked to have everything handy
      If something was missing
      Amid groaning and hissing
   He buried his head in the candy.

c There once was a church committee
   Which insisted on singing a ditty
      As each meeting progressed
      They became more distressed
   Because so little remained in the kitty.

Map – here be dragons?

This tool is one which some may struggle with since it invites you to reimagine whatever you are considering in spatial terms. Figure 12 provides an example to help you start. Don't attempt to find one-to-one correspondence between the different elements of the situation and what you put on your map. Let your map be more like a doodle – don't think about it, but just get on and do it. The map that you draw could be an island or part of the mainland, and probably needs to be an imaginary rather than actual location. You can put in roads and pathways, mountain ranges and passes, streams, rivers, woods, impenetrable forests, bogs, deserts and quicksands; you can name them as you wish, and also name towns and villages, houses, castles, ruins or whatever your imagination suggests. And of course, there will be parts of the land you are creating where particular dangers lurk, be they dragons, pirates or lawless militia. As your map takes shape, begin to label parts of it with features of your situation.

Figure 12: The map.

Decide where you are now, and where you want to get to, and identify goals and obstacles and what might help you along the route. Begin the journey in your imagination and notice which obstacles and opportunities become significant, and which hardly feature. When you have thoroughly immersed yourself, in this imaginative process, along with others involved if possible, gradually look again at the situation you began with, and see what insights begin to emerge.

Midrash

Chapter 4.4 describes this tool. It can be used with almost any passage of scripture or sacred text – though it works particularly well with narrative. Midrash can be adapted for use with the 'narrative' of any situation which has a written 'story'; and can be used over and over again, as it is as varied as the imaginative responses people make. It is well worth the time it takes in the early stages and can be fun bringing completely unexpected dimensions into play with juxtapositions that generate energy and new possibilities.

Music-making

Imagination, rather than musicianship or instruments, is needed for this tool, and it definitely works better in a group. Improvise with whatever materials may be to hand – glasses filled with varying amounts of water, combs and greaseproof paper, coffee tins and sticks for drums, wind chimes, anything that resonates. Then, as a one-person or several-person band, just let go! You may be agreeably surprised by the results, especially if you include quiet interludes. After about 15 minutes, see what you can relate from this experience to the matter you have been considering.

Negative space

Negative space is the space that lies between the things we focus on. In Figure 7, if we are focusing on the two faces, the negative space is the vase. Figure 13[28] appears at first to consist of strange characters, but if you focus on the negative

Figure 13: Negative space.

space you will find a very familiar word. Part of the skill in learning to draw is the ability to look not only at the shapes we are familiar with, but the shapes between them, since these also contribute to the beauty and balance of the drawing. In PTR likewise it is important to look at what is going on in between the main lines. At the board meeting, what was the other meeting that was going on? What is the unexpressed hope or fear between the words and ideas that someone described to you? As noted with Midrash, when reading a text like the Bible, you need to notice what is not said, and what that non-saying indicates.

Personal refreshment

This is listed as a separate tool from 'Recreation' which is used to refer to more obvious outdoor and restoring kinds of activity. What is suggested here is anything at all which helps you feel more whole and alive and in tune with the core of your being. It might be trainspotting or watching cricket, sitting in a garden listening to the background noises, visiting a favourite haunt or art gallery or going to a concert or listening to your favourite music – or indeed, music that you find challenging. Whereas the aim of 'recreation' in PTR is to free the muscles of the mind and enable wide-ranging non-linear thinking, 'refreshment' is valuable in PTR in that it can bring you an enhanced and rooted sense of yourself, so that you can be more present in the PTR and make decisions from an enriched and renewed perspective (see also Introduction 5).

Press reports

Write a brief press report about the events that have led up to the current situation and their imagined outcome in different ways. Choose a time in the future when matters have moved on and imagine and describe the outcome and how it came about. Press reports often involve oversimplification, distortion or significant omissions, or even all three, so feel free to make your reports for (a) and (b) racy rather than accurate. The report for (c) should be more measured. Write three different reports:

(a) one which celebrates you and your faith community as the 'heroes' who have done a wonderful job;
(b) one which vilifies you and your faith community as the 'villains' or scandal of the piece;
(c) one – perhaps written for your community newsletter – which offers a more balanced account, weaving elements from (a) and (b) into an integrated whole.

Playing cards

The cards offered here are not the familiar pack of 52, but a set of cards you can make by photocopying the images on pages 226–9 onto thin card and cutting them out. They are chosen as images found frequently in the Bible which also have a wider emotional resonance – and you can add others of your own. The idea is that having described your situation to yourself or a partner, you wait quietly until feelings come into focus. You then shuffle the pack and turn over the top five cards and choose the one that most corresponds with your situation and how you feel about it. If none of the cards draws you, discard them all, deal another five and repeat the process. There is no magic involved and the card predicts nothing: it is the very randomness of the card that can help you. And the card predicts nothing; far from taking away your autonomy, it is there to catalyse your reflection and suggest ways of linking to scripture and tradition, so that you can come to your own decision about future action. You will doubtless be able to think of other ways of using the cards which allow this same random-but-ordered engagement with scripture and tradition.

Figure 14: Image cards.

Figure 15: More image cards.

Recreation

Often when you have strained away at your desk trying to achieve productive PTR, simply relaxing and going away to do something you enjoy – taking a run or a bath, gardening, cooking, or whatever it is – can enable thoughts and insights to arise, or new aspects of experience to emerge. Longer and more focused recreation through sports, trekking, hillwalking or long-distance running has the additional advantage of exercise which enables you to be, for a time, in an all-absorbing and quite different context, while at the same time altering the chemical balance in your brain and enabling you to return to your reflection in a significantly different frame of mind.

Role play

Role play can be very a useful tool to help a group in thinking through a situation, particularly one in which the personalities of those involved seem to have significant impact on how it develops. Different members are designated to play the part of different people or institutions, or even different voices from scripture and tradition (see Chapter 3.2.c) and to engage in expressive dialogue with one another, even 'hamming it' if appropriate. The participants need to get completely into their roles, and express not their own views, but those appropriate to their assigned role.

Sculpting

This is a tool particularly suited for PTR groups, in which one member of the group is invited to arrange the other members in a way that expresses his feelings about the situation. For example, in a reflection on a situation in the NHS, different figures may express the relation of the different elements – nurses, doctors, patients, relatives, ancillary staff, managers and so forth. The arrangement of the figures may unite the members into a common pattern that expresses an idea, like a machine or a boat, or they can be disparate figures, crouching, standing, turning towards or away from each other, or up or down, or whatever. This obviously opens up a lot of non-verbal ways of reflecting on situations and relationships. The sculpt is best made in silence, and responded to initially in silence. Then each person can describe how they experience the situation from their identity with the group they represent, and from their particular position in the sculpt. This can be a valuable tool for understanding a situation as part of the thick descriptor.

Shifting bodily focus

This tool addresses the different centres from which we can experience things, as noted in the Enneagram (Chapter 7.4). Try experiencing or remembering the situation in turn from:

- your eyes and *head*, looking on as a detached 'scientist' analysing it all, but not relating emotionally or engaging with anyone involved;
- your *heart* or your middle: move into the centre of the experience, describing your loves, hates and fears, and your relationships with those involved;
- your *guts*, stomach, fists, legs: strut resolutely around the scene in your imagination, experiencing your gut reactions, instincts and impulses.

The order in which these different centres are explored does not matter in general, though you may find there is a right order for you. And you may well find some centres come naturally to you while others need to be worked at.

With practice you will be able to shift centre even in the midst of a real situation. For example, when your gut reaction is to hit someone, heart considerations of what it might do to your working relationship may be useful! Or when you sense that your talk or sermon is coming from a lean analytical place in your head, and people seem to be disengaged and nodding off, a shift to some heartfelt passion or some gut-level pulpit-thumping may enliven everyone. You will also discover that bodily posture, as well as expressing the centre you are experiencing, can also be deliberately changed to alter the centre. The heady sermon is probably largely addressed to the ceiling; get your head facing the people, move your shoulders to frame your heart, and you will start preaching differently. So in PTR bodily posture can be used as a tool to enable you to be a richer experiencer of situations, and a more effective agent within them.

Tape recorder

This is one of the simplest tools to use if you have a tape recorder (or equivalent). Just decide how long you will talk for and set an alarm to go off at the end of that period, then press 'record' and turn on your tape recorder, and talk freely about the matter being considered. Don't edit or attempt to restrict what you say – in fact, encourage yourself to say all the things you find yourself having to censor when in the company of others. Then go away and do something completely different, preferably leaving it for a day or two, or even a week – and then come back and listen to yourself. This new objective perspective can be extremely revealing of assumptions, blind-spots and presuppositions, and surprisingly liberating.

Further reading (and sources for some of the tools)

Ballard, D. (2005), *Explorations in Computer Mediated Theological Reflection*, MTh Thesis, Cardiff University (unpublished).

Berryman, J. (2002, 2003), *Complete Guide to Godly Play*, 4 vols, Denver CO: Living the Good News.

De Mello, A. (1983), *The Song of the Bird*, Anand, India: Gujarat Sahitya Prakash.

Kosko, B. (1994), *Fuzzy Thinking: The New Science Of Fuzzy Logic*, London: HarperCollins.

Pink, D. (2006), *A Whole New Mind: How to Thrive in the New Conceptual Age*, London: Cyan.

Reid, S. P. (2002), *How to Think: Building Your Mental Muscle*, Edinburgh: Prentice Hall.

Runcorn, D. (2006), *Choice, Desire and the Will of God*, London: SPCK.

Strong, D. (2003), *Complete Guide to Godly Play*, vol. 5, Denver CO: Living the Good News.

Notes

Preface

1 Particularly the Churches of St Aidan with St George, East Bristol, and St Barnabas, Knowle West, Bristol.
2 In *Theological Reflection: Sources* (London: SCM Press, 2007), Graham, Walton and Ward note that closing the gap between academic theology and concrete human experience 'asks the student to perform feats of intellectual and practical integration that no one on the faculty seems prepared to demonstrate' (p. 5).

Introduction

3 Cf. also V. Lossky, *The Mystical Theology of the Eastern Church* (London: James Clarke, 1957), A. Louth, *The Origin of the Christian Mystical Tradition* (Oxford: Oxford University Press, 1981) and M. MacIntosh, *Mystical Theology* (Oxford: Blackwell, 1998).
4 See note 2 above.

1 What Theological Reflection is – and what it isn't

5 'Marks of good practice in TR' are based on those provided by Dr Heather Walton at a conference on TR held in Manchester by the British and Irish Association for Practical Theology in July 2006.

3 Ways and Means: A Variety of PTR Approaches and Models

6   Delivered at a Symposium on Theological Reflection held at St Michael's College, Llandaff, in September 2004; unpublished as yet.

4 The Place of Scripture in PTR

7   The annual publication of the Retreat Association, *Retreats* includes 30–40 individually guided Ignatian retreats each year, and advertises several courses training participants in Ignatian spiritual direction.
8   Margaret Silf has a helpful chapter on consolation and desolation in *Landmarks: An Ignatian Journey* (London: Darton, Longman & Todd, 1998).
9   There are a variety of concordances and 'helps to Bible study' which can also be useful in building up such a list, as can A. Colin Day, *Roget's Thesaurus of the Bible*, San Francisco, HarperSanFrancisco, 1992.

5 God, Gaps and Glory – The *Kairos* Moment

10 This comment is often quoted; its origin seems to be a comment made at the time of the Second World War.

6 PTR in the Context of Daily and Community Life – *Chronos*

11 The distinction between 'left' and 'right' brain is a widely popularized assimilation of scientific discoveries about the way these two parts of the brain (which paradoxically control the right and left parts of the body respectively) operate. 'Left' brain is broadly associated with logic and analysis, 'right' brain with a more holistic, intuitive approach.
12 This requirement is specified in BACP literature, including the information sheet for the annual renewal of accreditation.
13 'Base communities' in Latin American churches, where liberation theology

originated, were open to all members of the community of a particular local church, meeting regularly to understand and take action on current issues affecting their lives and livelihood.

14 For a useful example see J. Heskins, *Unheard Voices* (London: Darton, Longman & Todd, 2001). Sr Anne Codd has also cited examples from the Roman Catholic Church in Ireland (verbal communication).

7 PTR and Personality: Differences in Thinking, Feeling, Learning and Doing

15 'Fallible cognitive indicators' is Ross Thompson's phase, intended to emphasize that emotions have a cognitive dimension without implying this is always objectively valid.

16 Jewish tradition is claimed to have specific prayers to this effect, though the authors have been unable to verify this.

17 The annual Covenant Service of the Methodist Church, usually used at New Year, has a valuable understanding on this:

> Christ has many services to be done: some are easy, others are difficult ... Some are suitable to our natural inclinations and material interests, others are contrary to both; in some we may please Christ and please ourselves; in others we cannot please Christ except by denying ourselves.

The Methodist Worship Book (Peterborough: Methodist Publishing House, 1999), p. 289.

8 PTR and Theology

18 This is said by some to characterize the Anglican tradition in particular, with its reservations about both the dogmatic claims of Catholicism and the 'enthusiasm' of radical Protestantism.

19 The watchmaker analogy is found in William Paley's *Natural Theology* (1802) and expresses a view derived from Aquinas' argument from design, based on the thought of Augustine and ultimately that of Plato and Aristotle, and current among seventeenth-century empiricists.

20 Irenaeus, *Against the Heresies*, 4.20.6.

9 PTR, Ethics, Institutions and the Wider World

21 I have tended to talk about rather concrete and local institutions here, such as schools, hospitals and prisons. But institutions can include less concrete forms of social organization and thought such as professions, instruments of government such as Parliament and ministries etc.

22 For a good source of methods and further questions that can be used to study organizations, see Cameron *et al.*, *Studying Local Churches: A Handbook* (London: SCM Press, 2005).

23 For a slightly more detailed discussion of what follows, see R. Thompson, *SCM Studyguide to Christian Spirituality* (London: SCM Press, 2008), ch. 12, on spirituality and ethics. And for more on the different ethical approaches, see N. Messer, *SCM Studyguide to Christian Ethics* (London: SCM Press, 2006), P. Singer, *A Companion to Christian Ethics* (Oxford: Blackwell, 1993), and P. Vardy and P. Grosch, *The Puzzle of Ethics* (London: Fount, 1999).

24 It was St Augustine who first proposed criteria to discern if a war was just, and Aquinas developed 'just war theory' around the notions of legitimate authority and just cause and intention. The theory has been developed further in the Christian tradition, the Catholic bishops in America in 1983 including notions of just cause, competent and legal authority, right intention, last resort, reasonable probability of success, and proportionality between the injustice prevented by the war and that caused by the war itself.

25 See note 13 above.

26 Prosperity gospel: a common belief in US 'televangelist' charismatic churches based on Deuteronomy 8.18 and the belief that God wants all the faithful to be successful in every way.

27 As was done, for example, by the Dutch Reformed Church in South Africa to justify apartheid.

A Toolkit for PTR

28 The original woodcut for this picture was made by Mrs Jayne Jones of Gorseinon, Swansea.

Core Texts

Ballard, P. and Pritchard, J. (2006), *Practical Theology in Action: Christian thinking in the Service of Church and Society*, London: SPCK.

Boff, L. (1997), *Ecclesiogenesis: The Base Communities Reinvent the Church*, Maryknoll NY: Orbis Books.

Bolton, G. (2001), *Reflective Practice: Writing and Professional Development*, London: Chapman.

Cameron, H., Richter, P., Davies, D. and Ward, F. (eds) (2005), *Studying Local Churches: A Handbook*, London: SCM Press.

Ford, D. (2007), *Christian Wisdom: Desiring God and Learning in Love*, Cambridge: Cambridge University Press.

Freire, P. (1996), *Pedagogy of the Oppressed*, Harmondsworth: Penguin.

Graham, E., Walton, H. and Ward, F. (2005), *Theological Reflection: Methods*, London: SCM Press.

Graham, E., Walton, H. and Ward, F. (2007), *Theological Reflection: Sources*, London: SCM Press.

Green, L. (1990), *Let's Do Theology*, London: Mowbray. Later editions published by Mowbray (2000) and Continuum (2001).

Gutiérrez, G. (2001), *A Theology of Liberation*, London: SCM Press.

Killen, P. and de Beer, J. (2002), *The Art of Theological Reflection*, New York: Crossroad.

Kinast, R. (2000), *What are They Saying about Theological Reflection?* Mahwah NJ: Paulist Press.

Moon, J. (2004), *Reflection in Learning and Professional Development*, Abingdon: Routledge Falmer.

Mudge, L. and Poling, J. N. (eds) (1987), *Formation and Reflection: The Promise of Practical Theology*, Philadelphia: Fortress Press.

Oliver, G. (2006), *Holy Bible, Human Bible*, London: Darton, Longman & Todd.

Pattison, S. (1989), 'Some Straw for the Bricks', in Pattison and Woodward (2000), pp. 135–45.

Pattison, S. (1997a), *The Faith of the Managers*, London: Cassell.

Pattison, S. (1997b), *Pastoral Care and Liberation Theology*, London: SPCK.

Pattison, S. (2000), *A Critique of Pastoral Care* (third edition), London: SCM Press.

Pattison, S., Thompson, J. and Green, J. (2003), 'Theological Reflection for the Real World: Time to Think Again', *British Journal of Theological Education*, vol. 13, no. 2, pp. 119–31.

Pattison, S. (2007), *The Challenge of Practical Theology: Selected Essays*, London and Philadelphia: Jessica Kingsley.

Ryken, L., Wilhoit, J. and Longman, T. (1998), *Dictionary of Biblical Imagery*, Illinois and Leicester: InterVarsity Press.

Schön, D. (1983), *The Reflective Practitioner: How Professionals Think In Action*, New York: Basic Books.

Ward, F. (2005), *Lifelong Learning: Theological Education and Supervision*, London: SCM Press.

Whitehead, J. and Whitehead, E. (1995), *Method in Ministry: Theological Reflection and Christian Ministry*, Lanham, Chicago, New York, Oxford: Sheed and Ward.

Wilson, M. (1988), *A Coat of Many Colours: Pastoral Studies of the Christian Way of Life*, London: Epworth Press.

Wink, W. (1992), *Engaging the Powers: Discernment and Resistance in a World of Domination*, Minneapolis: Fortress Press.

Woodward, J. and Pattison, S. (2000), *The Blackwell Reader in Pastoral and Practical Theology*, Oxford: Blackwell.

Index of Biblical References

Old Testament

Genesis
2.15	82
12.1–4	30
22	83
32.22–32	30

Exodus
1.11	66
18.22	66
19.16	47
24.16	47

Deuteronomy
| 8.18 | 236n |
| 10.19 | 42 |

1 Kings
| 8.10–11 | 47 |
| 19.1–2 | 47 |

Job
| 39.26 | 47 |

Psalms
19	167
32.11	42
55.22	66
63.1	46
104	47
124.7	47
139	167
148	167

Isaiah
19.1–2	47
13.15	46
43.19–20	42

Jeremiah
| 4.24 | 36 |
| 8.7 | 47 |

Ezekiel
| 37.1–11 | 99 |

New Testament

Matthew
4.1–11	46
5.28	131
6.25–34	14
11.30	67
14.13–21	87
18.20	13
20.1–16	109
23.4	67
23.9	4

Mark
| 6.30–44 | 87 |

Luke
1.52	4
6.40	55
9.10–17	87
9.48	55
13.29	42
14.15–24	42
15.4	46
18.9–14	38

Luke *continued*		Acts		Ephesians	
18.20	42	10	200	5.9	3
24.13–35	42	10—11	124		
				Hebrews	
John		Romans		13.1–2	42
1.1–14	165	12.15	43		
2	38			James	
3.5	199	1 Corinthians		1.22	3
4.21–25	38	13.12	167		
10.10	169			1 Peter	
13.34	42	Galatians		1.24–5	42
15—16	38	5.22	3	Revelation	
15.9–17	85	6.2	66	22.1–2	42

Index of Names and Subjects

Abraham 30, 42, 83, 161
abundance 42, 43, 169
active participant 51–2
Adam and Eve 82, 161
Aden 17, 33, 70
aggadot/aggadah 82–3
albatross 67
Alison, James 4, 14, 199, 207
alterity 30
Ancient Mariner (Coleridge) 67
Anglican 80, 171, 235n
apatheia 132
Aquinas 160–1, 203, 235n, 236n
Athanasius 5
Augustine 5, 161, 235n, 236n
authority 55, 82, 123, 163, 168, 172
    and power 55, 179

BACP (British Association for
    Counselling and Psychotherapy)
    121, 131
Ballard, Paul 98, 237
Ballard, Duncan 83, 95, 215, 218, 231
baptism 42, 199
    infant 5

Barth, Karl 31, 98, 163, 165, 168
base communities 123, 199–200,
    234n, 237
Bayne 133, 139
Beesing 133, 138, 139
Bentham, J. 189
Berryman, J. 218, 229
BIAPT (British and Irish Association
    for Practical Theology) 155
bisociation 100–1, 111
Blomberg, D. 83–4
bones, dry 42, 97–9
Boff, L. 23, 33, 201, 234
Boisen, A. 17, 33, 63, 70
Bolton, G. 51, 68, 70, 126, 234
Bonhoeffer, D. 207
bottom line 184
Brown, D. 80, 95
Browning, D. 193
buddhist, buddhism 161, 171, 191–2
Bunyan, J. 67
burden 66–7, 133

Cameron, H. 24, 33, 233, 234
Cavanaugh 205, 208

Christ 19, 43, 48, 82, 98–9, 162, 169, 201, 235n
Christology 180
chronos 73, 97, 111, 113–27, 190
Clinical Pastoral Education 17, 50, 58, 63–4
Codd, A. 235n
Coleridge, S.T. 67, 103, 111
community 151, 189, 198
    church community 113, 158, 201
    faith community 111, 121–6, 158, 169, 195–6, 198–9, 202, 207, 221
computer games 215
congregation 19, 124, 207
context 113–27, 177–9, 187,199, 202, 207
Continuing Professional Development 120–2
contradictions 3–5, 180, 196
Cornelius 200
correlation 19, 28, 98, 197
consolation 89, 231n
conversation 65, 79, 92, 99
counselling 22, 120, 121
creation 165–7, 173, 180, 197
critical conversation 61–4

Dante 160–1
dark night 90, 126
Davies, J. 118, 126
Day, A.C. 231n
deconstruction 77, 158
deductive theology 155–6
definitions of TR and PTR 7–8, 20, 27–9, 195, 198
de las Casas, B. 22, 33
Dennis, T. 46, 76, 95
deontolgoy 188

desert 42, 46, 132
desolation 47, 89, 231n
Despatches 54
Dewey, J. 18, 21, 33
dialogue 28, 57, 59, 92, 189, 218, 220
    inter-faith dialogue 7, 122, 172
Dillard, A. 65, 70
doctrine 5–6, 24, 162, 168–89, 184

Easter 87
ecclesiology 180–1
emic 175, 177, 183–7
emotion/s 9, 63, 100, 103, 128-133, 143, 168, 188, 225
emotional intelligence 129, 149
emotional literacy 132, 149
Enneagram 138–42, 147, 148, 149
etic 175, 177–81, 187
eucharist 118, 201, 205, 207
Evragius of Pontus 138

faith communities 3, 16, 122–3, 138, 172, 195, 101–5
faith of the managers 6, 14, 181, 194
fantasy 225
feelings 45–6, 61–2, 65–6, 70, 82, 88–9, 119, 129–33, 135–49, 211, 214, 225
Fischer, K. 65, 70
Fletcher 189, 204
Force Field Analysis 217
Ford, D. 76, 77, 95, 153, 159, 173
Foskett, J. 64, 70, 122
foundational narrative/myth 185–6
Francis of Assisi 42, 47, 55, 164, 230
Frei 95, 174
Freire, P. 23, 33, 234
Fresh Expressions 39

Fox, G. 31
fundamentalism 196, 203

Geertz, C. 53, 70
gentiles 210–11
Gerkin 64, 70, 126, 194
godly play 218, 231
Goleman, D. 129, 149
good practice, marks of 29–30, 110, 231
Gorringe, T. 149, 190, 194
Good Friday 87
Graham, E. 5, 14, 18–20, 24, 74, 233, 237
Green, L. 6, 14, 23, 33, 57–9, 82, 89, 95, 100–1
group/s 28, 68, 90, 122, 144–5, 145–8, 171–2, 209, 220, 227
Guigo II 92, 95
Gurdjieff, G. 138
guru's cat 5–6
Gutierrez,G. 23

Hauerwas, S. 190, 194
Hawkins, P and Sholet, R. 126
Hawkin, S. 167, 174
Heelas, P. 203, 207
Heitink, G. 153, 155–6, 174
hermeneutic 9, 76, 177
    of suspicion 77, 178
Heskins, J. 235n
Holloway, R. 192, 194
holy fool 55
holy week 87
homosexuality 62
Hopewell, J. 202, 208
hospitality 40–3, 81, 99, 102, 156
Hunter, R. 194

hypertext 218

Ichazo, O. 138
identity 48, 88, 112, 157, 178, 211
Ignatius of Loyola
    Spiritual Exercises 75, 76, 86–9, 94
image/imagery 48, 88, 112, 157, 178, 211, 226–9
incarnation 5, 89, 168, 169
indicator
    fallible cognitive indicator 129, 235
    Myers Briggs Type Indicator 135–8, 149
insight 52, 54, 57, 59, 100, 102, 103, 107, 119, 199, 200–1
inspiration 78, 97–111, 220
institutions 156, 159, 170, 176–87, 190–3,
interilluminatiion 27, 68, 73, 100–1, 132
interfaith 7, 122, 171–3, 205
Irenaeus 169, 232
Isaac 83, 161
Islam 54, 73, 138
    see also Muslim
Ivan the Terrible 55
Ivens, M 75, 86, 95

Jesus 4, 5, 13, 38, 42, 46–7, 67, 85, 87–9, 90, 131,136,155, 164, 169, 189, 194, 197, 220
journal/journalling 19, 120–1, 215, 216, 221, 147
Judaism 73, 76, 138
just war 233n

Kairos 57, 73, 97–112, 132, 161, 190
Kaufman, G. 174

Keats, J. 103, 112
Killen, P. 6, 14, 28, 34, 50, 65
Kinast, R. 14, 234
kingdom (God's) 42, 118, 179, 181
Koestler, A. 100, 112
Kolb, D.18, 21, 33, 51, 142
Kosko, B. 217, 229

Lambourne, R. 57
Lartey, E. 59–61, 70
Latin America 3, 18, 22, 123
learning style 128, 142–5, 147
lectio divina 76, 78, 85, 92–4
liberation theology 3, 14, 18, 21, 22–4,
    33, 123, 156, 158, 169, 170, 176, 180,
    194, 199, 234
lifelong learning 171, 196–8, 235
Litchfield, K. 9, 14
liturgy 5, 19, 168, 169, 172, 201
living human document 19, 63–5, 70,
    126
Loades, A. 80, 95
Lonergan, B. 58, 70
lost sheep 46–8
Loughlin, G. 174
Luther, M. 31, 153, 163
Lyall, D. 64, 70, 122, 126

managers/management 181, 228
    Faith of the Managers 6, 14, 181, 235
Marxist 23, 170
Maslow, A. 9, 14
Maundy Thursday 87
MacIntyre, A. 189, 194
McCurry, J. 81, 95
map/mapping 65, 98, 156, 217, 222
MBTI (Myers Briggs Type Indicator)
    135–8, 147

meetings 22, 25, 40, 45, 66, 85, 90, 220
Messer, N. 194
metanarrative 41
Methodist/Methodism 38, 232n
Miles, J. 76, 95
Midrash 68, 76, 81–5, 200, 223, 224
Milbank, J. 168
Mill, J.S. 189, 194
ministry 71, 90, 98, 113, 125, 133, 149,
    169, 177, 194, 201, 235
ministerial education/practice 6, 18,
    24–6, 122, 154, 196
modern 5, 54, 90, 91, 162, 165, 213–15
mood (theological) 159–64
Moon, J. 33, 120, 126, 237
Moses 46, 66, 161
Mothering Sunday 37
Mudge, L. 126, 237
Mumford 142, 149
music 103, 146, 223, 234
Mueller, J. 174
Muslim 54, 171 see also Islam
Myers Briggs see MBTI
mystical 76, 126, 162, 230
myth, reality shaping 184–6

narrative 19, 66, 68–9, 71, 81–4, 86–9,
    95, 186, 218 see also story
natural theology 165–7, 235
negative capability 31, 68, 102–4, 106,
    209
negative space 83, 223–4
Neusner, J. 82
New Age 139
newness of life 102, 107
Nietzsche 204
Northcott, M. 170, 174
Nyssa, Gregory of 131, 138, 149

observer 51–3, 140
Oliver, G. 78, 80–1, 95, 237
Osmer, R. 28, 34
Origen 76
original sin 5
Orthodox Church 168

Paley, W. 235
parables 19 89, 205, 207, 212–13, 218
paradigms 35–49, 92
passions 63, 131
pastoral cycle 56–61, 83, 85, 103, 158,
    166, 211
Parker, D. 95
Pattison, S. 6, 7, 20, 28, 61–3, 77, 130,
    154–5, 158, 168, 170, 175–87, 237–8
Paver 71, 184
pharasees 38, 67, 189
Piaget 51
Pilgrim's Progress 77
Pink, D. 112, 215, 231
Plato 55, 189, 203, 235
Peter's vision 210–11
poetry 67
Poling 34, 237
poor, bias to the 4, 23, 38, 42, 77, 170,
    176–7
post-modern 158, 204, 205, 207
power 4, 14, 55, 77, 123, 140, 1644,
    176, 179, 180, 204, 238
practitiioner 8, 21. 30, 34, 54, 63, 70,
    103, 115, 128, 138, 190, 197–9, 238
praxis 19–20, 23–4, 30, 85, 156, 157,
    161, 170, 191
prayer references to prayer are found
    throughout – see especially 117–19,
    and also 36–49, 85–9, 92–4, 98–111
pre-modern 203–4

Primavesi, A. 165, 174
Pritchard, J. 98, 111, 237
proof-texting 26, 78–80
prosperity gospel 199, 238n
PTR defined 20

Qu'ran 54, 73

Ramadan, T. 54
reality-shaping myth see myth
reason 103, 131, 158, 165, 167, 188,
    203, 213–15
recreation 8–9, 103, 214, 224, 230
refreshment 224
Reed, E. 78, 96, 134
reflexive 133
Reid, G. 142, 149
Reid, S. 232
retreats 55–6, 89, 231n
revelation 19, 20, 30, 43, 80, 98,165,
    168, 173
rhythm 92, 115–17, 121, 231
ritual 185, 205
role-play 81–2, 237
Romero, O. 31
Rohr, R. 133, 149
Runcorn, D. 214, 232
Ryken, L. 90, 96, 238
Ryle, G. 53, 71

sacramental 80, 95
sacred space 92, 102, 104–6
Scholet, R. 126
Schön, D. 22, 34, 238
Schreiter, R. 201 207
Schwartz, H. 96
Schweitzer, A. 31
scripture/s 9, 20, 35–49, 56, 75–95, 99,
    158, 168–9, 170, 199, 201

sculpting 230–1
Sharp, P. 129, 132, 149
Sheldrake, P. 102, 112, 149
Silf, M. 118, 126, 234n
Singer, P.194
soteriology 190–1
spirit 3, 4, 12, 32, 85, 99, 145, 193, 219
Spiritual Exercises see Ignatius
Stations of the Cross 87
story 19, 68, 80, 82–3, 174, 196, 215 see also narrative
Strong, D. 229
Suchocki, M. 126
supervision 121–2, 126–7, 198, 201, 238

Talmud 83–4
Tanakh 83
teleology 188
Temple, W. 109
Tempest, The 104
theology 153–74
    pastoral 52–3, 64, 154–7
    philosophical 165–7
    practical 6–8, 17, 18, 58, 98, 127, 154–7, 169–70, 174, 193, 200, 237–8
    systematic 18, 71, 168
thick descriptor/description 24, 35, 38, 45, 52, 55–6, 70, 130, 144, 160, 180, 214,
Thirty-Nine Articles 80
Thompson, R 90, 112, 154, 174, 201, 235n, 236n
Tillich, P. 58, 71, 98

Todd, A. 56–7, 97, 153
Tracy, D. 5, 58, 71, 98, 157–9, 184
transferability 32 see also 199–202
transformation 28–31, 106–10, 114, 118, 119, 158
trinity 5, 55, 162, 164, 169

Valdes, M.112
values 175, 179, 181, 185
Vardy, P. 194. 236n
verbatim 63–4
virtue 180, 188–90, 194

Walton, H. 30, 68, 71, 96,120, 127, 237
Walton, R. 33
Ward, F. 33, 68–9, 71,120, 196–7, 201, 237–8
Ward, P. 208
Ward, N. 46, 49
Watts, F 149
wilderness 46–8, 82, 90
Williams, R. 81
willing suspension of disbelief 103–4
Wilson, M. 5, 58, 153, 166, 168, 238
Wesley, J. 31
Whitehead, J. and E. 28, 57–8, 238
Wink, W. 4, 183, 194, 238
wisdom 20, 28, 65–6, 77, 151, 165–71, 190, 202–5, 237
worship 30, 48–9, 77, 113, 118, 181
Wright, S. 80, 96
word of God 79–80, 82, 155, 164
Wogaman, J. 194

Yoder, J. 194